Shih Tzu FOR DUMMIES®

by Eve Adamson

BICENTENNIAL
1807
WILEY
2007
BICENTENNIAL

W

Shih Tzu For Dummies®

Published by
Wiley Publishing, Inc.
111 River St.
Hoboken, NJ 07030-5774
www.wiley.com

Published by Wiley Publishing, Inc., Indianapolis, Indiana

Published simultaneously in Canada

For general information on our other products and services, please contact our Customer Care Department within the U.S. at 877-762-2974, outside the U.S. at 317-572-3993, or fax 317-572-4002.

For technical support, please visit www.wiley.com/techsupport.

Wiley also publishes its books in a variety of electronic formats. Some content that appears in print may not be available in electronic books.

Library of Congress Control Number: 2007920009

ISBN: 978-0-470-08945-3

Manufactured in the United States of America

10 9 8 7 6

About the Author

Eve Adamson is an award-winning pet writer and the author or coauthor of more than 40 books including *Labrador Retrievers For Dummies, Dachshunds For Dummies,* and *Adopting a Pet For Dummies.* She's the winner of the ASPCA Humane Issues Award in 2006 and a contributing editor and columnist for *Dog Fancy* magazine. She also writes the "Good Grooming" column for *AKC Family Dog* magazine and a holistic pet care column for Pet Product News.

Eve is a member of the Dog Writer's Association of America (www.dwaa.org) and the Cat Writer's Association of America (www.catwriters.org). She lives in Iowa City with her family, and you can find out more about Eve and her most recent publications on her Web site at www.eveadamson.com.

Dedication

This book is dedicated to our littlest dogs — they have the biggest hearts.

Author's Acknowledgments

Even as I sit alone at my desk writing about dogs, I am always aware of the many people so integral to the process. Thank you to all those who helped me with this book in so many ways: Tracy Boggier, Acquisitions Editor, who knew I would love to write about Shih Tzu; Chad Sievers, Project Editor, and Carrie Burchfield, Copy Editor, for their bang-up editing jobs; Victor Joris, Technical Editor, Shih Tzu expert extraordinaire, and a real force in the breed, for his thorough review of the manuscript; Dominique DeVito, for cheering me on and helping to keep me on task; and Caroline Coile, for keeping me just distracted and amused enough to make the days interesting (and for doing the same thing at the same time).

I also must thank Susan Chaney, Hazel Barrowman, Annie Shirreffs, Jackie Franza, Annamaria DiGiorgio, Carol Boker, Lisa King, Betty Liddick, and Tanya Bielski-Braham for giving me years and years of work that I consider my training ground for knowing all I know about dogs. Thanks to the Dog Writer's Association of America for keeping me tapped into the strange and wonderful community of people who write about dogs as a career. And finally, as always, to Ben for his great support of the work I do.

Publisher's Acknowledgments

We're proud of this book; please send us your comments through our Dummies online registration form located at www.dummies.com/register/.

Some of the people who helped bring this book to market include the following:

Acquisitions, Editorial, and Media Development

Project Editor: Chad R. Sievers

Acquisitions Editor: Tracy Boggier

Copy Editor: Carrie A. Burchfield

Technical Editor: Victor Joris

Editorial Manager: Michelle Hacker

Editorial Assistants: Erin Calligan, Leeann Harney, David Lutton, Joe Niesen

Cover Photos: © Ulrike Schanz / Animals Animals – Earth Scenes

Cartoons: Rich Tennant (www.the5thwave.com)

Composition Services

Project Coordinator: Erin Smith

Layout and Graphics: Joyce Haughey, Barry Offringa, Laura Pence, Erin Zeltner

Special Art: Photos by Isabelle Francais, Jean M. Fogle, Cathi Winkles, and Alamy

Illustrations: Jake Mansfield

Anniversary Logo Design: Richard Pacifico

Proofreaders: Aptara, Christy Pingleton

Indexer: Aptara

Publishing and Editorial for Consumer Dummies

Diane Graves Steele, Vice President and Publisher, Consumer Dummies

Joyce Pepple, Acquisitions Director, Consumer Dummies

Kristin A. Cocks, Product Development Director, Consumer Dummies

Michael Spring, Vice President and Publisher, Travel

Kelly Regan, Editorial Director, Travel

Publishing for Technology Dummies

Andy Cummings, Vice President and Publisher, Dummies Technology/General User

Composition Services

Gerry Fahey, Vice President of Production Services

Debbie Stailey, Director of Composition Services

Contents at a Glance

Table of Contents

Introduction

The world is full of dogs — big and small, short-coated and long, all of them with the potential to be devoted companions. When it comes to the Shih Tzu, even big-dog-lovers tend to admit after they meet one that Shih Tzu are hard to resist. That loving adoration, that sweet face, that gorgeous coat — few dogs compare to the Shih Tzu for pure and total commitment to the role of companion.

A Shih Tzu wants to please you, but he has his own personality, too. He loves the good life, and though he can be shrewd, or selectively deaf, or consciously naïve, Shih Tzu are big-hearted and have a certain Zen-like tranquility. They don't bark much. They don't get too hyper. They won't pester you all day to throw a tennis ball or go for a walk. But a Shih Tzu will stick by your side, serving as your companion through good days and bad. This dog specializes in *you.*

But be warned: Despite his wonderful qualities, the Shih Tzu can be challenging for individuals who aren't fully committed to a vigorous grooming regimen, who aren't home very much, or who don't have the space in their heart to nurture, love, and care for a dog who must be allowed to do his job as close personal companion to you.

If you're reading this book, you may have already decided on a Shih Tzu. If so, I provide you with all the info you need to start your life together. If you're still choosing a breed, you get the tools to make a sound decision. And if you've lived with a Shih Tzu for awhile now, I imagine you're already hopelessly in love. If your Shih Tzu is a true example of the breed, I can assure you the feeling is mutual.

About This Book

Because this book is about a particular dog breed, it has some special characteristics that distinguish it from some of the other *For Dummies* titles. This book is a tad smaller and more portable than larger *For Dummies'* guides. But it's just as comprehensive; you can find just about any Shih Tzu-related info you need in it.

Each section relates to different aspects of choosing and living successfully with a Shih Tzu. This book is unique because you can open it anywhere and just start reading. Find the topics that interest you or apply to your situation right now. You can find answers to questions such as

- What's a Shih Tzu really like?
- Is a Shih Tzu the right breed for me and my situation?
- Can I get a Shih Tzu if I have children or other pets?
- How difficult is grooming a Shih Tzu? Can I do it myself or should I hire a professional?
- How do I find a good breeder? What about a good vet?
- What should my Shih Tzu eat? How do I keep her healthy?
- Do small dogs really need that much training?

Conventions Used in This Book

I use the following conventions throughout the text to make things consistent and easy to understand:

- All Web addresses appear in `monofont`. ***Note:*** Some Web addresses may extend to two lines of text. If you use one of these addresses, just type the address exactly as you see it, pretending that the line break doesn't exist.
- New terms appear in *italic* and are closely followed by an easy-to-understand definition.
- **Bold** text highlights important terminology and the action parts of numbered steps.

Also, writers used to be told to call pets *it,* but to me, no Shih Tzu is an *it,* so I loosely alternate between *he* and *she* when talking about Shih Tzu. And just for fun, I've also invented two imaginary Shih Tzu named Samson and Lola.

What You're Not to Read

Throughout the book you see gray text boxes. These boxes are sidebars that contain extra info. If you skip over them, you won't hurt my feelings, and you won't miss anything crucial, but if you want to read them, that's okay, too. Of course, you don't have to read the copyright page or my acknowledgements of helpful people.

Foolish Assumptions

I don't know you, but I think I know a little about you, even though we've never met. As I wrote this book, I assumed the following:

- You're thinking about bringing a Shih Tzu into your home, or you already have a new Shih Tzu at home.
- You want to take the best possible care of your new little dog.
- You aren't quite sure if you're feeding the right food or grooming your dog the right way and you want more info.
- You suspect you should train your Shih Tzu, at least a little, but you aren't sure how to go about it.
- You just love to read about Shih Tzu.

How This Book Is Organized

This book is divided into five convenient sections. Here's where to find what you need.

Part I: The Quest for the Perfect Shih Tzu

In this part, you get the lowdown on what a Shih Tzu is, what this cute little guy is like to live with, and what kind of home makes the best sense for him. Find out how a perfect Shih Tzu is supposed to look (Chapter 2), the best sources for finding a Shih Tzu (Chapter 3), and the basics on choosing the right dog for you (Chapter 4).

Part II: Opening Your Home to Your Shih Tzu

This part focuses on bringing your Shih Tzu home. You get a shopping list (Chapter 5), info on safely Shih-Tzu-proofing your home (Chapter 6), and tips on introducing your family, including kids and other pets, to the new dog (Chapter 7). Chapter 8 helps you get through the first few days with your new pet.

Part III: Caring for Your Chinese Charmer

Your Shih Tzu needs special care, and this part tells you what to do to keep her healthy, happy, and beautiful. Chapter 9 discusses feeding your Shih Tzu. Chapter 10 shows you all about grooming. In Chapter 11, you discover the best way to manage and teach your new dog. Chapter 12 discusses how to keep your Shih Tzu at her healthy best, and Chapter 13 gives you the lowdown on specific health issues and emergency situations. Chapter 14 tells you everything you need to know about traveling with your dog.

Part IV: Training Your Shih Tzu

As well behaved as your Shih Tzu may be, this part helps you fine-tune that good behavior. Chapter 15 discusses some basic training rules for *you.* Chapter 16 gives you the housetraining lowdown. Chapter 17 covers basic verbal cues like Come, Stay, Sit, and Down.

Part V: The Part of Tens

From this trademark *For Dummies* part, you get quick, fun, and useful information. Interested in Shih Tzu legends? Check out Chapter 18. Think you have the next great show dog? Chapter 19 gives you ten tips for starting out in the world of dog shows.

Icons Used in This Book

To make this book easier to read and simpler to use, I include some icons that point you to some key ideas and information.

This icon points out helpful things to know — things you can actually do to help solve a problem or save you time or money.

Do your best to remember the info highlighted by this icon. The knowledge you gather here helps keep you and your Shih Tzu happy.

Pay close attention to the info at this icon. You're alerted to anything that may be potentially dangerous for you or your Shih Tzu.

I point out favorite products or services that I've used or tested. Consider them my personal recommendations.

Where to Go from Here

What are you waiting for? You can start reading now! But wait . . . where do you start? Wherever you want! I grant you the freedom to wander through the pages, but if you want some guidance, check in the table of contents or the index for some topics that interest you. Or, you can read this book from the first to the last page. The choice is yours. No matter where you start, I wish you and the beautiful, bright, and blissful little dog who fills your heart (or soon will) the very best journey together.

Part I
The Quest for the Perfect Shih Tzu

In this part . . .

Whether you know you want a Shih Tzu or you're still trying to determine whether a Shih Tzu makes a good match for you and your family, this part gives you all the info you need to explore the Shih Tzu's many qualities.

Chapter 1 helps you evaluate how Shih-Tzu-friendly your lifestyle really is, while Chapter 2 takes an up-close and personal look at how Shih Tzu should look and act. If you're looking for information about breeders, head to Chapter 3. That chapter contains questions for breeders and an explanation of the process of buying a Shih Tzu from a breeder. You also get tips on evaluating shelters and rescue groups, if you want to adopt a Shih Tzu in need. Chapter 4 guides you in choosing the perfect Shih Tzu: puppy or adult.

Chapter 1

Shih Tzu and You

In This Chapter

- Understanding the Shih Tzu
- Discovering what the breed needs
- Knowing whether you and the Shih Tzu mesh
- Determining what you want in a dog

He stares at you longingly, his big dark eyes glistening with love. She gazes at you, the god of her universe, and then shakes her long golden hair. Irresistible, coy, and flirtatious, yet passionately devoted to you . . . is this the love of your life?

Maybe a fluffy, cuddly, sweet-faced Shih Tzu would make the perfect dog for you. Maybe, just maybe, Samson really is the pet you've always dreamed of. Maybe spunky little Lola really is your canine match made in heaven. Or, maybe the little lion dog really isn't suited to be your next great love, because you aren't crazy about grooming or need a high-energy dog to go running with.

Whether you're still deciding on the right breed or you just want to know more about the little fella on your lap, this chapter serves as your broad survey of this most adorable of the toy breeds. Consider this chapter your crash course in Shih Tzu — Shih Tzu 101.

The Lowdown on the Shih Tzu

You don't have to bend over much to pet a Labrador Retriever on the head, but with a Shih Tzu (pronounced sheed-*zoo,* see Figure 1-1), you need to get down on the floor to pet him. His short legs don't get him much higher than about ten inches, so to admire all his wonderful features, you have to take yourself to his level.

© Isabelle Francais

Figure 1-1: A Shih Tzu is a small dog with a big heart.

The show-dog Shih Tzu has specific features (refer to Chapter 2), but show dog or not, all Shih Tzu have basic physical and personality traits in common, and the most noticeable trait is weight. Shih Tzu are heavier than they look and not as delicate as some finer-boned toy breeds. But despite the heft, Shih Tzu are perfectly sized for a lap or a handbag — not for hunting or tracking, pulling a sled, treeing a raccoon, or guarding a farm. Shih Tzu don't herd sheep or win races, and they certainly don't swim. Shih Tzu just don't have the body or the attitude for work, and although they can scare off a mouse in the house, chances are, they won't bother.

The Shih Tzu is built for one job and one job alone: to accompany you on your journey through life as your close personal friend. But having a Shih Tzu isn't all about you. Your Shih Tzu needs some very important things from her human caretaker in order to thrive and be a happy, healthy dog. Considering all she does for you, you must be willing, as a responsible and dedicated pet owner, to give back to your Shih Tzu the things she needs.

What Does a Shih Tzu Need?

This little dog's needs aren't complicated and can be summarized with one word: You! Okay, that's not very specific, so this section details your responsibilities to your little one.

Companionship, and a lot of it

A dog bred for companionship must be allowed to do his job, and his job is to be with you. You have to be available and present for him to feel like he has a purpose. When you aren't home, your Shih Tzu waits for you. If you leave him alone most of the day, he spends most of his time waiting for you. Shih Tzu don't like to be alone all the time, and being alone is no life for a companion dog.

Plus, Shih Tzu are social animals. They love to play and be with people, other dogs, and even cats. If you work all day, your Shih Tzu will be much happier with another pet friend, a visit on your lunch hour, or even spending the day at a nice doggy daycare facility. Spending time around other people and other dogs teaches the Shih Tzu about the world, and this kind of experience makes your Shih Tzu a more well-adjusted and friendly pet.

If you work at home, you can probably manage a schedule of work and play and potty breaks for your dog, but if you work away from your home, you need to make arrangements for someone to give your Shih Tzu a potty break. At the end of the day, be prepared for her to want to play and snuggle and just be with you.

Shelter . . . and a little luxury

A Shih Tzu needs warm, safe shelter. Just remember the following if you want a Shih Tzu:

- **Shih Tzu can't live outside.** Their short noses and heavy coats make hot humid weather dangerous, and a Shih Tzu stuck outside in the sun all day (or even in the shade when the humidity soars) is in serious danger of heatstroke (see Chapter 12 for more info on how to keep your pup safe and healthy).
- **Shih Tzu aren't suited for cold weather.** Shih Tzu may be descended from Tibetan temple dogs that lived in frigid, snowy climates, but those dogs were larger and heartier than today's dog, so forget about giving a Shih Tzu a doghouse and leaving him at the mercy of the elements. Sure, your Shih Tzu may enjoy a short romp in the snow, but be sure to dry him when he comes in (and maybe snuggle by the fire for awhile, too).

So you know your Shih Tzu needs a warm safe place indoors, but you can't just let your Shih Tzu lie on the cold, hard floor, can you? I suppose you *could,* but here's a head's up: This dog is a *royal* dog. She expects a little luxury in her life. Is that really so much to ask? For example, your Shih Tzu loves to lounge on soft furniture, and she'll probably prefer to sleep with you, if you let her. Whether you let your little dog into the bed or not, you also need other comfortable spots for your Shih Tzu to lounge when it's not bed time. Try out a soft dog bed, a safe crate or kennel, and access to other furniture (check out Chapter 5 for adding some luxury).

Healthy food

Everybody functions better on healthy food than on junk food, of course, but a nutrient-dense diet is vitally important for a small dog because every bite counts. Your Shih Tzu, especially as a puppy, can't hold much in that little stomach, so food must be full of good nutrition. Shih Tzu puppies also need to eat at least three small meals to keep that small-dog metabolism fueled. A young puppy that doesn't get sufficient nutrition could die.

Additionally Shih Tzu have potentially sensitive skin, and a healthy diet keeps both his skin and coat in good condition. Some pet food companies make food designed specifically for small-breed puppies. Or, you may decide to make a homemade diet for your Shih Tzu. (For more about feeding your Shih Tzu properly, see Chapter 9.)

Exercise

Move it or lose it! Despite Lola's small size, she needs exercise to keep her muscles strong and her heart healthy. Too many Shih Tzu become overweight from an excess of treats and too little exercise, and it doesn't take many extra calories each day to make an eight-pound dog tip the scales in the direction of too-hefty. Extra weight puts added stress on the Shih Tzu's joints and internal organs, compromising her natural good health. (Check out Chapter 8 for specific ideas on playing and exercising with your dog.)

Never exercise your Shih Tzu in hot weather! Her short nose and heavy coat aren't built for the heat, and she can suffer serious health consequences. See Chapter 13 for more info on heatstroke.

Training

He may be cute and charming. He may have great personal charisma. But that doesn't mean Samson knows that your new carpet isn't his personal toilet, or that children's fingers aren't for nipping, or that dashing out the front door isn't safe. All dogs need training, even the cutest and most naturally polite. Don't forget that your Shih Tzu is a dog and doesn't run the household. He needs to know the rules, and you need to enforce the rules. For more on Shih Tzu socialization, behavior, and training, see Chapters 11, 15, and 17.

Toy breeds

Ever since dog shows became popular in the 19th century, purebred dogs have been registered with organizations like the American Kennel Club (AKC), the United Kennel Club (UKC), the Canadian Kennel Club (CKC), and the Kennel Club of the UK. These registries divide purebred dogs into groups according to their purpose. The AKC — the largest registry in the United States — recognizes Shih Tzu as a Toy breed, along with these other little guys:

- Affenpinscher
- Brussels Griffon
- Cavalier King Charles Spaniel
- Chihuahua
- Chinese Crested
- English Toy Spaniel
- Havanese
- Italian Greyhound
- Japanese Chin
- Maltese
- Manchester Terrier
- Miniature Pinscher
- Papillon
- Pekingese
- Pomeranian
- Poodle (Toy)
- Pug
- Silky Terrier
- Toy Fox Terrier
- Yorkshire Terrier

The Toy Group includes 21 breeds (as of 2006), including the Shih Tzu. Although some other groups include smaller dogs, the Toy breeds have certain qualities in common:

- A portable size appropriate for many different living environments
- A big personality in a tiny package
- A propensity for companionship

Toy breeds have been bred to be companions to humans, some for thousands of years. A Shih Tzu may look a lot different from a Chihuahua, a Pug, or a Chinese Crested, but when it comes to skill as a companion, these little guys are all members of the same club.

Group names and classification systems differ among registries. The UKC has a Companion Group, which includes the Shih Tzu. The CKC and the Kennel Club of the UK also include a Toy Group, but neither organization groups the Shih Tzu as a Toy breed. The CKC considers him a member of the Non-Sporting Group, along with dogs like the Lhasa Apso, Bichon Frise, and Tibetan Spaniel. The Kennel Club of the UK states that he's a member of the Utility Group, along with the Lhasa Apso, Tibetan Spaniel, and Toy Poodle.

Medical care

A veterinarian who understands small dogs is one of your most important allies in caring for your Shih Tzu. These pups need regular check-ups and vaccinations (necessary parts of your commitment to your Shih Tzu), but a vet can also help you with pest control, skin allergies, behavioral issues, and any questions you may have about caring for your little dog. For more on Shih Tzu healthcare, refer to Chapters 12 and 13.

Grooming, grooming, and grooming!

I've saved the best for last . . . the best, or the most time-consuming, depending on your perspective. Most Shih Tzu have long, thick coats, which means they need grooming . . . a lot of it. Most pet owners have their Shih Tzu professionally groomed every four to six weeks. This timeline is a fine, but be prepared to pay for the service.

Even with professional grooming, you still need to brush and comb your Shih Tzu every day, or at least a few times a week, to keep mats and tangles from forming as the coat grows.

If you keep your Shih Tzu in a short haircut, you can minimize the work, but a Shih Tzu in full coat really should be thoroughly tended every day. Add to your brushing other routines, such as regular nail clipping, teeth cleaning, eye care, ear care, and all-over massage and you have quite the high-maintenance little pooch. You can't wait for a professional groomer to do these tasks (unless you want to take your Shih Tzu in weekly, which can get pretty expensive). For more info on grooming your Shih Tzu, see Chapter 10.

Are You a Match?

To spin off one of the world's greatest writers: To get a Shih Tzu or not to get a Shih Tzu? That is the question. Don't take this decision lightly. You're embarking on a lifetime (at least your dog's lifetime) commitment, and you want to make sure you, your lifestyle, your family, and your home all are good matches for a Shih Tzu. This section takes a closer look to see if a Shih Tzu is the match for you.

Why a Shih Tzu may be perfect

They're short. They're sassy. But are they right for you? A Shih Tzu might be your perfect dog if you

- **Love to brush dogs:** Shih Tzu need a lot of grooming!
- **Think flat-faced dogs are just *too* cute:** The Shih Tzu doesn't have a long slender profile. He has an adorable short nose.
- **Enjoy being worshipped:** Your Shih Tzu thinks you're *all that.*
- **Think pampering and cuddling a small dog is fun:** Your Shih Tzu needs a lot of one-on-one cuddle time to be happy.
- **Like to take your dog with you whenever you can:** Your Shih Tzu is always ready to hit the road with you.
- **Work at home or come home frequently during the day:** Bred to be a companion dog, the Shih Tzu needs to spend most of her time being a companion, not sitting alone.
- **Think lying around on the couch makes the perfect weekend:** Shih Tzu aren't athletic dogs. They prefer to hang out and relax.
- **Can't stand hot weather:** Your Shih Tzu can't stand it either. In fact, Shih Tzu are prone to heatstroke.

Or why a Shih Tzu may not be your ideal dog

Shih Tzu are cute, but that criterion isn't all that you should go on. A Shih Tzu probably isn't the best breed for you if you

- **Get impatient brushing your *own* hair:** If you don't like to waste time grooming yourself, you certainly won't have time to groom a Shih Tzu.
- **Don't like the sound of snoring and snuffling:** The Shih Tzu's short nose creates a certain amount of nasal noise.
- **Prefer an independent dog that isn't too clingy.** Shih Tzu want to spend time with you.
- **Think that because you have to work, your dog should make himself useful, too:** This dog's job is to be with you. She's not interested in retrieving or pulling a sled or guarding the house.
- **Aren't home very often:** Shih Tzu need people, not alone time.

- **Have several small children:** Do you really have time to take care of a Shih Tzu if you have small children? Probably not. Plus, small children can accidentally injure a small dog.
- **Like to go running, biking, swimming, or spend your weekends training for a marathon and think it would be fun for the dog to come along, too:** Unless you want to stick the Shih Tzu in a doggy backpack, you can forget your dreams of a marathon-training buddy.
- **Love the heat and can see yourself relocating to a tropical island:** Your Shih Tzu would prefer a cabin in the mountains. He doesn't *do* tropical.

Quick Questions to Ask Yourself

If you read the preceding section, you may think you've decided that a Shih Tzu is perfect for you, but wait! You still have a few more topics to consider. Ask yourself the questions in the following sections, and spend some serious time considering your answers.

Why do you want a Shih Tzu?

What about a Shih Tzu really appeals to you? If you want to replace a former Shih Tzu, you already have a good idea about what a Shih Tzu is like, so getting a new Shih Tzu puppy may not seem so scary. On the other hand, all Shih Tzu have their own, unique personalities, and your new puppy won't be exactly like your beloved former pet. Are you ready to accept your new dog?

If you haven't had a Shih Tzu before but you just love the way they look, that's a good start. Much of her appeal is in her charming and unique appearance. But you still have to be prepared for the grooming requirements and the attention your Shih Tzu needs.

If you know a Shih Tzu but never owned one yourself, then you already know how the adults look and act. Just remember that an adult Shih Tzu is more likely to be calmer and less likely to cause mischief than a feisty little puppy. Your Shih Tzu puppy will take at least a couple of years to grow up, and you need to be patient.

Are you a homebody, a couch potato, or an amateur athlete?

People often love the look of the Shih Tzu but just don't realize how physically limited this breed is. Shih Tzu simply can't exercise too long, run very far, or even stay outside for extended periods in hot weather.

If you like to be at home, however, your Shih Tzu will be your happy and enthusiastic friend, companion, and armchair buddy. And if you want to *watch* sports, your Shih Tzu will be more than happy to help you cheer for your favorite team.

One exception is the competition Shih Tzu — some people train their dogs to compete in obedience (a highly competitive sport that measures how well a dog can follow commands) or agility (a super-active obstacle course sport), but these dogs are like professional athletes (check Chapter 17 for more info). If you want an exercise buddy, consider a sporting or herding breed instead.

Is your home Shih Tzu-friendly?

You may like the idea of a Shih Tzu, but if you aren't the only one in your home, you have to consider the environment as a whole. Is your home Shih-Tzu friendly? The following sections help answer this overall question.

Do you have young children?

Your two year old wouldn't intentionally hurt a flea, but a young child can't understand that a Shih Tzu isn't a stuffed animal. If you have very young children, think twice about getting a Shih Tzu.

Young children can be too rough on a puppy, and a Shih Tzu may even feel forced to nip or bite to defend herself from a child's harassment. If a puppy is dropped or fallen on, the puppy can be seriously injured. Even an older Shih Tzu can be injured by a child or may be less patient with a child's poking and prodding, although older Shih Tzu who're used to children are a much better bet as a companion to children.

Older kids, on the other hand, tend to be great and helpful companions to Shih Tzu — if they're taught how to handle the dog safely and gently. They can walk, groom, and play with the dog. (Check out Chapter 7 for more info on children and Shih Tzu.)

Do you have other pets?

Although the friendly Shih Tzu loves to hang with other dogs or cats, some other breeds aren't so dog-friendly. Some dog-aggressive terriers and guardian breeds can attack a Shih Tzu or mistake her for a prey animal. Or, a large dog may injure the Shih Tzu during innocent roughhousing.

However, some large dogs do well with small dogs and often defer to their leadership. You must know your big dog very well before taking that risk, and supervision is extremely important. Shih Tzu normally get along with other small dogs, especially other Shih Tzu, as long as the other dog is friendly, too. Even so, the bottom line is your Shih Tzu would rather spend time with you than anyone else.

Some Shih Tzu may chase small animals like ferrets, hamsters, rabbits, or birds. Others ignore these animals completely or try to make friends. Be sure your home situation is safe for your new Shih Tzu, as well as for your other pets before bringing a Shih Tzu home. (Refer to Chapter 7 for more info on Shih Tzu and other animals.)

Do you like to do hair?

This book contains many references to the Shih Tzu's significant grooming needs, and that's no accident. You really do need to spend time grooming your dog every day. Even if you cut the dog's coat short, it continues to grow. You really have to like doing hair (or be able to afford a professional groomer) to appreciate a Shih Tzu as a pet. Check out Chapter 10 for more on grooming.

Can you afford a Shih Tzu?

A Shih Tzu is such a little dog, but he does incur some big expenses. The average dog owner spends about $6,000 on a dog over the dog's lifetime (which can be anywhere from 12 to 18 years), including the cost of the dog, food, supplies, and standard veterinary care. If you factor in the Shih Tzu's longer-than-average life span, the cost of monthly grooming, and any additional vet care your Shih Tzu may need if he ever gets sick, you can go well over that figure.

Even an adopted older Shih Tzu can cost a lot in vet care and supplies. Consider the price of your time, too, because your Shih Tzu takes up a lot of it. Can you afford all that? If it simply isn't in the budget, perhaps you should wait awhile until you're in a better position to afford a dog.

Despite the expense, the emotional, psychological, and physical benefits of having a loving companion dog offset the financial costs of pet ownership. Experts say petting a dog actually lowers your blood pressure, and pet owners are generally healthier and live longer than people without pets. Considering how much you get back, you may realize that your Shih Tzu is worth every penny.

Chapter 2

To Know a Shih Tzu Is to Love a Shih Tzu

In This Chapter

- Taking a peek at the proper Shih Tzu look
- Comparing real Shih Tzu to the written breed standard
- Understanding the true Shih Tzu personality
- Appreciating Shih Tzu history from ancient Asia to today

You can call your Shih Tzu a dog, or you can be more specific and call him a member of the Toy Group of dogs, or you can just call him your baby (don't even pretend you don't call him that), but do you really know what makes him a *Shih Tzu?* Knowing a little more about exactly what a Shih Tzu is helps you better appreciate and care for your new best friend.

For instance, do you know what kind of coat a Shih Tzu is supposed to have? What color of eyes? What shape of ears? Do you know how she's supposed to move, how she's been bred to behave, and where she came from? There's so much to know, but never fear. This chapter helps you answer all these questions and more. You take a closer look at what the Shih Tzu is all about, because to really know your Shih Tzu is to really love her.

Picturing the Shih Tzu: How Your Dog Should Look

While you're gazing at your pup in admiration, you may be thinking "Wow, she's the most beautiful little dog I've ever seen," and I'm not going to argue with you. But does she look the way a Shih Tzu is supposed to look? Does she display a true breed type or that unique look that cries out: *Now that's a Shih Tzu!?*

Whether your Shih Tzu measures up to show-dog standards is irrelevant to how well she fulfills her function as a loyal and loving pet, but understanding the breed standard may help you appreciate your dog's beauty all the more (or make her so-called faults all the more endearing). She may not be perfect, but she's *yours.*

The next sections give you a clearer picture of why Shih Tzu look the way they do, how certain desirable qualities are passed along through family lines, and what the detailed description of the technically correct Shih Tzu are, according to the American Kennel Club (AKC) *breed standard* — the written description of the theoretically perfect Shih Tzu. You also discover how differently the Shih Tzu in England looks, so you can differentiate between the two, just in case you should ever meet a Shih Tzu from across the pond (they're pretty popular over there, too).

Considering pedigree

You may wonder why your Shih Tzu doesn't look like the Shih Tzu in that dog show on television or even the Shih Tzu you know down the street. Differences in *conformation* — the official term for the form, structure, and shape of a dog — have a lot to do with *pedigree,* which is your dog's ancestry or lineage. And that means they have a lot to do with breeding.

Different breeders have different breeding priorities, and although good breeders try to improve the Shih Tzu and stick to qualities considered appropriate for the Shih Tzu, every breeder differs, and every pedigree differs. A breeder may get a pup with a great quality, like a particularly gorgeous coat. In an effort to pass that trait to the next generation, the breeder may sacrifice perfection in other areas.

Plus, individual genetic lines tend to have differences, and individual breeders see things differently, too. Some focus more on health and temperament or on the Shih Tzu look they believe is correct, while others may focus on certain aspects they want to improve, such as coat texture, expression, head shape, the front or back, or movement. Some breeders may prefer a larger, sturdier dog while others may want to breed for smaller dogs. Dog breeding is more of an art than a science, so you just don't see identical dogs being churned out like they came from a factory (check out Chapter 3 for more on what makes a good breeder).

Good breeders are proud to show you a puppy's pedigree, which may include dogs who've achieved titles in dog shows or dog performance events. Breeders who won't show you the pedigree or don't keep track of pedigrees may not be breeding as carefully.

Ask questions about the pedigree, if you have them. The dogs in that lineage determine how your dog looks as well as your dog's health and even her temperament. Don't leave the breeder without getting this documentation! Keep the pedigree on file with your dog's other important papers. (For more info on the paperwork involved and what you may see in the pedigree, see Chapter 3.)

AKC breed standard

The breed standard is a written document that describes the ideal dog of a certain breed. The Shih Tzu breed standard describes an imaginary, perfect Shih Tzu, and this standard is what dog-show judges study to pick the dogs that best match the standard. Dog breeders also use the standard to guide their breeding programs to nudge each generation of puppies toward perfection.

Why do you need to know about the Shih Tzu breed standard? Frankly, you don't. But, you may want to know about it just to see how closely little Lola measures up. On the other hand, just because Samson doesn't have the right ear shape or his nose is a little long doesn't mean he isn't perfect in your eyes. So feel free to skip this section. Or you can stick with me if you're curious about the breed standard, but don't want to keep looking up dog breeder terminology, which official breed standards tend to use. If I say *topline* or *pastern* or *undershot bite,* I clearly explain them.

If you have aspirations to become a dog show breeder, look carefully at this section, as well as the officially worded breed standard, which you can find on the AKC Web site: `www.akc.org/breeds/shih_tzu/index.cfm`.

General appearance

The first thing the Shih Tzu breed standard talks about is general appearance (see Figure 2-1). The Shih Tzu is a Toy dog, which means he's small, but he's also sturdy and lively. The Shih Tzu is no quivering, delicate flower! He should look a tad arrogant, like a member of a palace household, and feel solid and heavy for his size.

Size, proportion, and substance

Shih Tzu should be 9 to 10½ inches tall when measured at the peak of the shoulder down to the ground. If you plan to show your dog, make sure that he isn't less than 8 inches tall or more than 11 inches tall. Shih Tzu can't be disqualified for height or weight, but the judge can consider a too-small or large Shih Tzu faulty.

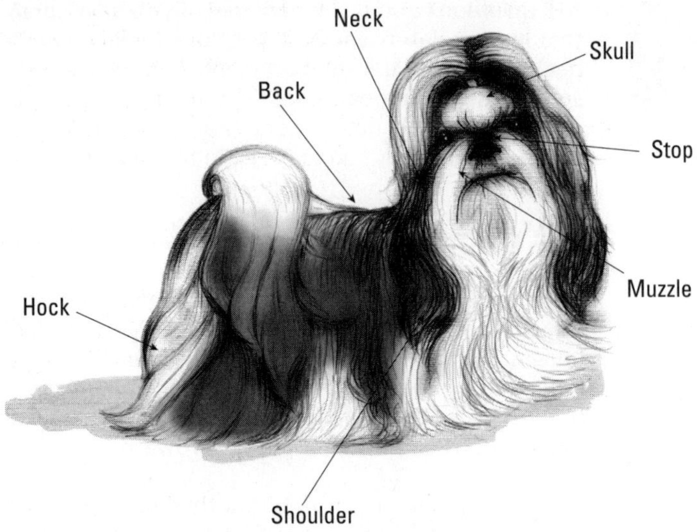

Figure 2-1: Highlights of the Shih Tzu breed standard.

Adult Shih Tzu typically weigh 9 to 16 pounds, and they should be slightly longer than tall. Shih Tzu aren't meant to be leggy. Instead, they should be compact and low without appearing squatty. You want your pup to look elegant and aristocratic, but regardless of size, he should always be compact and solid. Your Shih Tzu shouldn't look like he can blow away if a strong wind came along! (But he can stand in the wind, nose up, silky coat whipping dramatically around him, just to prove how gallant he is.)

Head

When you look at your Shih Tzu's head, you may just see the head of a Shih Tzu, but there's so much more involved in the judging of a Shih Tzu's head. For example:

- **Head:** The head should be round and broad with plenty of space between the eyes.
- **Expression:** Shih Tzu must have a characteristic sweet, warm expression that exudes friendly, affectionate warmth and trust.
- **Eyes:** The eyes should be large and round but not bulging. They shouldn't look ready to pop out of their sockets! The most desirable Shih Tzu eyes are very dark with open, friendly warmth. They'll be lighter on dogs with liver or blue coats.
- **Ears:** The Shih Tzu ears are large and set slightly below the crown, with plenty of long hair so the ears flow into the coat.

- **Skull:** The skull is domed with an obvious curve from skull to muzzle. There's a definite *stop,* which is the term for that place where the muzzle meets the head.
- **Nose:** Shih Tzu nostrils should be wide open for easy breathing, and all Shih Tzu should have a dark, black nose; black lips; and black eye rims; except on the liver and blue dogs. Pink noses, lips, and eye rims are considered faults.
- **Bite:** The Shih Tzu bite is *undershot,* meaning the top teeth fall behind the bottom teeth when the mouth is closed.

Some Shih Tzu tend to have crooked or missing teeth, and although that's technically not ideal, most judges don't consider it too problematic. However, the teeth and tongue shouldn't show when the mouth is closed and an *overshot* bite — the top teeth closing well in front of the bottom teeth, the way your teeth probably do — is a definite fault.

Neck, topline, body

The most important thing when looking at a Shih Tzu body — at least for a dog show judge or a breeder evaluating potential puppy parents — is that all the parts fit together in a balanced way. No one part should stand out. The neck should be long enough that the dog can look around easily and have a nice smooth line from head to tail. The *topline* (the line along the top of the back, when you look at it in profile) should be parallel to the ground, rather than sloping down or up toward the tail. The tummy shouldn't tuck up, but should flow smoothly from chest to abdomen, and the body should be just slightly longer than tall.

Shih Tzu have broad, deep chests, not barrel chests. They should have plenty of breathing room. The tail is set high on the back with a big fluffy plume of hair curled elegantly over the back. Low-set tails (tails placed down below the level of the spine) or droopy or flat tails don't look good in the show ring and can indicate that the dog isn't having a good time. A tail held proudly makes your Shih Tzu look great (and indicates that your dog's in a good mood).

Forequarters and hindquarters

Forequarters is the term referring to the front of the dog — the shoulders and front legs when you look at the dog face-to-face. The shoulders fit well into the dog with a nice deep angle so the dog can move easily. The legs should be straight and muscular with plenty of space between them for the broad chest, but the elbows should sit close into the body. The feet should be strong, nicely cushioned, and pointing straight ahead, not out or in. He needs a *front assembly* (another breeder term for the whole front end) that allows him to stand with sturdy confidence.

Hindquarters is the term for the back view of the dog, as you're facing his tail. The angles of the hips and rear legs as well as the feet should match the front, so the dog is balanced with strong muscular legs and plenty of sturdy bone.

Coat, color, and markings

The Shih Tzu coat is his most stunning and impressive feature. Luxurious and dense, straight or just slightly wavy, the coat has a thick undercoat beneath a longer overcoat. The hair on the head and ears is long and flowing and typically tied up on top of the head into a peppy little topknot. Thin, sparse coats are a fault, although females who haven't been spayed occasionally experience a thinning coat because of hormonal changes. (The Shih Tzu equivalent of PMS and a bad hair day all in one.)

Dog show exhibitors may neaten up the coat and trim the feet, rear end, and the very bottom of the coat, but too much trimming is considered a fault. The dog should look natural, not shaped like a Poodle. As for color and markings, Shih Tzu may be any color and any pattern with any markings. None of these are *technically* considered better or worse than any other, although the white and gold Shih Tzu is the most common and the most popular.

Gait

Gait refers to the way the Shih Tzu moves. He shouldn't race along or look like he has to be hauled around the dog show ring by the leash. The way he walks indicates not only how well he's put together but also his whole attitude. He should move on his own steam and with grace and power in a confident straight line. He shouldn't look like he's waddling or laboring to move. When he moves, the topline should stay parallel to the ground and his tail should stay gently swirled over his back — poetry in motion.

Temperament

If a Shih Tzu doesn't act like a lovable and adoring companion dog, calling him a Shih Tzu would be difficult. The attitude is what the dog's all about — his very essence.

Temperament matters (or should matter) just as much as coat or head shape or anything else in the show ring. Shih Tzu should be outgoing, happy, and trusting toward the judge. Your pup shouldn't act shy or withdrawn in the show ring (or at home or anywhere else, for that matter). A Shih Tzu should believe the world is a kind, friendly, and benevolent place where everybody loves him, and he should act accordingly.

What about Imperial Shih Tzu or Teacup Shih Tzu?

The Imperial Shih Tzu, also called the Teacup Shih Tzu, is a super-small version of a Shih Tzu. These names aren't official, and neither the AKC nor the American Shih Tzu Club (ASTC) recognize this so-called variety of Shih Tzu, but breeders who breed specifically for the small size claim that theirs is a legitimate type of Shih Tzu, even if the AKC doesn't recognize it.

Weighing in at just 3 to 6 pounds as adults (well below the official breed standard suggested weight of 9 to 16 pounds), these tiny dogs may look too cute to be controversial, but controversial they are. Some say they're runts of the litter and prone to major health problems, so they should cost less, not more, than a normal-sized Shih Tzu. Others say these tiny precious jewels are rare and special and just as likely to be perfectly healthy — and worth a premium price (I've seen them going for $3,000!). If you bring up the subject with Shih Tzu breeders on either side, you're likely to get an earful. However, if you want to be official about it, no breed club or official written standard existing today (at least, none I'm aware of) advocates these small Shih Tzu.

If you do decide to bring home an Imperial Shih Tzu or Teacup Shih Tzu, please be aware that you take on this size of dog at your own risk. Although your dog may be perfectly healthy and oh-so-adorable, you may end up spending a lot more money at the vet than you would with a normal-sized Shih Tzu. Also, dogs this small don't make a good match for homes with little kids, who can easily injure a small dog by mistake. And please, watch where you step! For more info on the AKC and ASTC, visit their respective Web sites: `www.akc.org` and `www.shihtzu.org`. To read the ASTC's position statement on Imperial Shih Tzu, look at `www.shihtzu.org/Info/imperial.asp?menu=Info`.

The Shih Tzu in England

The AKC categorizes the Shih Tzu as a Toy breed, but the United States is the only country that does. The Kennel Club of England groups the Shih Tzu with the Utility dogs — a group akin to what the AKC calls the Non-Sporting Group — such as the Boston Terrier, French Bulldog, Lhasa Apso, Miniature Schnauzer, and Poodles. The FCI — the organization most of the world other than the United States, Canada, and Great Britain adhere to when categorizing dog breeds — calls the Shih Tzu not only a Tibetan breed but also a Companion breed, rather than a Toy. (Even Canada considers the Shih Tzu a Non-Sporting rather than a Toy breed. Other countries may lump the Shih Tzu in with other larger, sturdier breeds because he's so heavy-boned and solid, instead of delicate like a tiny Yorkie or Maltese. Why do Americans have to be different? I guess it's just the American way.)

But much of the history of the Shih Tzu happened in England, so it's worth noting that Shih Tzu in England aren't only considered *Utility dogs* (meaning they have a *function* of some sort, although the breed standard doesn't specify what it is), but stand a tad taller and weigh a bit more than in the United States. Like any breed, Shih Tzu in England have gradually evolved to look slightly different, because of fashion and different genetic lines.

If you look at the Kennel Club of the United Kingdom's official breed standard (`www.thekennelclub.org.uk/item/174`), it allows for a slightly heavier, although not taller, dog at a height of not more than 27 centimeters (10½ inches) and about 4½ to 8 kilograms (about 10 to 18 pounds). The standard recommends an ideal weight of 4½ to 7½ kilograms, or 10 to 16 pounds. But in general, if you compared show dogs from both countries, the British dogs look a little bit bigger.

Other differences in the standard include

- A preference for a white *blaze* or white stripe of fur running down the forehead and between the eyes.
- A preference for a white tail tip in parti-colored dogs (parti-colored is a pattern of multi-colored patches). The AKC standard gives absolutely no official preference to any particular color or marking.
- A strongly recommended topknot, which isn't specifically recommended in the AKC standard.
- A reference to the word *short* when discussing the legs.
- A description of the Shih Tzu's face as chrysanthemum-like, an effect that comes from hair that grows upward on the nose.

How Shih Tzu Should Act: Personality

One of the Shih Tzu's most endearing qualities is his temperament. Shih Tzu have been bred for generations to be the ultimate companion dog, and this section looks more closely at why those magnetic personality traits make your Shih Tzu simply irresistible.

Hopelessly devoted to you

First and foremost, a Shih Tzu is devoted, wholly and completely, to you and your needs (check out Figure 2-2). Sure, sometimes he likes to play with a toy or romp around the living room, but you can't ask for a better listener, lap warmer, or sympathetic furry ear.

© Isabelle Francais

Figure 2-2: A cuddly Shih Tzu makes a great companion.

Your Shih Tzu can sit at your feet for hours gently snoozing, but he doesn't forget to occasionally gaze up at you in adoration. If you want a dog who does his own thing and only occasionally bothers to notice you, this breed may not be the one for you. But if you desire a pet who thinks it's all about *you,* then this is your dog.

No yip zone: The Shih Tzu's Zen-like tranquility

You've heard of those yappy little ankle-biting lap dogs, right? Well, the Shih Tzu isn't one of them. Calm and self-possessed, the Shih Tzu watches and waits. Sure, he may bark at the UPS guy when he comes right up to the door, but he's not bred to be a watchdog.

Your Shih Tzu is too focused on you to worry about anybody else who may be walking by outside, and if somebody else comes in the house, your Shih Tzu thinks it's obvious that this new friend has arrived for the sole purpose of petting and loving him. Sure, exceptions do exist, and you'll find some dogs who bark a lot, especially among dogs who were never properly socialized (check out Chapter 11 for more on socializing your Shih Tzu). Some people talk more than others, and some Shih Tzu bark more than others. But in general, this dog isn't yippy or suspicious.

"So this cat goes into a bar . . . ": Shih Tzu sense of humor

Part of being a good buddy is having a sense of humor, and your funny little Shih Tzu quickly discovers how to make you laugh. Whether he's flipping his stuffed mouse toy into the air and then spinning around to see where it landed, pretending to play fetch then darting just out of reach when you try to take back the ball, or gazing at you with an expression so serious and concerned that your bad mood dissolves completely, your Shih Tzu brightens your day and puts a smile on your face. Who can resist that?

Love the one you're with: The adaptable little dog

As devoted as Shih Tzu may be, they also adapt well to new owners. Don't be offended. It isn't that your Shih Tzu doesn't *worship you.* It's just that he loves everybody else, too. Anyone willing to feed, pet, groom, and love a Shih Tzu becomes that dog's new best friend.

This factor in their behavior makes considering an older Shih Tzu for adoption an excellent decision. Shih Tzu don't waste away pining for a former owner and ignore you. And an older dog may already be housetrained (not a bad bonus, eh?). If you have a warm lap and a treat to share, your Shih Tzu will adapt just to his new home. (For more info on adopting an older Shih Tzu, see Chapter 4.)

My crown, please: The Shih Tzu's natural arrogance

How can something so little and sweet also be so high and mighty? If your ancestors lived in the Imperial palace, you'd have a pretty healthy self-concept, too. The Shih Tzu reveals his natural arrogance in the way he stands, moves, and looks around with his flat little nose in the air. He may even look down his nose at someone he isn't quite sure deserves his attention — but probably not too often. Consider him a benevolent king.

And don't worry if you're not ancestry. Your Shih Tzu doesn't mind. He loves you just the same, and he's royal enough for both of you — he just has to show you who runs the castle once in awhile.

Looking Back at the Shih Tzu's History

Your dog may be all-American (or all-British, or all-Canadian, as the case may be), but her ancestors came from the far-away East. Discovering her past can be fun and interesting. You may look at your dog staring meditatively out the window and wonder, "Where *did* you come from?" In this section, I take a step back in time to show you where the Shih Tzu's relatives came from, starting way back in ancient Tibet. Also you can discover how the Shih Tzu came to the Western world and how today's Shih Tzu evolved.

This section is a no-yawning zone. The Shih Tzu history is fun, not like a boring high school history lecture on the Middle Ages, so stick with me, just for kicks (or don't, if dog lore really isn't your thing — I'm not going to make you read it!).

Ancient Shih Tzu: Tibet versus China

Ask Shih Tzu historians (yes, they exist) where the Shih Tzu originated, and you may get different answers. Not everybody agrees whether the Shih Tzu came from Tibet or China or even the Mediterranean. Most concede that dogs related to the modern-day Shih Tzu probably came from Tibet, but how long they were there and how much influence they had on the present-day Shih Tzu, may never be known. Some say that Tibetan dogs, given to Chinese royalty as gifts, were bred with Chinese dogs like Pekingese and Pugs, to create the Shih Tzu. Others suspect the Shih Tzu is a Tibetan original, not a Pekingese descendant.

I'm not going to get in the middle of that argument (dog historians tend to have very strong opinions!), so I'll just say that the Shih Tzu's ancestors *probably* came from Tibet, but the dog of today was *mostly* developed in China.

Lion-hearted

Shih Tzu means *lion,* and in both Tibet and pre-Communist China, the lion was a symbol of Buddhism. The Tibetan lamas supposedly bred their dogs to look like little lions; these dogs lived in the temples and were considered holy. In China, the *lion dog* was primarily a companion to royalty, but royal breeding programs continued to breed for the look of the lion.

You can see this influence in several other small Asian breeds from Buddhist countries, including the Lhasa Apso, the Tibetan Spaniel, the Japanese Chin, and the Pekingese. All have long flowing coats, flat faces, big dark eyes, and the sturdy bone structures one may expect from a miniature lion. Resemblances aside, Shih Tzu fans generally prefer to think that the Shih Tzu is the *original* lion dog.

The Shih Tzu's popularity in China

Back in the day, before dog shows, breeds didn't exactly have set names or breed standards. Dogs were often crossed or bred according to unknown goals, and the Shih Tzu type wasn't set for many centuries. Small long-coated dogs were a matter of fashion.

Depending on the emperor at the time, the look and style of these small dogs often changed. Sometimes the very small ones, called *sleeve dogs,* were fashionable, and at other times, larger shaggier dogs were more in favor and often bred to have particular markings. Some years, everybody loved the black Shih Tzu. Some years, the white. You know how fashion goes. One day you're in, the next you're out.

So even though you can't know precisely when the Shih Tzu became the Shih Tzu, you can be sure that *your* Shih Tzu (or the Shih Tzu you plan to bring home) has Chinese dogs somewhere in her bloodlines, and her ancestors really were very trendy in their time.

Dictator Dowager and her love for the Shih Tzu

Nobody embraced the quest for the perfect Shih Tzu more heartily than the Dowager Empress T'zu Hsi, who ruled China from the mid-19th century until her death in 1908. You can probably call her the great grandmother of the Shih Tzu because she's the first one to breed Shih Tzu with precision and purpose — or at least, the first one on record. Her vast kennels of Pekingese, Pugs, and Shih Tzu refined and cemented the type for these three Chinese breeds.

The Dowager Empress may not have been the most benevolent of dictators — in fact, history suggests that she was heartlessly ruthless — but she definitely loved her dogs, and her palace eunuchs made great strides in creating the modern Shih Tzu.

When the Empress died, however, the royal kennels fell apart. Dogs were sold or given away, and during the next few decades, fanciers in China bred the little lion dogs, showed them in dog shows under a variety of names, and exported some to the West. The Shih Tzu became a commoner! (And it's a good thing, too, because when communism came to China, dog breeding was abolished and the lion dog became, for all practical purposes, extinct in its native land.)

Go West, young Shih Tzu!

Dogs imported to other countries and regions as gifts during the 19th century and early 20th century kept the breed alive. Actually, all the Shih Tzu in the United States today came from just a few dogs rescued from China. By the middle of the 20th century, Shih Tzu were here to stay, having totally charmed the Western world.

The first dogs arrive in the United States

The first Shih Tzu imported into the States from England in 1938 were two females named Ding-Ling of the Mynd and Wuffles of the Mynd. More followed, but at the time they weren't distinguished from Lhasa Apsos and the AKC, who probably figured that all long-haired small dogs of Tibetan ancestry were the same, considered them Lhasa Apsos. In fact, well into the 20th century, the name still wasn't set. People called the Shih Tzu all kinds of names including Lhasa Lion Dog, Tibetan Poodle, and Lhasa Terrier.

In 1955, after breeders spent a lot of energy trying to convince the AKC that the Shih Tzu had a following (and was *different* than a Lhasa Apso), the AKC accepted the Shih Tzu as a distinct breed in the *Miscellaneous Class* — the step before final recognition as part of one of the AKC's seven groups of dogs. The Shih Tzu was official . . . sort of. But dogs in the Miscellaneous Class can't compete in dog shows, so the Shih Tzu had one more hurdle to overcome — full and total AKC recognition.

The American Shih Tzu Club is created

The American Shih Tzu Club (ASTC) formed in 1963 to promote the breed more actively. The club members wanted to show off their beautiful little lion dogs in the dog show ring! They approached the AKC relentlessly and followed all the rules and waded through the necessary red tape in an attempt to get official and full recognition. But one big problem remained: Someone crossed a Pekingese into the Shih Tzu in England in 1952, and the AKC required three generations of pure, unadulterated Shih Tzu breeding to accept the Shih Tzu as a full-fledged member of the AKC's Toy Group.

The AKC finally completely accepts the Shih Tzu

Popularity has its perks. The Shih Tzu got so popular so fast that nobody could stop its momentum and in 1969, the AKC finally accepted the Shih Tzu into the Toy Group. On the very first day the Shih Tzu was officially recognized, a little Shih Tzu named Canadian Champion Chumulari Ying-Ying won Best in Show at the New Brunswick Kennel Club, and Shih Tzu immediately swept the dog-show circuit, picking up Best Toy and Best in Show wins right and left. The Shih Tzu has remained a beloved and popular dog show competitor ever since.

Shih Tzu today

By the 1980s, the Shih Tzu had skyrocketed in popularity. Today, the Shih Tzu is the ninth most popular breed in the United States, according to the AKC, with more than 28,000 Shih Tzu registered — a pretty impressive journey from near-extinction.

Today, Shih Tzu owners in countries all over the world breed, show, and love the Shih Tzu. But the breed has had some problems. One of the downsides of popularity is overbreeding. People concerned more with profit than with health or temperament produced huge numbers of Shih Tzu throughout the second half of the 20th century, and many suffered health problems like renal dysplasia, liver disease, eye problems, skin problems, and allergies (for more on common Shih Tzu health problems, see Chapter 13), because breeders weren't paying attention to these health issues when making breeding choices. They were more concerned with volume. Another sad aftermath of this popularity was impulse buying, buyer's remorse, and abandonment, with many Shih Tzu ending up in shelters and rescue groups (believe it or not, that still happens today!). Some Shih Tzu developed bad temperaments — either aggressive or super-shy — probably from a combination of bad breeding and lack of proper socialization and training.

But the news isn't all bad. Shih Tzu remain incredibly popular, despite the fact that they need a lot of care and grooming. Why? Just look at that adorable face. Shih Tzu may not live in the imperial palace anymore, but they've been bred for centuries to be caring, affectionate, amusing, and endearing little companions with melt-your-heart eyes and heart-stopping beauty . . . and they still are. Many thousands of pet owners have brought Shih Tzu into their homes and given these little dogs long, happy, healthy lives full of mutual adoration. Shih Tzu have come a long way to be your companion, and aren't you glad?

Chapter 3

What You Need to Know Before You Buy or Adopt a Shih Tzu

In This Chapter

- Understanding why hobby breeders are the best source of good dogs
- Recognizing and finding the best breeders
- Considering an older or rescued Shih Tzu

Are you feeling confident that a Shih Tzu is the right breed for you? If so, the next step is to find one. But where do you look? Finding a Shih Tzu may seem pretty easy. The pet stores have them. The newspaper lists some. Maybe your neighbor even has a litter of puppies. But wait! I'm sure you're very excited to start your search, but before you open the newspaper to the classifieds section or run down to your local pet store, take the time to read this chapter.

You want your new Shih Tzu to be healthy and well adjusted, right? You want him to be friendly and cuddly, don't you? The best way to find a healthy dog is to start with a hobby breeder. Hobby breeders have the breed's best interest in mind. They breed carefully, selecting the healthiest dogs that are truest to the breed's qualities. They keep a close eye on the puppies that they produce and make a sincere effort to find the very best homes for each one. Plus, hobby breeders remain a helpful and interested resource throughout your dog's life. You won't get that kind of service, or dogs bred with such knowledge, love, and care, from inexperienced or accidental breeders, or (in most cases) from pet stores, no matter how well-meaning they may be.

I spend most of this chapter sharing what you need to know about hobby breeders, including what they do and how to find a reputable one. I also talk about how great it is to find a Shih Tzu at a shelter or in a breed rescue group, and give that Shih Tzu a second chance at a happy life.

How much is that doggie in the window?

How can you resist that roly-poly cuteness staring back at you through the thick glass? The answer is, you can't — or at least, that's what pet stores are banking on. Pet shops continue to do so well selling puppies, even at steep prices, because they play off your need for instant gratification.

If you buy a Shih Tzu puppy from a pet store, you may end up with a wonderful, healthy dog, as long as you're willing to follow through and do what it takes — training classes, daily grooming, vet visits, and so on — to take care of that puppy forever. On the other hand, that puppy may also develop some of the common genetic or other health issues that good hobby breeders work so hard to avoid in their breeding programs. Social issues may also exist because the puppy has been taken away from his mother and littermates too soon.

Where you buy a Shih Tzu puppy is, of course, your choice, but I want you to realize what comes with that high price tag. The following are just a couple of the risks you need to consider:

- **The puppy's secret, unknown past:** Many pet store dogs come from commercial breeders who breed large numbers of puppies for profit. This isn't a good start in life for a tiny, sensitive little toy dog. Behaviorists assert that the earliest weeks in a puppy's life are crucial for healthy behavior. How do you know what your pet store puppy's early weeks were like? Did he spend them getting shipped in a truck? Was he taken away from his mother too soon? Did he get the right kind of exposure to humans? With a pet store pup, you can't know for sure.
- **Potential health issues:** Large commercial breeders rarely do health tests or breed with health in mind. They breed for numbers, and for profit. Some do health tests, but because you can't see the parents of a pet store puppy, you can't know the genetic problems in his pedigree, or what diseases and other problems he's most at risk for developing. Without this info, it's anybody's guess what genetic fate may be in store for your new pup.
- **Looks aren't everything:** Not being able to see the parents matters not only for health reasons but also for behavior and appearances. You don't have as clear a picture of how your puppy may look and behave when he grows up, if you can't see the parents. Many pet store pups look awfully cute but grow up to be strange or 'off' examples of the breed. If you want to be sure your Shih Tzu looks like a Shih Tzu as an adult, reconsider the pet store impulse buy.

If you already have a Shih Tzu, well, frankly, you don't have to read this chapter. You can skip to Chapter 5 (or whatever chapter covers your current concerns). If you already have a Shih Tzu that you purchased from a pet store, a classified ad, or that neighbor with all those puppies, don't worry. Your Shih Tzu should be a wonderful, happy pet if he receives plenty of socialization, love, and care from you. But if you haven't made that big decision yet, stick with me. I help you make the best possible choice.

Understanding How Breeders Differ

Being popular has a downside. Some people use the Shih Tzu's must-have status as a way to make a quick buck, breeding Shih Tzu for profit and without regard to health or temperament. Some large for-profit breeding operations supply pet stores with their dogs, and these dogs sure are cute. But were they bred to look like Shih Tzu? Were they tested for genetic problems? Were they well socialized in the whelping box? How soon were they taken away from their mothers? What did their parents look like? A small hobby breeder can answer these questions for you, but in most cases, a pet store can't.

For-profit breeder, inexperienced breeder, accidental breeder, whichever — the result probably isn't what you had in mind when you pictured your perfect little portable pet, is it? That's why you and your potential pet benefit immensely from knowing how to pick out an experienced, knowledgeable *hobby breeder* — small noncommercial breeders who breed Shih Tzu because they love and care about the breed. (Check out the next section for more info on how to identify a reputable hobby breeder.)

Even those dogs bred by well-meaning folks who haven't really studied dog breeding, genetics, or the best ways to socialize young puppies, can turn out to have serious genetic problems or temperament issues. As for your neighbor and that accidental (or planned "so the kids can experience the miracle of birth") litters of puppies, those dogs need a home, and they may be just fine. But again, you don't enjoy the many benefits you get from an experienced hobby breeder.

Recognizing Good Hobby Breeders

Reputable and ethical hobby breeders devote their lives to producing better, healthier, more beautiful Shih Tzu. They pay close attention to each puppy, handling and socializing them from birth. Good breeders don't just breed puppies. They try to improve the breed by making each generation a little better. They pick out the right dogs for the show ring, the right dogs for families who are more active, and the right dogs for families with kids, for singles, and for seniors. They can help you pick just the perfect jewel for you and your family. They're *the* Shih Tzu experts.

A great way to identify a hobby breeder: His extracurricular activities

Ask your breeder about his or her extracurricular Shih Tzu activities, like being involved in clubs and dog shows. The following are some extracurricular activities a hobby breeder may be involved in:

- **Breed clubs:** A good sign of a hobby breeder is that he or she belongs to a local or national dog club where breeders and pet owners share info, take advantage of resources and networking, and build Shih Tzu camaraderie. Examples include the American Shih Tzu Club, a local Shih Tzu club, or an all-breed show or training club. Many of these clubs require that breeder members sign a code of ethics specifying good breeding practices.
- **Dog shows:** If a breeder participates in dog shows, she's working to improve the breed (or at least it's a good sign of that fact). If the breeder doesn't ever show her dogs, she may be into breeding for the money instead of the good health and temperament of the breed.
- **Competitive obedience and dog sports:** Shih Tzu like to have fun, and dog sports give them that chance. Breeders who participate in competitive obedience and other dog sports, such as agility, want their dogs to be versatile — both beautiful *and* smart.
- **Dog therapy:** A Shih Tzu can melt your heart just by looking at you, and some particularly gentle and intuitive Shih Tzu make excellent therapy dogs. Therapy dogs go through a training program with their owners to teach them appropriate behavior in a variety of settings. After both dog and owner pass the course, they can visit people in need of a warm puppy to pet, such as hospitalized children, home-bound seniors, psychiatric patients, people living in retirement centers, and children with terminal illnesses.

  If the hobby breeder you're considering has certified therapy dogs, you can bet she's committed to making a positive difference in the world (and probably has dogs with wonderful temperaments). For more details on getting involved in a therapy dog program, see Chapter 17.

How do you identify a reputable hobby breeder? Good breeders have a few important qualities in common. Good hobby breeders:

- **Pay attention to health and genetics issues:** Good hobby breeders study Shih Tzu physical and mental health. They know the health issues that are typical of the breed, and they work to weed them out of their dog's genetic lines. (For more information on specific Shih Tzu health issues, see Chapter 13.)

- **Want to know all about you:** Some breeders require visits to your home, and practically all good breeders require meeting every single family member, especially the kids. Breeders want to know where you plan to keep the dog, how often you're home, and make sure that you understand the grooming requirements.
- **Show you their digs:** Good hobby breeders breed their puppies indoors where they can safely care for and attend to the puppies, and they'll show you. Shih Tzu aren't kennel dogs!
- **Offer follow-up care:** Good breeders offer you follow-up care after you've taken your little bundle of joy home. If the dog won't stop crying or you can't figure out the best way to groom him, or you wonder why he won't eat his food, you can call the breeder and she'll help you. A problem you may not have a clue how to solve may be, to your breeder, an easy fix.
- **Provide appropriate documentation:** A good breeder provides you with the puppy's *pedigree* (his family tree), medical records including vaccinations, and the paperwork necessary to register your dog with the American Kennel Club (AKC) or United Kennel Club (UKC). Also, a good breeder provides a health guarantee and a contract. (Check out Chapter 4 for more info on the necessary paperwork.)
- **Maintain a waiting list:** The best breeders with the best reputations often have waiting lists because they breed for quality, not quantity. I know you want your puppy *now,* but a great dog is worth the wait.
- **Do more than just breed:** Good breeders almost always show their dogs in conformation dog shows or obedience. Check out the nearby sidebar, "A great way to identify a hobby breeder: His extracurricular activities" for more info.
- **Don't breed for the money:** Hobby breeders rarely, if ever, make a profit from breeding dogs. They do what they do out of passion for the breed and for a hobby, not because it's a business.

The classified ads: Shih Tzu for sale

You're in the market for a new dog, and every week you see a smorgasbord of Shih Tzu listed for sale in the classifieds, either online or in your daily newspaper. Does that mean that these are good sources? Not necessarily. Most reputable hobby breeders don't advertise in the paper because they have more than enough buyers for their carefully planned litters.

Sometimes, you can find a good puppy through the newspaper, but don't act on impulse. Evaluate breeders who advertise in the newspaper exactly like you would evaluate any breeder. (See the section "Recognizing Good Hobby Breeders" in this chapter for more info.)

If the newspaper says "Free to Good Home," just remember: Free puppies often end up costing even more than expensive puppies from good breeders because of health and/or temperament problems. That dog is free for a reason.

Searching for a Good Breeder

Although you have many options in finding your new Shih Tzu, including a pet store (check out the nearby sidebar, "How much is that doggie in the window?"), from the classifieds (check out the nearby sidebar, "The classified ads: Shih Tzu for sale"), and from auctions and flea markets (refer to the nearby sidebar, "Going once, going twice: Auctions and flea markets"), a hobby breeder is still your safest bet.

If you're serious about using a good hobby breeder, you may be wondering where on earth you find these wonderful hobby breeders. Well, you've come to the right section. Start with the following useful resources that can point you in the right direction:

- **The American Shih Tzu Club (ASTC):** The American Kennel Club (AKC) recognizes this club as the national guardians of the Shih Tzu. Many of the best hobby breeders are members, and they have a breeder referral committee. You can find a list of the current members on the Web site (`www.shitzu.org`) with contact information. Under the ASTC menu, click *Breeder Referral Committee.*
- **Dog shows:** These shows are great places to meet good breeders in person and see how the adult dogs look. Find nearby dog shows on the AKC Web site: `www.akc.org`. Go to the *Events* tab and click *Events and Awards Search.*

- **Dog clubs:** The AKC can refer you to local and national Shih Tzu and all-breed dog clubs, many of which keep lists of good hobby breeders. Join a local club and you may also make some great friends who love Shih Tzu as much as you do. To find this info, head to `www.akc.org`; then click *Clubs*.
- **Phone a friend:** Ask for a reference from someone you trust who's bought a Shih Tzu. If she found a good breeder and had a great experience, she'll probably be glad to share that info.

If you want to find a good Shih Tzu breeder, you may consider searching online. However, if you do, you'll get a lot of for-profit breeders and breeders with less experience along with the good ones, and the best breeders in your area may or may not have Web sites. In other words, search online if you want, but don't rely solely on an Internet search to find a good breeder. Dog clubs can usually give you more reliable, and more local, info than the Internet, or at least help you narrow down your list.

After you've found a hobby breeder (or two or three) you want to visit, don't just dive right in and snatch up the first puppy you see. Take your time and be selective. This section arms you with important pointers to remember when investigating breeders.

Ask the appropriate questions

When you first contact a breeder on the phone, a few pointed questions can reveal a ton of information. You may already have some questions in mind, but here are some others that can reveal much about a breeder's quality. Ask the breeder these questions before you even make a visit.

- **Do you specialize in Shih Tzu?** You want a breeder who breeds Shih Tzu, not seven different kinds of dogs that happen to be the most popular. If the breeder answers yes, ask some more in-depth questions:
    - **How often do you breed a litter?** Good hobby breeders usually don't breed more than a litter every year, or even less often. Commercial and for-profit breeders have puppies available all the time, and may breed six, seven, eight, or more litters per year.
    - **How long have you been breeding Shih Tzu?** New breeders can be great, but people who have been breeding Shih Tzu for a long time probably have a lot more knowledge and experience. The puppies may be healthier and better pets because of that experience.

- **Are you a member of the national or local club?** This question indicates a commitment to learning about Shih Tzu and breeding in an organized and ethical fashion.
- **Do you show your dogs? If so, how many dogs of your breeding are champions?** Breeders who show and whose dogs win championships are likely producing excellent pets, too. If your puppy's parents are both champions, that's a good sign you're working with someone who really understands the breed, and how Shih Tzu look and act.
- **Where do you raise the puppies?** Shih Tzu aren't kennel dogs, and good breeders raise them inside a warm house, often in a box in the kitchen or the living room so they can be part of the family from the very start.
- **Can I come out to see the litter or the parents of the litter?** Expect the breeder to want to meet you and interview you, so the answer, of course, should be yes. If the breeder doesn't want to let you see the parents, consider that a red flag. The parents may not look or act the way a Shih Tzu should. Many breeders don't have the father on the premises but you should be able to see the mother, and at least see a picture of the father and his pedigree.

  Also, some breeders ship Shih Tzu puppies, and on occasion, with reputable breeders and older puppies, doing so may work. However, as a general rule, this isn't a good idea for the heat-intolerant and sensitive Shih Tzu, particularly when he's young or very small. The plane trip can be not only physically difficult for the puppy, subjecting him to jostling and extreme temperatures, but also could be frightening. The traumatic experience can cause future behavior problems, such as separation anxiety or fearfulness (for more on Shih Tzu behavior issues, see Chapter 11).
- **When will you have puppies available?** Because good hobby breeders don't breed constantly, they often don't have puppies available. When you find a breeder you feel good about, get on a waiting list. You can ask for a referral to another breeder who may have puppies right now. However, doing so makes you look impatient, so be careful how you approach this subject. If you seem primed to make an impulse purchase — you want a Shih Tzu and you want her *now* — the breeder won't want to refer you to *anybody.* Breeders who truly care about Shih Tzu won't want impulsive types to snap up — and possibly later regret — a Shih Tzu.

Asking about price before meeting in person makes a bad impression. Breeders think you're only interested in a good deal, instead of a good dog. Save that question for when you pay a visit.

Going once, going twice: Auctions and flea markets

You may have seen a Shih Tzu sold at a dog auctions that sell to pet stores and others, at a flea market with boxes of dogs next to the bric-a-brac, and even out in front of the grocery store. However, as adorable as these puppies may look, these are some of the worst sources for dogs. These dogs often have serious health problems and are usually taken away from their mothers too early, which many animal behaviorists believe has serious consequences for the puppy's future behavior. These puppies don't normally receive good healthcare or socialization, don't come with any health guarantees, and after you buy, the seller is usually long gone. You could be in for a host of problems.

It may seem almost impossible to avoid "saving" a puppy from a situation like this, if you happen to encounter it. I understand that impulse, I really do. But remember, you're taking a big risk buying a puppy from this kind of source.

Pay a Visit

After you make initial contact with a few breeders, pay a visit either to meet the parents of the litter-to-be or to visit the puppies. In most cases, you won't bring home a puppy on this first visit. This visit is a get-to-know-each-other trip. (Just keep telling yourself that instant gratification isn't a good thing!)

The breeder should be happy to give you a tour and show you how he cares for the dogs. In that tour, make sure that you see where the dogs are kept and that the breeder is up-front about the conditions. Before you actually think of selecting a dog, look around, pay attention, and get to know the breeder as well as the dogs.

Be inquisitive

When you meet the breeder, expect him to ask you a lot of questions about you, your home, and your situation. The breeder wants to make sure you'll make a good and suitable guardian of his precious puppies. You should ask the breeder some questions, too. Don't agree to a puppy purchase until you find out the following info:

- **What should I know about Shih Tzu before deciding this breed is for me?** Even if you've already read all about Shih Tzu and have a good idea of the answer, it can be enlightening to see what the breeder says. A breeder who emphasizes the challenges, such as the amount of grooming required, housetraining, and some of the health issues, may be more honest than a breeder who has nothing but reports of how easy and perfect Shih Tzu are. Shih Tzu are awesome, make no mistake — but no breed is effortless, and a good breeder wants to weed out pet owners who won't be a good match.

- **When you breed, are you trying to produce any particular traits?** You want a breeder who is working for better health and behavior as the most important priorities. However, keep in mind that dog show breeders are also working toward a Shih Tzu that not only acts but also *looks* perfect, so these breeders may be specifically focused on issues in their own lines — a nicer coat texture, a more appropriate head shape, a better front-end, or various other appearance-related concerns. This is fine, as long as health and behavior come first. An answer you don't want to hear: "Larger litter sizes." Or "What do you mean?"
- **Are there any health-related issues or concerns in your dogs? What health problems and genetic issues have you encountered in your experience?** If a breeder tells you that his dogs have never had any health problems, he doesn't test because his Shih Tzu are healthy, or he doesn't know what you're talking about, tuck *your* tail and run the other way. Consider these statements *huge* red flags and keep looking for a more reputable breeder who is honest with you about the perfectly normal occurrence of certain health issues in his breeding program.
- **Can I see the vaccination records and any records of any veterinary care the puppies have had so far?** The breeder should be happy to share this info with you.
- **What guarantees do you offer? If so, under what circumstances do they apply?** Reputable breeders usually have a contract that includes some sort of health guarantee, to protect the dog, you, and the breeder. Make sure you understand exactly what you're signing and what your rights are, as well as what the breeder expects of *you.* If the breeder doesn't require any kind of contract and doesn't guarantee anything, keep looking.
- **Do you have references?** Your breeder should be proud to give you names and numbers of others who know him and have had good experiences. Check the references. You never know what you may hear when someone speaks to you confidentially.
- **Are you available for follow-up if I have questions in the future?** A good breeder wants to be available to you throughout the puppy's life to ensure all his dogs thrive.

- **If for some reason I ever have to give up the dog, can I return him to you?** If the breeder thinks you have any intention at the outset of not sticking with the dog through thick and thin, he probably won't want to sell you one of his puppies. On the other hand, if unforeseeable circumstances happen and giving up the dog is a necessity, a good breeder wants you to bring back the dog instead of taking it to an animal shelter. The contract often states that you *must* return the dog to the breeder if you ever have to give it up.
- **What do you do to socialize the puppies?** Responsible breeders already have a plan for handling and socializing puppies from the very beginning of life, to help those pups become accustomed to gentle human handling.
- **How soon do you let puppies go home?** Puppies need to stay with their mother and littermates for at least eight weeks, but many breeders prefer keeping smaller breeds, including Shih Tzu, until 12 or even 16 weeks. That's a sign the breeder cares (even if you want to take home that puppy *now*).
- **Do you have any questions for me?** Responsible breeders have plenty. You probably won't even have to ask. (Check out the "Expect to be grilled" section later in this chapter for more on what the breeder may ask you.)

Be observant

You can talk to the breeder until you're blue in the face, but sometimes, a little silent observation is equally informative. When you visit the breeder, pay attention! This is the time to notice everything you can about the breeder, the home, and the dogs. Do you get a good feeling from the breeder? Does he or she seem trustworthy and forthcoming? Is the home clean and well cared-for? Are the dogs healthy, friendly, and clean?

If you spot or smell diarrhea or vomit anywhere in the kennel, don't just assume the breeder has a problem. Ask about it, or let the breeder know. Puppies poop a lot, and sometimes they have stomach distress. Or, maybe an individual dog has a problem and the breeder already knows about it. But if it looks like the dogs are generally sickly, excuse yourself politely and move on!

If a breeder only brings you puppies from another room and won't let you see where they're kept, he may have something to hide. Likewise if you see a mess, poor housing, or a mommy dog with a bad look or temperament, these conditions are also indications of poorly raised dogs. Ask about anything you think seems strange or suspicious. The breeder may not want your germs around the puppies, but you really need to get a feel for the conditions so you can feel good about the health of the dogs.

Meet the parents

At the very least, you need to meet the mother of the litter and preferably the father, too. If the breeder doesn't have the father — very often, the father comes from another breeder and lives elsewhere — ask for pictures or even a video of that dog. The breeder should be able to show you the father's pedigree and health documents, too. You can also ask the breeder for the name and phone number of the father's owner to arrange your own visit or at least a phone conversation (sometimes the father lives far away).

Meeting the parents lets you know how the puppies may grow up to look and act. If either parent doesn't look like a Shih Tzu and/or has a bad temperament, those flags can also indicate a less-than-ideal situation to avoid.

Expect to be grilled

A hobby breeder spends most of her time gently nurturing puppies brought into the world but only after careful study, research, and consideration about how best to improve the breed. Those puppies, softly handled, cooed at, coaxed to accept humans as kind gentle beings, gently groomed, played with, and adored, are like children to the caring hobby breeder. Do you really think that she's going to let her puppy go to just anybody?

When searching for a reputable hobby breeder, the breeder may have tons of questions. She isn't being rude or intrusive by asking. Her job is to ensure that her beloved little Shih Tzu pups go to only the very best possible home. The following are the types of questions you can expect a breeder to ask:

- **What's your dog experience?** The breeder wants to know how many dogs you've had in the past, whether any of them were Shih Tzu or similar breeds (like other toy breeds or breeds with significant grooming needs), and what happened to the dogs you had before.
- **How familiar are you with the Shih Tzu breed?** You want to be sure the breeder knows her subject, but she wants to be sure you know yours. Have you looked into the breed before rushing out to buy?
- **Do you have other pets?** Shih Tzu get along well with most other pets, but some other pets won't get along well with a Shih Tzu. The breeder wants to make sure the puppy will be safe, and also that you have enough time, space, and resources to add a Shih Tzu to your menagerie.

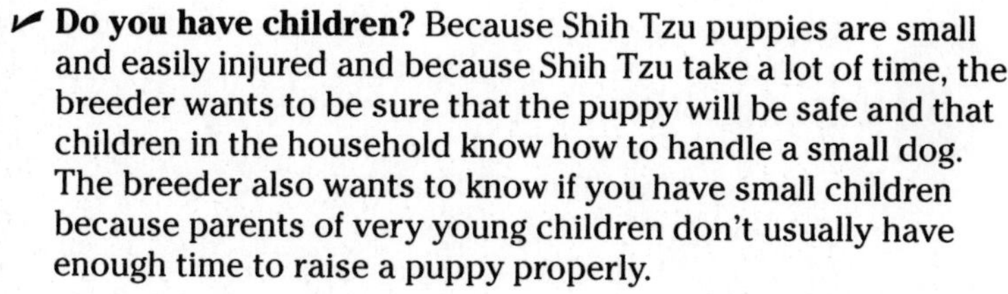

- **Do you have children?** Because Shih Tzu puppies are small and easily injured and because Shih Tzu take a lot of time, the breeder wants to be sure that the puppy will be safe and that children in the household know how to handle a small dog. The breeder also wants to know if you have small children because parents of very young children don't usually have enough time to raise a puppy properly.

  Some Shih Tzu breeders won't sell a puppy to families with young children. Don't be offended — the breeder is just doing what she feels is right for her dogs.

- **Where will you keep the dog?** Shih Tzu must be kept inside, and the breeder needs to be sure you're prepared for this.
- **How often are you home?** What good is a companion dog to someone who never needs a companion? The breeder doesn't want to send her precious puppies to a house that's empty.
- **Are you willing to do the necessary grooming?** The breeder needs to know that you're willing to do and/or pay for the grooming necessary to keep your Shih Tzu puppy healthy and comfortable. (For more on grooming, see Chapter 10.)
- **Do you plan to show the dog?** The breeder handles the sale of a show dog much differently than the sale of a pet dog. The breeder may want to retain co-ownership (this is fairly common) and may be willing to mentor you in this competitive and interesting world. If you want to show and potentially breed a Shih Tzu, the breeder has to make sure that you're able to do this the right way, with plenty of knowledge and guidance, so you aren't bringing unwanted or unhealthy Shih Tzu into the world. Otherwise, she'll prefer you to have a spayed or neutered pet Shih Tzu instead of a show dog.
- **What's your vet's name and phone number?** Your breeder should be willing to share her own vet's name and number with you, and you need to do the same. Your vet can assure the breeder that you're a good pet owner.

Be cautious if a breeder is eager to send a pup home with you as soon as possible without asking any questions. That's a sign of a breeder who may not have the dog's best interests in mind.

Talk about price and other costs

Buying a Shih Tzu pup from a breeder isn't cheap. In fact, it can run on average anywhere from \$500 to more than \$2000, depending on the breeder, the dog, and the area of the country.

Consider not only the price of the dog but also the cost of other aspects of having a puppy, such as veterinary care, vaccinations, food, grooming, pet supplies, training classes, and the time you'll spend raising, training, caring for, and grooming the dog. Dogs cost a lot, especially if they have heavy grooming needs (like the Shih Tzu does) or health problems. Older dogs need more vet care and often need treatment for age-related diseases, so the costs keep coming. When visiting the breeder, also ask her about the cost of registering the puppy with the AKC and how to do that. (For more on registration and paperwork, see Chapter 4.)

The point of talking about price and other costs is to let the breeder know that you're serious and responsible about the financial commitment necessary to take care of your puppy. The breeder wants a careful and dedicated pet owner.

All these costs may seem a little daunting or more than you expected, but keep in mind that a pet store dog or a dog from a commercial breeder is likely to cost on the high end of that scale at the beginning. (I've seen tiny undersized Shih Tzu for sale on the Internet for more than $3,000!) These dogs potentially cost more down the road, if they end up with health and behavior problems.

If you feel comfortable with the breeder and the breeder thinks you would make a good owner for one of his puppies, ask the breeder about when you can bring home a puppy. If the breeder has a litter now, you and the breeder can begin to discuss which puppy may be best for you (for more about selecting a puppy, see Chapter 4). Some breeders ask you to return for another visit to meet the puppies, so they can review your information and check your references. You can use this time to prepare your home (see Chapter 6) and check the breeder's references, too.

Adopting an Older Shih Tzu

You may be excited about getting a Shih Tzu, but you're not really into the whole puppy thing (housetraining, accidents on your living room floor, those little needle teeth, and so on). If so, you may want to look for an older dog. An older dog is more likely to be housetrained, used to people, calmer, and even do a few tricks. An adult Shih Tzu is, in other words, probably more like what you imagine when you think of a Shih Tzu as a pet.

When adopting an older Shih Tzu, you have two main options: a Shih Tzu rescue group or an animal shelter. This section takes a look at your options and helps you navigate the waters.

Shih Tzu rescue groups

A *rescue group* is a privately run, volunteer organization that rescues animals and finds new homes for them. They often specialize in a particular breed, and work with animal shelters who call them if a dog of that breed comes into the shelter. They pick up the dog, put him into a foster home, evaluate him, and work to find him a new, permanent home. Rescue groups like to call this new home the dog's *forever home,* because they work hard to be sure they don't place a dog with someone who'll just give the dog up again.

Many rescue groups raise money, and often the individuals use their own money, to give the rescued pets medical care, to spay or neuter them, and even to put them through basic obedience training, to make sure they're adoptable and successful as pets.

For the right owner, these Shih Tzu can be perfection. There are benefits to rescuing an older dog:

- Many dogs are already housetrained and have learned how to behave in the house.
- They get along with kids and other pets, or the rescue workers know if they don't because the dogs are carefully evaluated.
- These dogs often know simple cues like Sit and Stay.
- Many pet owners say their dogs seem to know they were rescued and have a particularly strong bond with their new owners.
- You know how the dog looks and acts because he's already fully grown. Because rescue workers have screened the dog, you'll also get a lot of info from them, and from the dog's foster parents, about what it is like to live with the individual dog, and that can help you make the right choice.

Finding a rescue group

You may be wondering where you can find a rescue group in your area. Here are a few places to help you get started. (For more general info, check out my book, *Adopting a Pet For Dummies* [Wiley].) The last three give you lists of rescue groups as well as animal shelters near you:

- **ASTC:** They have a rescue committee with many members all over the country. Check them out online at `www.shihtzu.org/ASTC/rescue.asp?menu=ASTC`.
- **PetFinder:** This source is my favorite Internet resource for finding adoptable pets. The user-friendly Web site allows you

to select any kind of animal and breed and enter your zip code to get a list of all currently adoptable animals near you. Their database is huge and comprehensive. Find them at www.petfinder.com.

- **The American Society for the Prevention of Cruelty to Animals (ASPCA):** The ASPCA has a great Web site (www.aspca.org) with tons of info about adopting pets, and a search engine to find rescue groups and shelters near you.
- **Pets911:** Another good Web site for searching locally or regionally is Pets911, a group that's partnered with the Humane Society of the United States (HSUS) to provide local shelter information. Go online to www.pets911.com.

Adopting a rescued Shih Tzu

Even though the policies and procedures may vary from one organization to another, the process for adopting a rescued dog is usually about the same. Here's what to expect:

1. **You complete an application.**

   You fill out an application and specify if you have a particular dog that interests you, or if you're looking for a dog in general. Rescue groups are extra picky about who they allow to adopt a dog, because they want to make absolutely sure you won't give up the dog and are willing and able to keep the dog for the rest of his life. Expect to supply a lot of info about you, your home, your schedule, your family members, your other pets, your financial resources, how much time you have for the dog, your pet experience, and references.

2. **The rescue group interviews you and visits you.**

   Expect questions about your application and a home visit, so the rescue workers can see that the info on your application is true, and that you live in a suitable environment. The rescue workers want to meet everyone in your family.

3. **You wait to see if you're approved.**

   If you're approved, you get to visit some dogs or spend time with the dog you want to adopt. If you aren't approved, don't be offended. (See the sidebar in this chapter, "Why did they turn me down?")

4. **You bring home your new pet.**

   After all the questions, visits, and paperwork, you finally get to bring home your new rescued pet. Congratulations! You've done a good deed, and you'll be richly rewarded.

Why did they turn me down?

Some people with great intentions try to adopt a dog from a rescue group or shelter, and the rescue group or shelter says: Sorry, but no. Huh? Aren't you trying to do a good deed? Don't the dogs need homes? Why won't they give you one?

Rescue and shelter workers have seen a lot of very sad situations, dogs coming back again and again, and plenty of irresponsible and tragic human behavior. They want to make very sure that if they let you adopt a dog, you'll keep that dog for life.

They may have turned you down for a number of reasons, such as you don't have a good place to keep the dog, you aren't home very much, you have a lot of other pets, or they get the impression you aren't responsible in some way. If you rent, they'll need a letter from your landlord saying it's okay for you to have a dog. If you have small children or other pets, they may know the dog you want doesn't do well with children or other pets. If you're a student, the rescue group may not let you adopt a dog because so many students abandon their pets at the end of the semester.

The bottom line is if a rescue group or shelter turns you down, there's probably a good reason. Ask the workers what the reason(s) is, and then either fix the problem or wait awhile to adopt a dog. They may be right that you aren't ready for a dog yet, or aren't suited to a rescued or shelter dog. The rescue or shelter workers aren't trying to be nasty, so don't take it personally. They really are doing what they believe is best for the dogs they care so much about.

Animal shelters

Shelters are often city- or county-run facilities that take in many animals, and they're another great way to adopt an older Shih Tzu. Of course shelters have all types of dogs, but if you're diligent, you never know when a Shih Tzu may show up.

In many cases, shelters work with purebred rescue groups (see the previous section) and shuttle any purebreds directly to them. If you're really keen on a purebred Shih Tzu, start with a rescue group. However, if you're open to the idea of a Shih Tzu mix (a dog that's part Shih Tzu, part something else), a shelter may be exactly the right place for you. Get to know the shelter workers, or even volunteer at the shelter, and you'll be among the first to know if a Shih Tzu or Shih Tzu mix comes through the door.

If you do decide to adopt from an animal shelter, consider these points:

- **Adopting a shelter Shih Tzu can bring you joy, but it also comes with its challenges.** You may need to start back at square one with housetraining, socialization, and trust.
- **You may have limited info about the dog.** You won't know for sure how your dog has been treated in the past or if he's had any medical issues. Shelter workers can often help you decipher the clues, but many shelters don't have the time or resources to evaluate every detail about every dog. You and your Shih Tzu may have some things to work out.
- **The shelter must approve you for adoption.** Most shelters require lengthy application forms because the shelter wants to make sure the dog doesn't wind up right back in the shelter when you find you aren't able to handle the situation. If the shelter turns you down, see the sidebar, earlier in this chapter, "Why did they turn me down?"
- **Shelters are affordable.** Adopting a dog at a shelter usually runs around $25 to $200, a lot less than the cost of buying a purebred Shih Tzu. *However,* remember that because you don't know the dog's history, you may end up spending plenty at the vet and/or for training, to fix health and behavior problems. Also, an adopted shelter dog still costs the same as any other Shih Tzu for food, supplies, and grooming.

Shih Tzu want nothing more than your love and trust, and they're adaptable little dogs, so treat your new Shih Tzu, no matter his age, as a puppy. He can learn everything from you, including trust, and you'll be off to a great start.

Chapter 4

"I Want That One!": Finding *Your* Shih Tzu

In This Chapter

- Knowing what to do *before* you get your dog
- Choosing a Shih Tzu for your family
- Considering doggy temperament as well as gender
- Wading through the red tape

If you've found the breeder or the rescue group of your dreams (if not, check out Chapter 3), now you may find you're faced with the cutest, fuzziest bunch of Shih Tzu puppies you've ever seen. Which one is yours? Or, maybe you're on a waiting list for a litter to be born, or you have a list of adoptable rescued Shih Tzu to consider. How do you choose?

Every puppy, like every person, is a little bit different — a unique combination of genetics, environment, and personality. Some dogs may clearly be unhealthy or overly shy or have other qualities that don't make for a good pet, but most often, especially after you've found a great breeder, all the puppies look pretty darned charming.

This chapter helps you narrow down which puppy really is best for you. From trusting chemistry (you just know *that's* the one) to tapping the breeder's wisdom to filling out the final paperwork, I help you close the deal so you can finally bring home your dog.

Basic Questions to Ask Before You Start Looking

Step away from the litter! That's right, you heard me. Before you even look at, or especially *touch,* those fuzzy little puppies, you need to make some rational decisions. After you pick up a puppy, you're going to fall in love, and objectivity flies right out the window. At this moment, use your head. Before you select the right dog, you want to ask yourself a few important questions.

This section highlights some of the more important questions to ask. Furthermore, you need to remember a few important considerations, such as the dog's health, temperament, and personality (check out "Beginning the Inspection: What to Look For" later in this chapter for more info on health, temperament, and personality).

Puppy, teenager, or grown-up?

When choosing a new Shih Tzu, your dog's color and gender may be somewhat important to you. However, what age do you want? This question is most important because getting a puppy is a lot different than getting an adolescent or a senior dog. Read on for some important considerations.

Puppy love

People often automatically want a puppy. However, bringing home a puppy involves a lot of responsibility, work, and expense. With a puppy, you have to think about the following:

- **Housetraining and obedience training:** Although puppies are cute, they know next to nothing about living in a human household. How are they supposed to guess that the carpet isn't a bathroom and your bunny slippers aren't chew toys? Puppies need a lot of training and patience. Are you willing to put in the necessary time and stay calm when she has *another* accident?
- **Size:** Shih Tzu puppies are tiny, and although they can be tougher than some toy breeds, they can also easily be injured by a rough child, another dog, or a misstep. You need to keep their protection in mind at all times.
- **Socialization:** Puppies don't know much about other people, other dogs, and new places, and the wrong kind of exposure to the world can turn into behavioral problems such as fear, anxiety, or even aggression. Having a puppy means taking on the responsibility to socialize the dog so he grows up well-adjusted. (For more on socializing a Shih Tzu, see Chapter 11.)
- **Energy:** Shih Tzu are relatively calm, but all puppies have energy to spare. If you get tired just thinking about wild puppy antics, maybe a puppy isn't the best choice for you.

Thinking of a teenager

Adolescent Shih Tzu — those teenaged years from about 9 to 18 months — have some benefits (and some disadvantages) when you compare them to a puppy. If you have the opportunity to bring home a Shih Tzu teen, don't forget these important traits:

- **Adolescents can have an attitude, but it doesn't last long.** By the time your Shih Tzu reaches 2 years old, she should be calm and sweet again just like when your teenager turns 20!
- **Adolescents may need training just like puppies, but they often learn faster, too.** They may challenge you to make sure that you really mean what you say about all those silly human rules, but they have better concentration. Furthermore, they're probably housetrained or can learn more quickly than a puppy.
- **Adolescents may already be well trained.** Depending on the dog's past, you may get a Shih Tzu who already knows all about humans and even knows basic cues like Sit and Come. That makes your job a lot easier. In fact, sometimes you can get adolescents from good breeders who reserved a puppy they thought would be a good show dog but who turned out to have some faults that would be incidental to a pet owner. Having gone through puppyhood with a Shih Tzu expert, these dogs are usually well mannered, well trained, and well groomed. They just need someone to make them the center of their universe. That could be you!
- **Adolescents bond easily to their new owners.** Shih Tzu adapt well to new situations and loving people, so even if you adopt a dog who's no longer a puppy, your teen should quickly bond to you, as if you've known each other forever.

- **Adolescents need a lot of grooming.** During adolescence, the puppy coat sheds, and the adult coat grows in and needs a lot of maintenance. If the adult coat hasn't quite grown in, you may bring home your new dog just when the puppy coat is falling out. This time period requires some tough, high-maintenance grooming. You need to brush and comb the shedding coat every day or you'll end up with a seriously tangled dog.

Contemplating an adult dog

Adult and senior Shih Tzu sometimes lose their homes through no fault of their own, and you can adopt them from shelters or rescue groups. Some adults are raised by show breeders, ready to retire after a successful career and spend their golden years being pampered in a pet home. Either way, older Shih Tzu can be absolutely delightful with a lot of good years left. Don't discount this wonderful option.

To show or not to show: That is the question

So you have an adorable, beautiful Shih Tzu. Do you want to just snuggle him all day, or are you contemplating entering him in the exciting and glamorous show dog arena? Well, showing dogs can be a fun and interesting (and expensive) hobby, but deciding whether to show your dog can be a complicated question involving you, the breeder, and your dog.

Whether you want a show dog makes a big difference in which puppy to pick. The breeder can help you select a pup with good show potential, but even then, she may grow up to have some physical trait that will keep her from doing well in the ring. You won't know for sure until she's a little older. Also, the original purpose for showing dogs was to evaluate breeding stock, so keep in mind that if your dog competes, you can't have your Shih Tzu spayed or neutered. (Check out Chapter 12 for the importance of spaying and neutering.)

Also, most people in dog shows are committed dog breeders (or their hired professional handlers) looking to perfect the breed. The breeder may want to retain co-ownership of a good show prospect. Talk to your breeder and other breeders, visit dog shows, look into professional handlers, and do your research before you choose a puppy and before you decide to go this route. Then, if you still love the idea and you have the time and money to commit, let an experienced show breeder guide you in finding the right dog and discovering how to show. Also check out the American Kennel Club's (AKC) helpful Web page on dog showing for beginners: `www.akc.org/events/conformation/beginners.cfm`.

Peruse the following list when deciding whether an adult dog is right for you:

- **Adults may already be well trained and used to life in a pet home.** Adult Shih Tzu may need little, if any, training, so no worries about having to housetrain or teach them what not to do.
- **Adults are usually accustomed to grooming and are well socialized.** Adult dogs know the ins and outs of grooming. They also typically get along well with children and other pets, if they've been raised with them.
- **Adults bond easily to new loving owners.** Sure, they may take a short while to adjust to a new home, but with patience, plenty of love, and good care, adult Shih Tzu can quickly bond to you. An older Shih Tzu just wants a warm lap and pampering.

- **Senior dogs (8 to 10 years or older) can be particularly calm, sweet, and companionable.** Just because a Shih Tzu slows down a bit in old age doesn't make him less of a good friend.
- **Rescuing an older Shih Tzu who needs a new home can be a deeply rewarding experience for both you and the dog.** Many people report that the adult or senior dogs they've adopted turned out to be the best pets they've ever had.

Do you want a male or a female?

In many ways, gender doesn't matter when it comes to Shih Tzu. Experienced Shih Tzu folks may tell you that some subtle differences exist between the sexes, but the individual health and temperament of the dog is more important (see "Beginning the Inspection: What to Look For" later in this chapter).

First and foremost, before you select a dog based on gender, talk to the breeder about individual personalities of the puppies. Personality trumps gender any day of the week. But some general differences do exist. Not every Shih Tzu fits into these stereotypes, but you could say that when it comes to Lola (or, the girls) and Samson (or, the boys), Table 4-1 sums it up.

Table 4-1 Understanding the Different Sexes

Lola's Behaviors	*Samson's Behaviors*
Lola's a little more independent and strong-willed. (I didn't say "bitchier.")	Samson's a little sweeter and more lap-doggish and more likely to go along with anything. Just stick him in a Sherpa bag and off you go!
Lola demands attention. She likes to be in charge. You *will* worship her.	You can't help giving Samson attention because he's so darned charming.
If you don't socialize Lola, she may get a little bit protective of her favorite person.	Samson's more likely to love the one he's with, no matter who it is.
Lola can be harder to housetrain. You use an inside bathroom, so why can't she?	Samson's a little more sensitive. You didn't raise your voice, did you?

(continued)

Table 4-1 *(continued)*

Lola's Behaviors	*Samson's Behaviors*
Lola may have a little more drive and be able to pick up tricks and sports like agility or competitive obedience a little faster. She likes to do something.	Samson's favorite daily schedule: Sit on your lap. Have treats. Stare at you with adoration and worship. Take a potty break. Sit on your lap again.
Lola's number one reason for living is to make sure she's pleased with you.	Samson's number one reason for living is to make sure you're pleased with him.

These points are merely generalizations! Plus, the differences between boys and girls may be more pronounced in dogs who aren't spayed and neutered, and as a pet owner, you're certainly planning on spaying or neutering your pet, right? (For more info on why these procedures are so important, see Chapter 12.) *Your* Lola may be the sweetest, most lap-doggy dog in all of creation. *Your* Sampson may be a little firecracker and a whiz at agility, with a big dose of attitude. It's really about the individual.

Do you care about color?

Some people think all Shih Tzu are gold and white because that's the most popular color, but Shih Tzu actually come in many different colors, such as black, red, liver, blue, silver, gold, and white. They also come in patterns, like *bi-colored* (black and white), *masked* (gold with black mask), or *brindled* (striped). Gold and white Shih Tzu with black tips may be easiest to find right now because it's currently the most popular color, but it certainly isn't your only option. You can see how all these different colors look on a Shih Tzu at `www.shihtzu.org/Info/colors.asp`.

Color does *not* affect personality or structure. That jet-black Shih Tzu should be indistinguishable from that gold-and-white Shih Tzu when the lights are out. You may believe a particular color is beautiful, but health and temperament are much more important.

Beginning the Inspection: What to Look For

Having a picture in your mind or an idea of the type of dog you want is one thing. Getting down on your hands and knees and really looking at the actual puppies to determine which one is right for you is a totally different matter. If you're ready to begin your inspection of a litter (or of a couple dogs at a rescue shelter), now it's time to get down on your hands and knees.

If you're seriously looking for a puppy, please keep this important point in mind: The worst possible time to buy a new puppy is at Christmas or around the holidays where large numbers of people are around and when there's a great deal of activity. The puppy needs time to adjust to his new surroundings.

This section helps you evaluate the dog's health, determine the dog's temperament, and check to see if you and the dog have good old-fashioned chemistry. Most importantly, get the breeder's or rescue person's input on which pup may work best for your personality, family, and lifestyle.

Checking the dog's health

Naturally, you want a healthy puppy or dog, and you need to look for certain signs when picking out your pooch. When you examine the puppy, pick him up carefully (with the breeder's permission), pet him, lift his fur, and check for the following:

- Bright, shiny eyes with no discharge
- Clean, sharp, white teeth
- Sweet smelling breath with no sour or foul smell, which could indicate a poor diet or an oral infection
- Clean, soft fluffy coat with no mats, tangles, or bare patches
- Soft clean nose and clean ears with no discharge, redness, or swelling.
- Clean rear-end with no dirt, oozing, redness, swelling, rashes, discharge, feces stuck in the fur, or bugs
- Neat, clean feet with short nails and firm soft paw pads
- Clean skin with no red patches, rashes, wounds, fleas, ticks, or lumps

After you select your dog, take your Shih Tzu to the vet, right after you take possession, for an expert opinion (check out Chapter 12 for more info about a visit to the vet). Your health guarantee should state that if the vet finds a problem that you can return the dog. (For more on health guarantees, see the last section of this chapter.)

Rescuing a sick puppy

Trying to rescue a sick puppy can be incredibly tempting. He looks so helpless and adorable. However, be aware that even with treatment, many sick puppies — especially small breeds — don't make it. If the pup has a contagious disease like Parvo and you have other pets, bringing that puppy home can put your other pets at risk. If you still insist on bringing home a sick pet to save, such as a rescued or shelter animal that needs special medical care, a health evaluation by a vet lets you know what you're getting yourself into.

Some less-than-ethical breeders may try to sell you a puppy for a discount that isn't doing as well as the others. You'll more than make up for that so-called bargain in future vet bills and heartache! Some puppies in pet stores may also be in less-than-glowing health, and the pet store employees may not know enough about dog health to know they shouldn't sell you that dog. Even a Shih Tzu from a shelter or rescue group can have health issues that nobody knows about or mentions to you. That's why you need to pay attention and look carefully for signs of good health.

Evaluating for temperament

A healthy looking puppy is important, but temperament matters, too. Evaluating temperament can be tricky because much of temperament is learned and comes out later depending on how you raise the puppy. However, some aspects of temperament are inherited.

Some books give you specific temperament tests to try on dogs, but I'm not a big advocate of these for Shih Tzu. They can be too rough for the naturally trusting Shih Tzu. Instead, find a good breeder or rescue group (see Chapter 3) to advise you, and pay attention to how the dog acts when you meet him. The following questions may help.

How does the dog relate to other dogs within a group?

You can discover a lot by watching how he acts around his littermates. Does he jump on the others and wrestle or stay back and watch? The breeder knows the litter best and can point you to the most active and the most mellow pups in the whelping box. (See "Tapping the wisdom of the experts" later in the chapter.)

If you're looking at a rescued or shelter dog, how does the dog respond to animals in the environment? Dogs that seem interested or playfully interactive should get along well with other friendly pets. Those who shy away or try to attack may have some issues with other pets. These Shih Tzu may do fine in a home without other pets, but you'll have to be responsible for future animal interactions.

How do you relate to the dog?

As you survey the possible dogs, ask yourself a few questions to figure out what dog is right for you:

- Do you like a spunky or serene Shih Tzu?
- Do you like a dog who wants to be on you or in your arms all the time, or do you prefer a little more independence?
- Which puppy seems most like the dog you imagine living with for the next 12 to 18 years?
- Which puppy seems most interested in *you?*

How do the parents behave?

You should be able to meet at least one of the parents. In many cases, the father of the litter (breeders call him the *sire*) lives somewhere else and came to visit during courtship as part of a planned breeding. But the mother (the *dam*) should be right there with the breeder, nurturing the puppies. What's she like? If she's sweet, friendly, curious, and trusting, she's probably passed down the potential for these traits to her pups. If she's nippy, nervous, excitable, or fearful, she may have passed on those qualities, too.

If you can't see the sire, ask to see pictures, and ask the breeder for the phone number of the person who owns the father. Give that person a call to ask about the father's personality. Even if you can't meet him in person, you may get further assurance that the mother's good temperament is complemented by the father's.

In the case of rescued dogs, you won't get to see the parents, so you have to rely on other measures of temperament, such as seeing how the dog relates to his environment and the people who care for him, as well as the way he relates to you. The foster parents or shelter workers can tell you a lot, too. As with many aspects of rescued dogs, you take a slight risk. However, because the environment determines a lot of the temperament and because Shih Tzu are naturally sweet, loving, and trusting, chances are you'll be okay.

How does the dog interact with you?

You can tell things about a puppy's natural temperament by interacting with the puppy. All the puppies should be basically curious, energetic, and interested in you and shouldn't cower or shy away from your hands. Follow these easy steps to determine how the dog interacts with you.

1. **Take the dog into a safe, familiar place but away from her mother, littermates, or other household pets.**
2. **Hold her while sitting down, pet her, and play with her.**

   If she seems interested in you and interactive, that's a great sign. If she seems afraid of you or shies away from your hand, you may be dealing with a dog that has a temperament problem and takes much longer to train and socialize.

Tapping the wisdom of the experts

Nobody knows the puppies like the breeder, who has, ideally, been handling and interacting with the puppies every day since they were born. If you find a Shih Tzu through a shelter or rescue group, the volunteers for the group can also give you a good idea of the personality characteristics of that dog.

Ask the breeder, shelter, or rescue worker the following types of questions tailored toward your needs to help narrow your choice:

- **What is this dog's personality?** If you want a more outgoing pup, a mellower pup, or something in between, tell the breeder, who can probably point out the exact dog for you.
- **Has the dog been introduced to children?** Rescue groups and shelter workers may have firsthand experience regarding the dog's compatibility with other pets and/or children. Breeders with kids can give you a thumbs-up on this one, too.
- **Has the dog been introduced to any other animals?** Some dogs love other animals. Some don't get along with them at all. Most Shih Tzu find other pets interesting, but just in case, ask.
- **I really like *this* puppy (or dog). From what you know of her, would this one be a good match?** If you really just love a particular pup or dog, ask. Unless the breeder, shelter worker, or rescue group knows a good reason why the match wouldn't be made in heaven, you may get the thumbs-up, with a blessing.

If you spend time talking to the breeder (or the rescue or shelter worker), he can get to know you better and can be in an even better position to match you up with the dog of your dreams. The better he knows you, the better he can help you.

Chemistry and intuition: Letting the dog choose you

Sometimes, one particular dog just speaks to you — and I don't mean by barking. You look at a dog, he looks at you, and sparks fly. But listen to the experts. If a breeder or rescue worker has strong objections to the match, you should probably listen. If a dog is very shy and you want to bring him home to a big, loud family with other pets and young children, you're probably dizzy and irrational due to the cute-fuzzy-puppy factor. But if the breeder or rescue worker thinks you would be a good match, then listen to your own intuition. You may have just found *the* one.

Dealing with the Paperwork

Petting and playing with puppies is fun, but it isn't the only part of buying a dog. Yes, you inevitably have to deal with the red tape. Legally you *are* making a purchase, so you should research getting your new dog like you would purchasing a car or home, making sure that everything is in order before you sign on the dotted line. And yes, you'll be asked to sign.

Even if you're adopting a dog from a shelter, you still have paperwork and a lot of it. This section looks at all the paperwork and helps you understand what it means and how it protects you, the breeder, the shelter or rescue group, and of course, the Shih Tzu.

Sign on the dotted line: Contracts

You probably won't have to sign a contract if you take a puppy from your neighbor's litter of Shih Tzu, but if you buy a puppy from a breeder or a pet store, or if you adopt a dog from a shelter or rescue group, you may be required to sign a contract. Don't worry. Signing a contract is good because it protects both you and the seller.

The trick is to make sure that all the info you need, including your protections, are spelled out clearly in the contract. The contract typically contains the following:

- **The breeder's (or the shelter or rescue group's) contact info:** This info includes the name, address, phone number, and e-mail address (if she has one).
- **The parents' info:** This info includes the complete names of the sire and dam, their registration numbers, their dates of birth,

sex, and of course the breed, if the puppy comes from a breeder.

- **Breeder requirements regarding the puppy, in the case of a purchase from a breeder:** If the breeder doesn't think the puppy should be bred or shown in dog shows, she may require you to have the puppy spayed or neutered. The contract may state that you may register the puppy on a *limited registration only,* which means the dog is a registered purebred dog, but can't be bred. If the breeder is selling you a show prospect, then the breeder will probably require, in writing, that you register the dog with an organization like the AKC, and may want his kennel name as part of the puppy's name or may even want to retain co-ownership. Ask the breeder to explain any conditions like these to your satisfaction.
- **The purchase or adoption price:** All fees should be explained.
- **A health guarantee:** Check out the next section for more info on health guarantees and what they cover.
- **All health information:** Any vaccinations that the dog has received and any other info on veterinary visits, tests, or other procedures, such as if the dog has already been spayed or neutered, should be included. The contract may also stipulate what veterinary visits and vaccinations you're required to have done after taking possession of the dog.
- **A spay/neuter agreement:** Many breeders and virtually all shelters and rescue groups require that you have your dog spayed or neutered. Some give you a voucher to have this procedure done at a reduced rate or even free. Some breeders won't release registration papers until you come back with proof of this procedure. When they say to have your dog spayed or neutered in writing, *they mean it.* (For the many reasons why it's important, see Chapter 12.)
- **A clause that you must return the dog if you aren't able to keep the dog:** Good breeders and diligent rescue workers always want to know where every single puppy they've brought into the world is at all times, and they don't ever want their precious pups to end up in a shelter or in a bad home.

  Some rescue groups may stipulate, as part of the contract, that you promise *never* to give up the dog to anyone else, no matter what (a tough promise, but one rescue groups take seriously).

If you don't find some of the previous items in your contract, you can ask that they be added. Your contract may contain other info, too. But whatever you do, make sure to read the document carefully and understand everything it says before you sign on the dotted line.

Put your mind at ease: Health guarantees

Health guarantees are a part of the contract that protects the dog, you, and the breeder in case the dog develops a health problem. This documentation is essential and yet a misunderstood part of the red tape involved in buying or adopting a dog. Sometimes a dog gets sick or develops a genetic problem, and you can't blame anybody. Even if the breeder does everything possible to ensure good health in his puppies, health problems can happen.

If the vet finds a problem in a new puppy or newly adopted dog, you should have the legal right, as stated in your health guarantee or contract, to return the dog for a refund or a replacement. But if the dog gets sick later, at some point the care and treatment is *your* responsibility, not the breeder's or anyone else's. That's just part of pet ownership. The health guarantee should specifically state where the breeder's, shelter's or rescue group's (or pet shop's) responsibility ends, and where yours begins. *Be sure you understand this before agreeing to purchase or adopt the dog!*

Some people feel shocked and betrayed when a dog gets sick. "But I had a health guarantee!" they often say to the vet. Unfortunately, a health guarantee doesn't and can't *guarantee* good health. The breeder does her part to maximize the possibility for good health, and you do your part to promise to care for your pet if it gets sick.

Whether or not the breeder promises (in a contract) to help you with health problems, always tell the breeder if your Shih Tzu develops a health problem. This info is valuable for a breeder working to produce healthy dogs. If the breeder never knows your dog ended up with luxating patellas or liver disease (genetic issues in Shih Tzu which you can find out more about in Chapter 13), he can't use that info for making smarter breeding decisions next time. Consider it your duty to all future Shih Tzu.

The proof is in the pudding: Registration papers

Registering your purebred Shih Tzu means your dog is on record as being a purebred with an official pedigree. This pedigree is required for show dogs but optional for pets. Many pet owners like to do it just for the fun and prestige of having a registered purebred.

If you buy a purebred dog, the breeder should give you all the necessary paperwork *on the day you bring home the dog* to send to the

AKC — or other registry, depending on the breeder — to register your dog. A good breeder always gives this paperwork to you and explains what to do, unless she wants proof that you have spayed or neutered the dog first. That's the only valid excuse to delay giving you the registration papers.

If you think snail mail is *so* 20th century, you can register your dog online at `www.akc.org`. Click *Registrations* and then *Register a Dog Online.* This option is convenient, but you'll need your credit card. Basic registration costs $15.

Some breeders may sell you a puppy on *limited registration only,* which means the puppy is pet quality and not for breeding. The contract states that you should have the puppy spayed or neutered, and then you can register the dog. This kind of registration allows for a purebred dog to be registered while ensuring that you won't breed puppies indiscriminately. Good breeders often insist on it.

Tend to your Shih Tzu: Care info

Both breeders and rescue groups typically send home other info, too. This paperwork may involve care, vet, grooming, socializing, and training info. If the info isn't already in the contract, the care info may include some or all of the following:

- What food the dog's been eating (you may even get a sample to take home; see Chapter 9 for what to feed your Shih Tzu)
- What to do if you want to switch foods (see Chapter 9)
- A recommended supply list (check out Chapter 5)
- Puppy-proofing information (refer to Chapter 6)
- Grooming information (look in Chapter 10)
- Housetraining information (see Chapter 16)

Future guidance from the breeder: Get those digits!

A good breeder provides follow-up support, and a good rescue group is willing and happy to help with any problems, too. Make sure that you get the thumbs-up about calling with questions and problems (and cute stories and holiday cards) before you leave the breeder, shelter, or rescue worker. Get a full name, address, phone number, and e-mail contact, if available. You're now a team, along with your vet and groomer — all of you work together to keep your new Shih Tzu healthy, happy, and loved for the rest of his life.

Part II
Opening Your Home to Your Shih Tzu

"Okay, before I let the new puppy out, let's remember to be real still so we don't startle him."

In this part . . .

You've done it! You've really done it. You've brought home a new Shih Tzu. Now what? This part helps you prepare your home and give you the lists of supplies you need (check out Chapter 5). In Chapter 6, you discover the art of Shih-Tzu-proofing your home, so your new dog stays safe and comfortable. In Chapter 7, you can find info about bringing your dog home safely from the breeder and introducing him to your family.

In this part, you also figure out how to schedule a vet visit and introduce your new Shih Tzu to your family and other pets in a safe and friendly way. Chapter 8 helps you with those first few days in establishing a solid routine, so your Shih Tzu knows exactly what to expect.

Chapter 5

Stocking Up: What Every Shih Tzu Needs

In This Chapter

- Identifying the right pet supplies
- Finding the fancy stuff

You can't wait to bring home your new dog, but before you do, you should do a little shopping. And if you like to shop, this chapter is for you! Your Shih Tzu needs some stuff (just like any new baby would) and you — the responsible pet owner — have to get what your baby needs.

You may feel like I've listed a lot of stuff in this chapter, but you don't need all of it. I clarify which items are non-negotiable and which are pure luxury and up to your discretion (and the level of pampering, spoiling, and coddling you plan to do).

Eyeing the Necessary Supplies

Whether you like to shop or not (you can always order stuff off the Internet — I give you some good sources later in this chapter), the tricky part is knowing what to shop for. The next sections fill you in on everything from food to bedding, grooming tools to toys, and the fancy stuff like hair accessories and party dresses. (Yes, I said party dresses. Don't worry, Samson, they make doggy tuxedoes, too.)

The right food

First and foremost on your list should be a good-quality dog food. Forget that cheap junk-food kibble. Toy dogs don't eat much and every bite counts, so you want a premium food with high quality meat (not by-products) listed first on the ingredients label and preferably a few other meat sources in the first five ingredients. (For more on choosing the right food and other nutritional concerns, see Chapter 9.)

Fortunately, the best food is also the best deal, even if the price tag doesn't look that way. Cheap food may cost less up-front, but the problems the food can cause cost more down the line, and a good quality food makes cleaning up after your Shih Tzu easier, because good food going in comes out the other end smaller, more compact, and less stinky.

Your local grocery stores and discount stores carry dog food, but the really good, premium brands are usually only available at a pet store or vet. Find the store near you specializing in quality pet food, or ask your vet what brand she recommends. You may also find a good brand in your local health food store, particularly if you want to feed your pet organic food or a raw diet.

The right dinnerware

No need to spend a lot of money on a fancy artistically sculptured set of food and water bowls, unless you love the way they look. Your dog won't care. A few things do matter when choosing food and water bowls:

- **Make sure bowls offer plenty of room for your Shih Tzu to get his mouth to the food and water.** Shih Tzu have hairy faces so they tend to get food and water all over themselves and the floor.
- **Consider keeping a placemat or some other washable mat under the food and water bowls to make clean up easier.** For water, consider a bottle instead of a bowl.

When choosing food and water bowls, also consider the following:

- **Size:** Remember that Samson is a little dog, so a small- to medium-sized dish is fine for his food. Buy a deeper bowl for his water, if you aren't using a water bottle, so you don't have to refill it as often. But don't just top it off — at least daily, dump the water, rinse the bowl, and refill.
- **Type:** Bowls come in three main types (ceramic, plastic, or stainless steel), and you can offer water in a bottle. Each option has its advantages and disadvantages:

Water bottles for small dogs

Some Shih Tzu owners train their dogs to drink from water bottles, much like the ones hamsters and gerbils drink out of, only larger. (See the photo at right.) Shih Tzu are easily trained by rubbing a small amount of chicken or beef baby food on the nozzle. Water bottles keep Shih Tzu faces dry and clean, and eliminate splashes on the floor, too. Also, the water stays cleaner. These bottles come with a bracket for installation in a crate or near the food bowl. You can purchase water bottles for small dogs from vendors at dog shows, dog product catalogues, online, or in pet stores.

Jean M. Fogle

- **Stainless steel:** They're the sturdiest and easiest to clean. They don't break when you drop them, and your dog won't chew on them.
- **Ceramic:** These bowls are sturdy and easy to clean. You can even customize a bowl with your dog's name. However, ceramic is heavier (don't drop it on Lola's toes or your own), and it breaks easily.

  Stay clear of ceramic bowls made outside of the United States. The bowl's glazing may contain lead.

- **Plastic:** You can find a wide assortment of colors and sizes, and they're inexpensive, but I don't recommend these. They scratch easily and harbor bacteria. They're also lightweight, so they can skid across the floor as your dog's trying to eat his food.

Grooming supplies

Other than training (if you choose to do this) and spending time together, you may spend more time grooming your Shih Tzu than doing any other aspect of his care. To groom, you need the right supplies. Chapter 10 gives you a lot more info about these grooming tools, but your basic shopping list should include a few necessities:

- Pin brush
- Natural bristle brush
- Steel comb
- Mat splitter, grooming scissors, and electric clipper
- Dog shampoo
- Dog crème rinse
- Spray conditioner
- Moisturizing eye drops (if your vet recommends them)
- Tear stain remover
- Toothpaste and toothbrush made for dogs
- Nail clippers made for dogs
- Bows, barrettes, and other hair accessories (optional but fun)

Kennels and crates

Some people object to the idea of keeping their Shih Tzu in a kennel or crate, but to your Shih Tzu, this little den is a safe spot where nobody can bother him. The crate also acts as a place to travel, to sleep, and to escape from people or other pets when your dog just isn't in the mood. This valuable haven also helps you housetrain your Shih Tzu (see Chapter 16 for more info on housetraining).

You can find crates and kennels in any pet store or online, and they can range quite a bit in price depending on how basic or fancy you get and what brand you choose. The most important consideration is that your Shih Tzu should be able to stand up, lie down, and turn around easily inside the crate, but it shouldn't be so big that your Shih Tzu is tempted to use one end as a bathroom and the other as a bed.

You can choose between two types of crates:

- **Plastic crates:** This type is good for feeling secure because the sides are solid and perfect for traveling in the car or by air, but they have vented sides so your dog can breathe. Check out Figure 5-1. Some fancy versions even look nice in your home.
- **Wire crates:** Wire crates allow your Shih Tzu to see everything but don't feel as comfortable and cave-like. You can fix that, though, by draping a blanket over the wire, leaving only the front end exposed.

Either way, line the crate with soft bedding (see more information about this in the next section).

© Isabelle Francais

Figure 5-1: Your Shih Tzu feels safe in his kennel.

Bedding for a good night's sleep

Your Shih Tzu may sleep in bed with you, in her kennel, or in a fancy dog bed, but whether your dog sleeps in that kennel or not, you need to place soft bedding in the crate for when your dog does go inside for a nap, a rest, or for travel. Your Shih Tzu doesn't want to lie on the cold plastic, or worse yet, a wire grate.

Choose a soft cushion, pad, pillow, fleece mat, or folded blanket to line the crate. You can also cut a piece of foam and wrap fleece or a blanket around it or slip it inside a pillowcase. Whatever you choose, the cover should be washable and allow space for your Shih Tzu to get in the crate and change positions.

You may also choose to purchase a comfy dog bed. You can spend a little or a lot on a dog bed, and there are many to choose from. Shih Tzu tend to enjoy smaller beds that make them feel safe and surrounded, such as doughnut-style beds or beds with padded sides. Some even like covered cat beds they can crawl inside.

Collars and harnesses

Every dog needs a collar to hold identification tags and to have somewhere to clip a leash when you take your dog on a walk. However, because Shih Tzu sometimes have breathing problems and trachea problems (see Chapter 13 for more info about these health issues), some Shih Tzu do better with a harness, especially if they tend to pull on the leash. A harness puts pressure on the dog's chest instead of the neck, so this option is safer and more comfortable. If your Shih Tzu doesn't pull or walk on a leash much, a collar is fine.

When choosing a collar or harness for your new Shih Tzu, make sure you pick one that's comfortable and soft so it doesn't wear away at your dog's coat. Nylon, plastic, and other soft materials are lightweight and often adjustable. Leather collars cost more but are more durable, and some are quite beautiful.

You should be able to fit two fingers between the collar and your Shih Tzu's neck or between the harness and your dog's chest, but not much more, or she could slip out on a walk and run into the street. Adjustable collars and harnesses offer room for growing. Or, buy a less expensive collar or harness for your puppy, keep checking it for the correct fit, and then invest in a nicer, more permanent version when your Shih Tzu is fully grown around his first birthday.

Never use a metal training collar or choke chain. Because Shih Tzu's tracheas are vulnerable to collapse, the compressing action of these training collars is too harsh and dangerous. Besides, your Shih Tzu doesn't need you to jerk on him. There are kinder, gentler ways to train him. (See Chapters 15 and 17 for more info on training.)

Leash

Even if you don't think your tiny puppy could run away from you very quickly, a *leash* (or *lead*) can keep your Shih Tzu safe when you go on walks or venture outside your fenced yard. If Samson sees something like a squirrel across the street and dashes out in front of a car, you won't be able to stop him if he isn't on a leash.

Choose nylon or a lightweight leather leash because a big, heavy, leather or chain leash can be too cumbersome for a small dog. Leashes generally come in four-foot and six-foot lengths. Either one is fine, depending on what's more comfortable for you.

Some people like retractable leashes — the kind that let your dog go out on a long leash to explore, but that wind up automatically into a plastic case as your dog gets closer to you again. These leashes are fine as long as you can keep control over the dog in case a larger dog with aggression on his mind suddenly shows up on the scene.

Toys and playtime

Puppies need to play, and plenty of adult dogs enjoy playtime, too. Play is good exercise and it lets dogs release the hunter, retriever, or tug-o-war champion inside. Get your Shih Tzu a few toys to treasure, and rotate them if your Shih Tzu loses interest.

Choose toys without small parts that could break off and become a choking hazard.

Make sure that your shopping list has one or two of the following types of toys:

- **Chew toys:** Puppies need to chew as their adult teeth come in. You may have to offer your Shih Tzu a few different chew toys to find the one she really likes.
- **Stuffed toys:** Some dogs may rip out all the stuffing, and some Shih Tzu will ignore stuffed toys completely, but if your dog gets attached to his stuffed toy, it could become his second best friend (after you, of course). You may want to have a spare!
- **Squeaky toys:** Some Shih Tzu think toys that squeak are a hoot and love to paw them and even toss them in the air. Others ignore them, but if you squeeze the squeaker, you can probably get them interested.

  If your Shih Tzu breaks open the toy, take the toy away. You don't want her to choke on the squeaker.

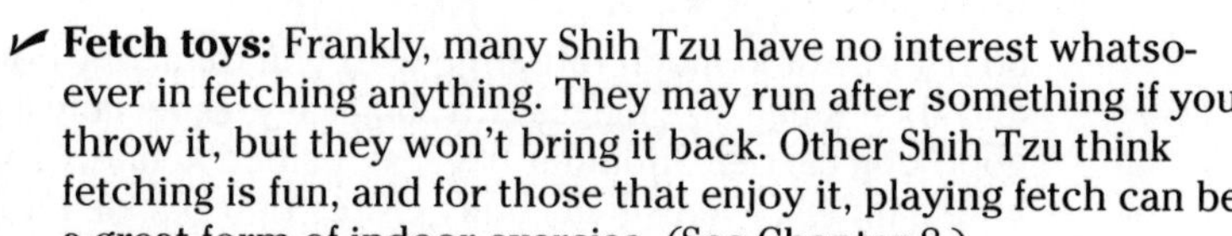

- **Fetch toys:** Frankly, many Shih Tzu have no interest whatsoever in fetching anything. They may run after something if you throw it, but they won't bring it back. Other Shih Tzu think fetching is fun, and for those that enjoy it, playing fetch can be a great form of indoor exercise. (See Chapter 8.)

Baby gate

You may want to buy a baby gate if you leave your Shih Tzu inside the house when you have to leave for awhile and can't take your Shih Tzu with you. The gate can either keep your dog in one area or keep him out of other areas of the house.

A baby gate is especially helpful during the housetraining period, when you need to confine your pup to one place to pee, and when there are doorless rooms or staircases you don't want your Shih Tzu to go. (See Chapter 16 for more on housetraining.)

When you buy a gate, keep the following in mind:

- **Size:** Shih Tzu aren't jumpers or climbers. They're more likely to want to keep all four paws on the floor, so shorter baby gates usually work just fine.
- **Style:** Pick a style that's easy for you to use, but sturdy enough to stay put. Look for well-made, solid gates. Cheap, rickety gates are a pain to operate.
- **Safety:** Make sure the baby gate doesn't have openings that your dog's head can fit through and get stuck in. Avoid gates made of anything that can snag your Shih Tzu's coat or collar.

Yard pen and fence

Sometimes you may want your Shih Tzu outside with you, so you can both enjoy the nice weather or get out of the stuffy house. If you have a fenced yard, that's great! But if you don't, buy a small portable pen or dog run.

Shih Tzu simply aren't outdoor dogs, period. Never keep Shih Tzu outside unsupervised, because they don't tolerate temperature extremes, and they'll be vulnerable to theft, dog attacks, and rough children. There's also a strangulation risk if Samson is left unsupervised tied to a line.

Travel bags and carriers

Shih Tzu would much rather go with you than stay home alone, and their small size makes traveling easy, especially if you have a good dog carrier. Shoulder bags, soft-sided kennels on wheels with long handles, even small comfy crates that buckle into a seatbelt can all facilitate taking your Shih Tzu with you, whether on vacation or just out to the mall. And don't forget the dog seatbelt! (See Chapter 6 for more info on dog seatbelts.)

For carrying your Shih Tzu around town with you, I particularly like Sherpa bags. They come in many cool styles and the quality is great for the price. Check them out at `www.sherpapet.net`. I also love the puppy purse, which you can see at `www.puppypurse.com`.

Some people even sneak their Shih Tzu into malls, shopping centers, and restaurants because the dogs are so good, and they snooze quietly in a roomy shoulder bag, knowing they're close by their owners. Of course, I would never officially recommend taking your Shih Tzu into a place where dogs aren't allowed. (But if you do it, I promise not to tattle.)

Other important stuff

Your supplies list isn't complete without a few of these odds and ends:

- **Identification:** Your dog's ID tag needs to include your address, phone number, and your dog's name. (Check out Chapter 12 for identification ideas.) You can order them in your local pet store or find hundreds of options online.
- **Stain and odor remover:** When a dog smells the place where he previously peed, he's likely to pee there again. Remove stains immediately and ramp up your housetraining efforts to prevent repeat offenses (Chapter 16 has more on housetraining). Your local pet store has effective stain and odor removers.
- **Bitter Apple or other chew deterrent spray:** Although Shih Tzu aren't notorious chewers, some do like to chew on shoes, clothing, and furniture, especially when teething. Keep plenty of acceptable chew toys around and spray off-limits areas like furniture legs with Bitter Apple or another safe chew deterrent spray. Find this product in your local pet store or online.

Living in the Lap of Luxury: Fun, Extravagant Supplies

If you're so inclined, you can spend a lot on goodies for your dog. Small-dog people are notoriously prone to frequenting pet boutiques for gourmet treats, jewelry, or canine couture. Just search *pet boutique* on the Internet and see what you find.

Your Shih Tzu really doesn't care one way or the other, but if you really want to shower your Shih Tzu with the best, this section has some supplies to consider for your Shih Tzu.

Fancy food and high-end treats

A good-quality premium kibble may be all your Shih Tzu needs, but some people like to go all out and buy frozen raw food; fancy, canned food; organic food; or even home-cooked food. Some of these options really are healthier than regular kibble, while others are just packaged to *look* fancy. For more on feeding your Shih Tzu appropriately, see Chapter 9.

Even more fun are dog bakeries that are popping up all over the country and offering healthy and even gorgeous pet treats for pets who only snack on the very best. Some of my favorite places include

- **Three Dog Bakery:** This place is the market leader in the dog bakery business. Check them out online: www.threedog.com.
- **Good Dog Express:** This company has all the supplies to throw the doggy bash of the year! Go to www.gooddogexpress.com.
- **Canine Confections, Inc.:** The company sells treats for the organically minded dog owner. The treats even come in candy boxes. *Very* swanky. Find them at www.canineconfections.com.
- **Central Bark Bakery:** They sell toys, pet supplies, and other dog goodies. Go online at www.centralbarkbakery.com.

Fancy grooming

You can buy plain old regular dog shampoo, or you can buy dog shampoo full of sweet-smelling botanicals and other natural ingredients in fanciful bottles. Some products contain glitter, milk and honey, or candy colors. Some companies also sell bath toys, terry towel wraps, and dog perfume. You can even buy fingernail polish for dogs! Because Shih Tzu need more grooming than many other breeds, you can really go to town with this stuff if you desire.

Home furnishings

Would you believe that you can get Shih-Tzu-sized furniture to match your home décor scheme? It's true. From frothy, pink canopy beds in miniature to red, velvet sofas, leopard-print

Expressing the Shih Tzu in *you*

Why should Lola and Samson have all the fun? You can buy plenty of Shih-Tzu-inspired merchandise made just for you. Some companies sell matching sweaters for dogs and their parents. You can buy Shih Tzu charms, pendants, paintings, sculptures, and folk art, or if you're a little more budget-minded, you can purchase flags, T-shirts, and bumper stickers. Everybody loves their breed and many companies make it easy to prove it to the world.

Hundreds of companies exist with Shih Tzu stuff for sale. To find more on your own, just search *Shih Tzu gifts* on the Internet. Try these Web sites:

- `www.shihtzu.org`: The American Shih Tzu Club (ASTC) has an online store that sometimes features cute Shih Tzu paraphernalia and gift ideas.
- `www.akc.org`: The American Kennel Club (AKC) has a store that features books, prints, ornaments, and decorative art.
- `www.danburymint.com`: The site has a huge selection of merchandise: figurines, clothing, ornaments, throws, decorate plates, and more.
- `www.k9gifts.com/dog-gifts/shihtzu.html`: Find mailboxes, stained glass, gift bags, leash holders, and much more.
- `www.dogdecor.com/shihtzu.html`: Find holiday stuff and more.
- `www.krittersinthemailbox.com/animals/dogs/shihtzus/index.htm`: Find figurines, luggage tags, key chains, watches, cell phone holders, and so on.

chaises, and smart-tweed loveseats, you can find just about any style and your Shih Tzu can have a space just for her. Of course, she may prefer your lap, but just think how cute she'll look sprawled dramatically, movie-star-style, on that lime-green puppy-sized beanbag chair.

Your local boutique pet store may have some great choices in dog furniture, but you can get some outrageous and gorgeous stuff online, too. Companies change often so just search *dog furniture* or *dog beds* and see what you get.

Bling and couture

Crystal or studded leather collars, anyone? Delicate party dresses or fleece hoodies? Leather motorcycle jackets or faux fur wraps? Charms to hang on the collar or rhinestone chokers? Hair accessories *galore?* Whatever your delight, you can find it all. In fact, this category is so big that New York even holds Pet Fashion Week in August with a full-scale runway event featuring supermodels of both the two-legged and four-legged varieties.

DUMMIES APPROVED

I love this stuff for my dog, so I have a few favorite companies:

- **High Maintenance Bitch:** Don't be offended by the name — everybody in the dog world uses this word and nobody thinks anything about it. This company is one of my favorites for bling. They have magnetic earrings, feather boas, kimono wraps, furniture, and even elevated food and water bowls shaped like martini glasses. Go online: `www.girlmeetsdog.com`.
- **Charming Pet Charms:** They specialize in charms and jewelry, but they also sell pet clothing. Wouldn't Lola look cute in that pink furry scarf? Find them at `www.charmingpetcharms.com`.
- **Kool Dawg Tees:** Your pup doesn't have to be delicate. Check out the hard-core biker wear on this site: `www.kooldawgtees.com/DOG_MOTORCYCLE_CLOTHES.html1`.
- **Doggie Foo Foo:** Pink fur jacket? Party dresses? Look no further: `www.doggiefoofoo.com`.
- **Doggie Designer:** They have sweatshirts and motorcycle jackets and wedding dresses. You never know when Lola may meet *the* one. Visit `www.doggiedesigner.com/clothing/clothes.htm`.

Chapter 6

Prepping for Your Shih Tzu's Arrival

In This Chapter

- Preparing the people in your life for the new dog
- Making your house and yard Shih-Tzu-safe
- Getting the vet on board
- Celebrating the joyous homecoming at last
- Buckling up for safety

You have the crate; you have the collar; you have the comb. (If you don't have the necessary supplies, check out Chapter 5.) All that's left is bringing home your new canine companion, right? Actually, you have a few more things to think about and take care of before you bring your Shih Tzu into your home. Do you have areas set up for your new family member to be comfortable? Have you thought about safety? Have you told the kids what to expect? Does the vet know you're coming?

So many questions but don't worry; this chapter helps you get all your ducks in a row so when you do finally bring that puppy home, everything (and everyone) is ready.

Making Sure Everyone Is Ready

Other than knowing how to say "Awwwwwww," you and your family may not think you need to know a ton of info before bringing your Shih Tzu home with you. But there are plenty of steps to take before bring the new addition home. Keep these general tips in mind about introducing your new dog to the family:

- **Give your pup some space.** No matter how adorable little Lola is, no matter how much you want to scoop her up and carry her around with you all day, you need to give her some space. She's experiencing a major adjustment period and needs time to get her bearings, explore a little, and find out about her new life.

- **Know your puppy-free zones.** Make sure that your family knows of any people-only zones in your house. If you don't want the dog to go to certain places, such as downstairs or into certain rooms, everybody in the family must be aware of this policy and get in the habit of keeping doors shut and baby gates in place (see Chapter 5 for info on baby gates).
- **Have a talk with the kids.** Prepare your kids for your new family member. Children must understand that even though little Samson looks like a toy, he isn't a toy. Shih Tzu puppies are sturdier than some toy breeds, but they can still be injured if a child drops the dog or falls on the dog. Every home with small children and Shih Tzu should live by a hard-and-fast rule, which must apply not only to the children in the house but also to any visiting children: *Small children must only play with Shih Tzu puppies while sitting or lying on the floor. No carrying a Shih Tzu while standing up!* (Check out Chapter 7 for more detailed info about introducing children to Lola or Samson.)

Shih-Tzu-Proofing Your House and Yard

Your family is ready for your new family member, but is your home ready? Even if you have a small apartment, every human household has potential dog hazards — poisons, choking, strangulation. But you don't have to live in fear for your new puppy, and I don't want to freak you out, either. As long as you're aware of these dangers, you can prevent something bad happening to little Lola and Samson.

Just as you would childproof a home if you were bringing in a toddler, you must puppyproof your home and yard before bringing in your new puppy. This section can help you start.

Avoiding poisons

Every year, many pets visit veterinary emergency clinics because of poisoning. Poisons come in surprising forms from spoiled food to that innocent looking houseplant. All puppies chew on things and explore the world with their mouths, so you must put all potential poisons out of reach from your new dog. You can either place these poisons on shelves where your Shih Tzu can't reach them

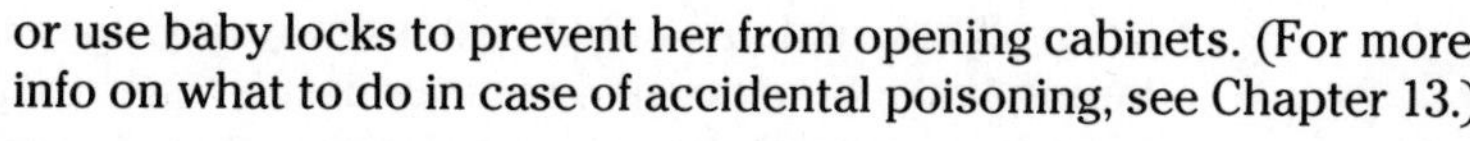
or use baby locks to prevent her from opening cabinets. (For more info on what to do in case of accidental poisoning, see Chapter 13.)

Before you bring home your puppy, make sure you do the following:

- **Cover all garbage and put it out of reach.** Even though your Shih Tzu looks little, you'd be surprised what a motivated small dog can do to tip over that trash.
- **Keep all household cleaners, laundry detergent, and other chemicals in a locked cabinet (or at least in a cabinet that a dog can't nose open).** You never know what a curious puppy may try to sample. Don't use rug deodorizers or carpet cleaners when you have a dog, or keep the dog out of the room when using them. They can be hazardous if ingested or inhaled.
- **Keep certain human foods away from dogs.** Some regular foods humans enjoy can be toxic to dogs, including onions, raisins, chocolate, and some spices. Even though junk food isn't necessarily poisonous, it can make your Shih Tzu sick or just overweight. Your pup should only eat high quality pet food, healthy treats, and occasional healthy people food like meat, fish, veggies, fruit, and the occasional spoonful of plain yogurt or cottage cheese. (For more on feeding, see Chapter 9.)

  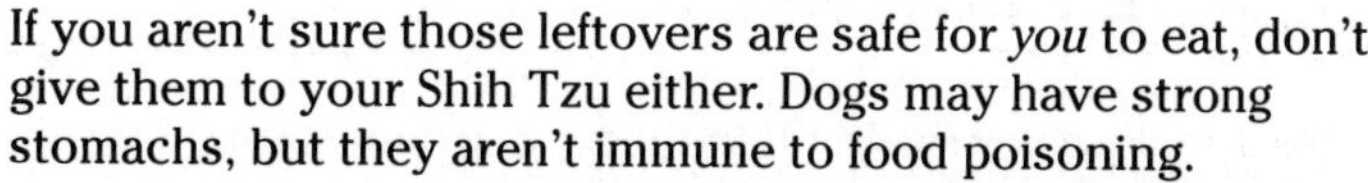
  If you aren't sure those leftovers are safe for *you* to eat, don't give them to your Shih Tzu either. Dogs may have strong stomachs, but they aren't immune to food poisoning.
- **Store human medications out of reach.** Human medications can poison dogs. If you accidentally spill aspirin or any other pill or liquid medicine, make sure you pick up or mop every bit.
- **Lock away all pesticides.** Pesticides in the form of roach traps, ant bait, rat poison, or any other chemical in the house or yard can pose a serious threat. If you must use pesticides, be sure that your Shih Tzu can't get anywhere near them.
- **Stash antifreeze away (and clean it up immediately).** Antifreeze smells and tastes sweet to dogs, but it's a deadly poison. Make sure that your car doesn't leak antifreeze in the garage or driveway, and never leave your Shih Tzu unsupervised in any area where cars park and potentially drip toxic fluids into tempting puddles on the ground.

  If your little Samson drinks even a bit of antifreeze, call the vet immediately, or go straight to the clinic. If your dog staggers around or acts drunk and you suspect he ingested antifreeze, go immediately to the vet. Pets can seem to recover but can suffer kidney failure, coma, and death within 12 hours if untreated.

- **Keep all houseplants out of reach.** Many dogs won't chew on houseplants, but some do. Some houseplants are harmless, but others can kill. According to the American Society for the Prevention of Cruelty to Animals (ASPCA), the ten most common poisonous household or yard plants are marijuana, sago palm, lilies, tulip and narcissus bulbs, azaleas and rhododendrons, oleander, castor bean, cyclamen, kalanchoe, and yew. For a more extensive list of toxic plants to avoid in your home or yard, check out the following Web site: `www.hsus.org/pets/pet_care/protect_your_pet_from_common_household_dangers/common_poisonous_plants.html`.
- **Watch your dog at all times outside.** Many items in your yard can be harmful to your pet, from mulch in the garden to flowering plants to lawn chemicals. Never leave your Shih Tzu outside unattended, especially if she likes to chew on things, and never let a Shih Tzu play on a chemically treated lawn.

If you think your Shih Tzu has swallowed poison, contact your emergency veterinary clinic immediately or call the ASPCA Poison Control Center hotline at **(888) 426-4435.** A $55 consultation fee may be applied to your credit card.

Eyeing other potential dangers

Puppies can get into plenty of trouble around the house. Curious and interested in the world, they explore — often with their mouths. Also, because they're small, they can get lost, stuck, or stepped on.

Here are some ways to keep your puppy safe from harm.

- **Cover or tape all exposed electrical cords.** Puppies need to chew, and if they see an electrical cord, they may gnaw.
- **Reduce all potential strangulation hazards.** A Shih Tzu can get caught in a mini-blind cord, drapery tie, or even a baby gate, and strangle himself when nobody's watching.
- **Never, ever leave your Shih Tzu unsupervised and tied on a leash outside.** Doing so leaves your pup vulnerable to strangulation, attack by other animals, heatstroke, frostbite, and theft. Your Shih Tzu is a companion, so keep him with you.
- **Check for unsteady furniture and low-hanging tablecloths or runners.** Your Shih Tzu can bump or pull them, accidentally knocking over heavy objects, or breaking things.
- **Watch your feet!** Your Shih Tzu wants to be with you and will most likely follow you around, so if you aren't watching where you step, you may step right on him.

- **Always check inside dryers, cupboards, and other small spaces before closing them.** Your Shih Tzu could be inside. Also be careful of recliners, baskets of laundry, and other snuggly places your Shih Tzu may wiggle into.
- **Prevent drowning!** Their heavy coats and heavy bones don't suit Shih Tzu for swimming, and if a Shih Tzu falls into a swimming pool, fish pond, hot tub, bathtub, bucket of water, or even the toilet, he can drown. Keep Shih Tzu away from *all* water (and keep the toilet lid *down*).
- **Puppyproof all rooms.** If you haven't puppyproofed a room, keep your Shih Tzu out. Close the door or erect a baby gate.

Protecting your belongings

You didn't really care that much about your favorite shoes or that imported cashmere sweater did you? Sure, many dogs chew much more vigorously and destructively than a Shih Tzu, but that doesn't mean little Lola doesn't have a destructive set of choppers, too.

The best way to protect your belongings is to put them away, and make sure that kids keep their toys off the floor, too. A Shih Tzu may only chew a tiny hole in your gorgeous new silk skirt, but a tiny hole is a still a hole. For items you can't put away, like couch cushions or the corner of the Oriental rug your Shih Tzu favors, spray them with a bad-tasting chew-deterrent spray (nontoxic) such as Bitter Apple.

Putting Your Home in Order for Your Shih Tzu

Just because your home's safe for a Shih Tzu doesn't mean it's ready. Your Shih Tzu feels most welcome and can adjust quickly to her new environment if you have her space mapped out and set up. This section moves from room to room and helps you make your home Shih Tzu-friendly.

Her boudoir: The kennel, the dog bed, or your bed

Where will your Shih Tzu sleep? This consideration is important. Sleep takes up a big chunk of life and establishing good habits matters. Deciding where your Shih Tzu is going to sleep may be a hard decision for you. You want to make a choice that you can stick with because changing your mind later sets the stage for inconsistency, which confuses dogs. Before you decide, consider the pros and cons (in the next sections) to each of your options.

Choice #1: The dog den (kennel or crate)

Having your new dog sleep inside his dog den, especially during the first few weeks or months in your home, is arguably the best choice. You should have a kennel or crate already (check out Chapter 5 for what to look for when buying a kennel or crate) for housetraining, travel, and other times when you need to keep your dog enclosed. This kennel also makes a great sleeping spot.

Having a dog sleep in an enclosed space has the following advantages:

- **When the dog sleeps better, you may sleep better.** When comfortably lined with soft bedding, the kennel feels like a den. This place feels safe and secure. Even your sociable Shih Tzu sometimes wants to be alone.
- **Dens serve as great housetraining tools.** Check out Chapter 16 for how to use a kennel and crate for housetraining.
- **Dens make little Samson feel safer.** A den gives Samson a place to rest when you can't watch him. He can't get out, which he may not always like, but others can't get in either, which he *will* like. The trick is to make the den seem like the best place in the world to little Samson.

  Here's how:

  - **Hide yummy treats in the crate.** Whenever he goes in, he'll find little snacks buried in the bedding of the kennel.
  - **Locate the den next to your bed.** This placement gives your dog some comfort to know that you're right there beside him during the night. During the day, you can move the crate to your office or wherever you spend time, or you can leave it in a secluded spot Samson prefers. After you find a place for the den, keep it there so Samson always knows where it is.
  - **Maintain an open-door policy during the day.** Leave the den door open so Samson can go inside for a peaceful break from the family whenever he wants. Before you know it, he'll probably hang out in there when he isn't busy with his very important job of being your companion.

Don't use a child's room or play room to place the kennel for seclusion. Children can be tempted to take Lola out of her cage and play with her when you aren't watching.

Choice #2: The dog bed

Dog beds come in many shapes and sizes. Some are simple, basic dog beds, while some are quite luxurious. But no matter what type of bed you choose for your new Shih Tzu (check out Chapter 5 for more info), the trick is to get her to actually *sleep* in the bed. Unlike a kennel with a door that closes with a latch, a dog bed is used voluntarily. If Lola doesn't want to sleep there, she can always get up and go somewhere else.

You can, however, make the dog bed more appealing to your Shih Tzu with a few easy tricks:

- **Hide treats in the bed.** "Look what's in here, Lola!"
- **Put the bed next to your bed.** "Don't worry, Lola. I'm right here."
- **Place her in the bed and praise her.** Whenever she goes to the bed on her own, praise her! "What a good dog, in her own bed!" Never scold her for leaving the bed. She may associate the scolding with the bed and then she'll never want to go back.

If Lola consistently chooses a different space other than her dog bed for sleeping, such as under a chair, under the bed, or under a desk, you can put the dog bed in that spot, or you can get her a dog bed that's more enclosed and private. She may be seeking a space that feels safer and more like a den.

Choice #3: Your bed

My guess is that many Shih Tzu owners let their dogs sleep curled up beside them in bed. If you decide that your Shih Tzu can sleep in bed with you, just remember to take her out for a potty break several times during the night to make sure she doesn't find a nice potty spot under your covers!

Some people teach their Shih Tzu to sleep in the kennel until housetraining is complete and then let the dog come into the bed later, if she so desires. (See "Choice #1: The dog den [kennel or crate]" earlier in this section.) That's fine, too. But doing things the other way around may hurt your dog's feelings, and she won't understand why she's being banished from a place she was welcomed before.

The downside of bed sleeping: You can injure or even smother a very small puppy if you happen to roll over on him during the night. Plus, Shih Tzu can get overheated under a lot of covers. Keep your dog on top of the blanket, and if he's a very small puppy, keep him in his crate or dog bed at least until he's big and strong enough to fend for himself.

And of course, some people don't want the dog in the bed at all and for good reasons:

- **Insomnia:** Many people suffer from insomnia because their pets keep them awake in the bed.
- **Snoring:** Some Shih Tzu snore, which may keep you awake.
- **Dog hair:** Some people don't want dog hair in the bed.
- **Allergies:** Allergies can worsen at night for some people.
- **Private time:** Some people just like to sleep alone (or alone with another human companion).

If you don't want the Shih Tzu in your bed, that's perfectly fine. Samson can be just as happy in a dog bed or a kennel — eventually.

Daytime quiet area

The doggy boudoir is a nice place for a Shih Tzu to sleep, but also it serves as a useful tool for housetraining and enforced quiet times when you can't supervise. Most dogs sleep a lot and sensitive types can get over-stimulated by too much activity. Sometimes, a Shih Tzu really needs to get away and calm down or nap undisturbed.

However, not every Shih Tzu owner ultimately uses a kennel or crate for rest time and housetraining, preferring to set aside a special area for unsupervised rest times during the day. This practice is particularly common among pet owners who decide to paper- or litter-train their pets instead of training them to go outside.

The space you choose for your Shih Tzu should be small, puppy-proofed (see "Shih-Tzu-Proofing Your House and Yard" earlier in this chapter for more info), inaccessible to small children, escape-proof, and comfortable. You can use a baby gate to section off a small portion of the kitchen with newspapers or a doggy litter box in one corner and food and water dishes in another corner.

The space shouldn't be too large. Don't give your Shih Tzu puppy the entire run of the house — or at least, not at first. Dogs feel much more secure in small spaces, preferably partially enclosed. It's the den instinct, and even though Shih Tzu don't much resemble wolves, they still feel safer and more comfortable in smaller spaces.

The dining area

One of the most important things to keep regular in a Shih Tzu's life is his eating area and schedule. Dogs like routine, so you should set up the food and water bowls in a place your Shih Tzu can get to easily and at all times. Many people feed their pets in the kitchen or dining room, before, during, or after the family meal. Where you feed your Shih Tzu matters less than always feeding him at the same time and in the same place.

If your dog has a special quiet area or gated area where he stays while you can't watch him, put the food and water in this area, so he always has access to water. Avoid choosing places like bathrooms where a door may get closed and block your Shih Tzu's access to water. Be sure the water bowl or bottle (see Chapter 5 for more info on selecting a water bowl or bottle) is clean with fresh water, and fill the food bowl the same way, at the same time, every day.

To keep the dining area clean and sanitary, you can use a large plastic placemat under the dishes. Shih Tzu beards tend to slop water around, so this can keep your floor from getting stained. Also, locate the food and water away from the bathroom area, for sanitation and because Shih Tzu don't like to have these areas too close together. If they are, the dog may decide to relocate his bathroom spot, with or without your knowledge.

The pooping and peeing area

Decide where to locate your dog's bathroom area *before* you bring home your Shih Tzu because you spend some time establishing this very important habit on your first day together. Do you want your Shih Tzu to use a special spot in the house as her personal toilet, or would you prefer she use the great outdoors? After you decide which way to go, switching is very difficult and disruptive to your dog's routine, so think about this carefully.

Choosing that special place

If you decide to paper- or litter-train your Shih Tzu, choose an area inside your house where your puppy can go:

- **The daytime quiet area:** If your Shih Tzu gets a daytime quiet area, you can set up papers or a litter box in one corner (see "Daytime quiet area" earlier in this chapter).
- **The kitchen:** Some people don't like to see dog waste in the kitchen, but for others, the floor is the easiest to clean.

- **Bathrooms:** Bathrooms make sensible areas because your Shih Tzu is smart enough to tell that the bathroom is where *you* do *your* business. Some dogs have been trained to use shower stalls as their personal potties.

If you do choose the bathroom as your Shih Tzu's potty spot, be sure everyone in the family knows to keep the toilet seat down at all times (except, obviously, during use). The toilet bowl is a very real drowning hazard for Shih Tzu.

Paper training (or doggy litter box training) is ideal for people in high-rise apartments, people who are homebound and have trouble getting outside, those who can't walk a dog or don't live in an area where they can easily or safely walk a dog, and those who live in climates with harsh conditions. For the lowdown on housetraining, check out Chapter 16.

Going outside

If you choose to train your Shih Tzu to poop and pee outside, pick an area in your yard or patio where you teach your Shih Tzu to go. The area should be where people don't walk in the yard or in a spot that's easy to clean and not unsightly.

Shih Tzu are small so they're easy to clean up after, and some pet owners find the Shih Tzu's waste virtually disappears into the grass and doesn't really need to be picked up. This method applies only to your own yard. Of course, you must pick up after your Shih Tzu on walks when she poops on other peoples' property.

Yard training is ideal for people with fenced yards, easy-clean patios, or who don't mind taking a dog out on a leash multiple times every day, not only for walks but for short potty breaks.

Scheduling the Vet Check-up

Every new pet should visit a vet within the first 48 hours in a new home. Most breeders and pet stores require, by contract, that you take a new dog to a vet to check the dog and give her health a thumbs-up (or thumbs-down). So make sure to arrange for a vet and make an appointment *before* you bring home your new puppy.

Plan ahead and tell your current vet (if you have one) that you're getting a new family member. Then when you pick up your new arrival, your vet is aware that you need to schedule an appointment and can fit you in.

What if you really aren't sure which vet to use? First, check with your breeder or friends and neighbors for a recommendation. If you don't find any useful info, check out Chapter 12 to find a vet.

Picking Up Puppy

Are you really ready to pick up your new Shih Tzu puppy and bring her home? If you have all the supplies, if the house is ready, if the family is prepared, then . . . yes! Make arrangements with the breeder (or shelter or pet store or wherever you're getting your dog) to pick up the puppy, so they can prepare all the paperwork and supplies (see Chapter 4 for more on the essential paperwork and Chapter 5 for the necessary supplies). Be sure you bring a car-safe kennel or dog seatbelt with you (check out the next section to help you make the decision).

Before you leave the breeder (or place you get your dog), be sure you have all the necessary, important stuff:

- The purchase or adoption contract (see Chapter 4)
- The health guarantee (if separate from the contract — see Chapter 4)
- Vaccination records and other records of any veterinary care your Shih Tzu has already had (see Chapter 4)
- All necessary registration paperwork to register your pure-bred dog (if relevant) (see Chapter 4)
- Written info on care, grooming, and training
- A small bag of the food that your Shih Tzu has been eating, if you plan to switch his food (for more info, see Chapter 9)
- Information on microchipping and how to send in the paper-work to have your dog's microchip registered (for more on microchipping, see Chapter 12)
- The breeder's contact info
- The dog! (If you walked out without her, you wouldn't be the first flustered new pet owner to do that.)

At this time, you can also ask any remaining questions you've thought of while preparing your home. And then off you go . . . home sweet home, here you come, with a Shih Tzu in your arms and a song in your heart. Wait, did I just say "a Shih Tzu in your arms?" Perish the thought. All Shih Tzu should travel to their new homes safely buckled up or crated. (Check out the next section for important info.)

Buckling Up: Making the Trip Home

You're finally ready to take your new dog home, but remember, your dog may never have ridden in a car before. She may be scared. Also, if the drive is long, you'll want water for her, and a leash and collar so you can safely take her out for potty breaks.

Before you load Lola into the car, make sure she's safe. The following advice can help your trip home go more smoothly.

- **Secure your puppy in her crate.** If you've brought along a crate that buckles into the car, put her in the crate first, and then put the crate into the car. Don't buckle a crate into the back of a pickup truck or any other open-air space. The temperature extremes, noise, wind, and being far away from you can be too traumatic and even dangerous.
- **Use a dog seatbelt.** A seatbelt you say? Your Shih Tzu is so little. He absolutely needs a seatbelt. What if you get in a car accident on the way home? A dog can be seriously injured or killed in a car accident, and he can also act as a missile inside the car, injuring you or other passengers. Plus, a loose puppy can easily bolt out of an open door and into oncoming traffic.

  Most well-stocked pet stores have dog seatbelts, or you can shop online. The following Web sites provide essential products to keep your new Shih Tzu safe while riding in a car:

  - `www.ruffrider.com`
  - `www.batzi.com`
  - `www.seatbeltsfordogs.com`
  - `www.doginfopoint.com`
  - `www.petsafetybelts.com`
- **Keep your dog confined at all times when the car's moving.** You probably want to take her in your arms and cuddle her on the drive home, but this simply isn't safe. What if you were in a car accident? Talk to her, assure her, but if you absolutely must take her out of her crate or seatbelt, stop the car, park in a safe place, and then offer those cuddles (and a bathroom break, if it's been awhile).

Chapter 7

Welcoming Home Your Shih Tzu with Open Arms

In This Chapter

- Showing your Shih Tzu around the house
- Introducing your Shih Tzu to the family and other pets
- Making it through the night

To your new puppy, your home isn't home sweet home at all. At least, not yet. A strange, unfamiliar, possibly even scary place awaits your little Lola, and she isn't at all sure she likes the idea of leaving her mother and fuzzy little brothers and sisters for a big, unknown world.

This chapter can help you help Lola transition from life in the whelping box (or the animal shelter) to life with you and your family in your home. Your house will quickly become home to your Shih Tzu if you introduce her gently and with guidance.

Introducing Your Dog to the New Digs

There you are, pulling up in the driveway with poor little Samson in the backseat. He's probably wondering what the heck is going on and why these giant two-legged creatures have taken him away from the place he thought was his home. Not to worry, Samson. Everything will turn out just fine. But remember how your little puppy probably feels when you take him into that place you know so well. He probably feels a little bit lost.

To help him feel a little less lost, introduce him to his new home by showing him around. This section covers the important areas of your home to show your new family member, as well as what to remember when allowing your Shih Tzu a chance to explore your home on his own.

Showing your Shih Tzu the important areas

Dogs like to know where they are. If you walk in the door and everybody starts shrieking and cooing at the cute little puppy, Samson is going to feel even more overwhelmed, so tell everybody to step off for just a few minutes. Put other pets in their kennels or closed in other rooms, and ask the kids to *step away from the Shih Tzu.* You're going to help Samson feel right at home by taking him to the important areas in your house first and letting him use all his doggy senses to get a feel for the place.

Taking a potty break

After the stress of driving in a car with you, Samson probably needs to relieve himself. Young puppies, in particular, need to pee quite often. Before you go anywhere else (and that includes putting your puppy down on the living room carpet), take the dog to the spot you have chosen to be his own personal Shih Tzu bathroom.

The place a dog relieves himself is very important to you and to the dog. This spot marks the dog's territory, and after he's put his scent on the spot, he'll remember where it is he's supposed to go. That's why taking your new Shih Tzu to his potty spot first thing — before he makes the leg of your new couch his new pee spot — is important. (For more on choosing the right spot, see Chapter 6).

Getting your new dog to use the bathroom isn't overly difficult. Just remember these steps:

1. **Put on his new collar and leash.**

   Doing so is very important because you'll have better control over Samson when you get to the pee spot. You want to send a clear message: *This is the bathroom.* The only way to do that is to keep your Shih Tzu from wandering away before he does his business.

2. **Go to your dog's potty spot.**

   If you've chosen a spot outdoors, go there before you go inside the house. If you plan to paper-train your Shih Tzu, take him inside. Either way, carry the dog to the pee spot and don't put him down until you've reached that special spot. He gets to sniff here first.

3. **Allow your Shih Tzu to explore the potty area all he wants, to the end of the leash.**

   Because your dog is in new territory, he has an instinct to make his mark. This is just what you want! He can sniff; he can scratch; he can sit down and look at you as if to say, "Why are we still here?" No matter. Talk to him gently and encouragingly. And wait. Don't be in a hurry. Let the dog get situated. Eventually, he'll squat and do his business.

4. **After Samson finishes his business, praise him by saying, "Good dog!"**

   Don't scare your little guy with too much enthusiasm, but let him know he just did pretty much the most amazing thing you've ever seen. Mission one accomplished. Now you can move on to the next interesting site (see the next section).

If Samson simply won't pee, don't despair. Show him his kennel next, and let him take a little rest, for about 15 minutes. (See the next section on introducing your dog to his sleeping area.) Then, take him back out and try again. (Also check out Chapter 16 that covers housetraining more in-depth.)

Introducing the sleeping digs

Dogs sleep a lot, and your Shih Tzu will probably spend a lot of time snoozing on your lap, at your feet, in your arms, or somewhere nearby, where he can keep an eye on you. Much of the time, however — when you can't keep an eye on *him* — your Shih Tzu will be snoozing in his crate or dog bed, so be sure to spend some time introducing him to his boudoir as follows:

1. **Take your Shih Tzu to his dog bed or kennel/crate.**

   If it's a kennel or crate, open the door.

2. **Toss a tempting, tiny treat or two onto the bedding.**

   He may not be hungry, so don't worry if he ignores it.

3. **Put your Shih Tzu next to the bed or kennel/crate and see if he climbs in to get the treat or just to explore.**

   Some dogs climb right in, curl up, and look at you as if to say, "Okay, I can hang out here for awhile, I'm good." Others may not be so interested, or may even seem shy or fearful about this strange new place. Don't worry, all these reactions are normal. Most importantly, don't force your Shih Tzu into the bed or kennel/crate right now. The point is, you've introduced the area, so the next time your dog sees it, it won't be new anymore.

Hankering for a nibble

With all the excitement, your Shih Tzu puppy may not be very hungry just yet. However, the next spot you may want to visit is the dining area. You can let your Shih Tzu find the dinner dishes on her own, or you can escort her to the dining area.

To show the dining area for your pooch, check out these tips:

- Put a tiny bit of dog food in the food bowl, and fill the water bowl with fresh clean water.
- Let Lola have a sniff and a bite or a sip if she likes.
- Don't force it. If she drinks or eats or both, praise her. *Good girl.* If she doesn't, don't worry about it.

Now she knows where her dinner dishes are located. If she does have a snack, check a clock. In about 15 minutes or so, she'll probably need to go back to her potty spot. But for now, she can explore a little bit more.

Letting your dog explore safely

As your puppy explores the house, keep a few things in mind. Too much territory can be intimidating, so if your puppy seems overstimulated or scared — shaking, whining, hiding, or sticking to you like glue — keep the exploration limited to one room where you and your dog will spend a lot of time, such as the family room or kitchen.

These pointers can help as you allow your dog to explore:

- **Follow her around, just to be sure she's safe and doesn't get into anything she isn't supposed to.** As Lola explores, remember that you want to set the rules right from the beginning. Don't let her do anything on that very first day that you don't want her to do later, like nibble on the edge of the rug or play tug-of-war with the curtain fringe. If she goes astray, redirect her attention to something else, like a toy or a treat. Don't scold harshly or yell. You don't want to scare her before you've really gotten to know her. Distraction works better.

- **Keep an eye out for signs that she has to go potty again.** If she starts to circle, sniff intently in one spot, or obviously squat, then whisk her back to the potty spot. Don't scold! Praise her after you get there. Check out Chapter 16 for all the signs.

After she has had a chance to explore the new smells of her new home for awhile — five minutes, 20 minutes, or as long as she remains interested — you can start introducing her to her new roommates. The next section shows you how.

Making Proper Introductions

Imagine if someone took you out of your home one day without any warning and took you to a whole new place to live, where you were suddenly bombarded with five giants trying to pick you up and pet you and talk right in your face. Yikes!

In the same way, your Shih Tzu can be scared and intimidated by too many people trying to meet and handle her all at once. That's why carefully introducing other pets and family members is important — one at a time, under controlled conditions — so the whole experience is positive (or at least not traumatic). The following sections tell you how.

Meeting your other pets

Fortunately, Shih Tzu tend to be pretty easy-going and not aggressive or territorial with other animals. But even so, the sweet temperament of your Shih Tzu is no guarantee that your resident cat or dog will take kindly to this new addition.

Here Kitty, Kitty

Most cats happily leave a new dog alone, and the most likely scenario in a home with a resident cat is that the new puppy will harass the cat, instead of the other way around. Cats generally are independent, but they aren't above getting jealous. So if all your attention gets showered on your new little Lola, then Miss Kitty may have good reason for revenge.

Keep the following pointers in mind when introducing your cat with your new Shih Tzu:

- **When you bring Miss Kitty out of hiding to meet Lola, keep firm control over both pets.** Let both animals have a look at each other, but if either pet reacts negatively, let them go their separate ways. They'll work out their peace on their own, as long as everybody has their personal space.
- **Make sure Miss Kitty always has at least a couple of escape routes, just in case Lola gets feisty.** Some Shih Tzu chase cats, and others simply keep trying to play with them long after the cat has lost patience. Your cat should be able to dash out of the room or jump up above Shih Tzu level.

  A cornered cat can be dangerous, and if the cat thinks she can't escape any other way, she may injure your puppy with a swipe of the claws — and your Shih Tzu's eyes are particularly vulnerable to scratches from a cat.

- **Keep the cat's litter box, food, and water out of Lola's reach.** Your cat has been with you for awhile, and she shouldn't have to endure trespassing into her territory by some canine upstart. Plus, some dogs like to play in cat litter or even eat those little treats they find in the litter box. Dogs can even get intestinal impactions from eating kitty litter.
- **Be sure to give your cat plenty of attention and affection when she wants it.** As long as she knows she's not out of the loop, she probably won't have a problem with her new roomie. Shih Tzu are ultimately agreeable and aren't a breed prone to dashing after cats as if they were some kind of vermin. Your cat probably doesn't care much one way or the other whether Lola wants to hang around way down there on the floor.

Most Shih Tzu really do get along fine with cats, and even if the first meeting isn't love at first sight, Lola and Miss Kitty will get used to each other eventually. That is, as long as the cat can get away and both pets are getting plenty of attention and care.

Other dogs: Friend or competition?

Shih Tzu see other pets, whether dogs or cats, as potential friends and interesting companions. Other dogs may not always see a Shih Tzu that way, however. Some breeds can be very territorial and will feel threatened by the presence of another dog. Other breeds have a strong prey drive and can even see the Shih Tzu as something to chase! These dogs aren't generally good companions for Shih Tzu, although there are exceptions.

Many dogs, however, are just as friendly and open to taking on a dog sibling as the Shih Tzu is, and these friendly fellows can be wonderful companions for Shih Tzu. In particular, Shih Tzu love other Shih Tzu, and many people keep two, three, or more together quite happily. That doesn't mean your resident dog won't be jealous or a little put out by the presence of a new dog in the house. The way you introduce your new dog and your old dog can go a long way toward easing the tension and making your two best friends, well . . . best friends!

To ensure that the initial meeting goes smoothly, try the following steps when introducing your new Shih Tzu to another dog. If you have more than one dog, introduce your new dog to each one separately, so they can work out their own relationships without too much chaos:

1. **Clip a leash on both dogs and bring the resident dog out for an introduction.**

   Introduce your dogs in a room that doesn't contain your resident dog's bed, crate, food, or water, and keep all toys somewhere else during this first meeting, to eliminate any sense of competition over resources. Neutralize the territory as much as possible so your resident dog doesn't feel threatened. If your dog likes to hang out on your bed or the couch, don't hold the meeting near these areas, either. You may try to hold the meeting outside in the yard.

2. **Keep both dogs on the ground and on their leashes at first, just to test their reactions.**

   Let your dogs meet with all four paws on the floor so they don't feel possessive of, or possessed by, you. They need to work out their relationships on dog terms. Also keep them both on leashes just in case you need to reel in anybody — if somebody lunges, you need to have control. (Doing so is easier if someone else is helping you, so each one of you has responsibility for one of the dogs.) Be aware, however, that some dogs become more defensive on a leash just because they know they're on a leash. Keep the leash loose — hold it firmly but make your dog feel like you're pulling on it — so neither dog feels restrained. Only use the leash (to pull a dog away from the other dog) if somebody becomes aggressive or threatening.

3. **Let the dogs sniff each other and greet each other.**

   Stay positive and praise all friendly interactions. Chances are, your two dogs will be fast friends right away! But if they aren't, or if you get a growl or a little fight, separate the dogs again for awhile and try again in a few minutes. Let them know that these fights won't be tolerated. If they want to interact, they have to play nice. If they growl, they get separated (and separated from you — the ultimate doggy punishment!).

Even if the dogs get along great, be sure to supervise all interactions for at least the first few weeks. Dogs can be unpredictable, especially when they're adjusting to a new situation, and you want to be sure you're there to manage any sudden incidents. Keeping everybody playing nicely and gently is your responsibility.

Problems may be less likely with a puppy — your resident dog may just write him off as inferior. But even if your larger dog is ecstatic about *his* new little puppy, he may get too rough, just out of sheer exuberance. However — and this is important — don't scold your older dog for friendly interactions, even if you think they're too rough! Your dog could interpret your scolding as a message that it's wrong to be friendly with the Shih Tzu. Instead, keep hold of him and encourage gentle interaction.

Many a resident dog has been interested and excited by a new puppy at first, but when the pet owner (yes, you) gives the new puppy all the attention and neglects the resident dog, the dog then becomes dejected and feels jealous or confused about why he's no longer important to you. Please don't let this happen! Give both dogs plenty of attention and love and one-on-one time, too. Your old dog needs to know you still love him just as much as you always did, even if you have a new furry little sibling in the family.

Meeting the kids

The children have been bouncing off the walls in the background, eager to descend on the new puppy with all their explosive energy. And that's wonderful! Kids and Shih Tzu go great together . . . with a few precautions.

First of all, small puppies are fragile, just like human infants. You can't step on them, drop them, pull on their ears, or tote them around like dolls without hurting or traumatizing them. Unlike human infants, puppies have teeth like sharp little needles, and because puppies explore the world with their mouths, children's fingers and toes may easily come into contact with those teeth. To prevent anyone from getting injured or feeling traumatized, follow these steps:

1. **Place the dog in an adult's lap and ask the kids to sit by the adult, *one at a time*.**

   Too many kids at once can frighten and overwhelm the new dog. Tell the child not to rush over squealing, but to walk over quietly and calmly as not to scare the new dog.

2. **Allow the child to pet the dog.**

   Teach the child to be quiet and not to grab the dog. Remember to be gentle with soft pats and soft words. An older child can hold the dog on her lap, but remind her to be gentle.

3. **After a couple of minutes, take a break and let the dog rest.**

   A new puppy can become overstimulated by too much wild kid energy. Let Lola be the guide when she's had enough contact. If she shies away or starts to shake or growl, the interaction has gone on for too long. Chances are, however, that this won't happen and dog and child will love each other immediately.

Adults are in charge. Pay attention and don't allow children and dogs to hurt each other. If children understand at a young age to treat a dog with gentle kindness, they've learned a valuable lesson.

Naming your new Shih Tzu

In this book, I talk a lot about Samson and Lola, but of course you can name *your* new Shih Tzu anything you want. Naming a pet is fun and the whole family can get involved. Whatever you name your dog, consider that shorter names are easier for a dog to master. He can pick up "Here, Puff!" faster than "Here, Mister Puff-n-Stuff!" or "Here, Sean Puffy Shih Tzu!"

Of course, that's what nicknames are for. Your dog can have a long fancy name like Elizabeth Barrett Browning, but you can call her Lizzy for short. In fact, most show dogs have long fancy names, such as Champion Rapunzel's Gold Plaited Mischief, and also *call names,* like Goldy — the show-dog term for a nickname.

A lot of people give their Shih Tzu Chinese names to reflect their origins, and others give them names that make reference to their long fluffy coats, but you can be as creative as you want. Confucius? Fluffy? Steve? Have fun choosing.

After the child and the Shih Tzu have met, be sure the child understands some basic rules about handling the dog:

- **Show the child the correct way to pick up and hold the dog.** The child should put one hand under the dog's chest and the other around the rump, and then hold the dog against the chest. Remember, children should always hold the dog while sitting on the floor, until they're old enough that they won't accidentally drop the dog. I recommend a child be at least 10 before carrying around a Shih Tzu.
- **Tell the child *not* to let the dog chew on fingers.** Any contact of canine teeth on human skin should be met with a "No!" and pulling the hand away. (*Not* a slap.) Have the child pet little Lola and talk gently to her
- **Depending on the child's age, enlist him in the care of the puppy.** Teens and mature elementary-age kids can be a big help. Kids can walk the dog, brush and comb the coat, practice basic training cues, and even feed the dog. However, remember that ultimately, an adult should be responsible for making sure these important jobs are accomplished.
- **Instruct children in Shih Tzu safety.** Just because the neighbors allowed their Golden Retriever to go swimming doesn't mean little Lola can go swimming — her heavy coat and bone structure make swimming very difficult, and the result could be a disaster. Furthermore, Samson can't run in the heat. That long coat and short nose make him susceptible to heatstroke! You can't tie his leash to a bicycle and expect him to keep up. You can't take Lola outside without her leash on or expose her to dangerous situations such as interactions with large aggressive dogs or rough children. You can't put Samson outside and forget about him, especially in hot weather. (For more on Shih Tzu safety, see Chapters 12.)
- **Keep a close eye on children to ensure they're taking care of the dog.** Older children are still learning how to be responsible and no child should be solely responsible for the care of a dog. If the Shih Tzu belongs to an older child (say, an adult gave the dog to the child as a gift), that's great, in theory. In many cases, a dog that supposedly belongs to a child quickly figures out that he really belongs to the parents, because they're the ones who feed him, walk him, and spend time with him.

Older kids need guidance, too. They're still kids and still learning how to manage life in the world. Keep a watchful eye out and make sure little Samson and older children both stay safe.

Getting Through the First Night

Even if you've had smooth sailing with all the other steps so far (see the previous sections in this chapter), you may be in for a difficult night. If you think about it, this stage is perfectly natural. When the house goes dark, your Shih Tzu is bound to feel the loss of those snuggly siblings and her mother's warmth.

But nighttime is a routine, and the best time to start a nighttime routine with a new dog is on the very first night. Use these tips so Lola's first night (and the following nights) in her new home are calm and soothing:

- **Take your dog on a last-minute potty break.** Doing so allows your dog (and you) to sleep comfortably for awhile before she has to go out again.
- **Ensure that your dog has a full tummy — but not too full.** Your Shih Tzu should have had her evening meal, but also her evening potty break after that meal. You don't want to feed her and put her straight to bed or she'll just have to go out again.
- **Leave a soft dog toy with your dog.** A little cuddly toy can comfort your dog, especially on her first few nights in a new home. It may feel like one of her siblings.
- **Make your dog's boudoir comfy.** Place soft padding in your dog's bed so she's comfortable and warm. (Check out Chapter 5 for the right type of bedding.)
- **Stay nearby.** Remember, your dog doesn't want to be alone. If she knows you're near, she'll feel safer.

The whining and crying is only a test

Whimper, whine, whimper, whine . . . and you thought it was time for sleeping? Most new puppies and even many adult dogs spend some time whining and crying on their first night in a new home. Remember, your Shih Tzu has been thrown into an entirely new existence. Now it's bedtime and your pup feels awfully nervous. Where are her littermates? Where is her mother? And so starts the whining! Wouldn't you whimper a little, too? But (and this is a *big* but) . . . you have to be strong.

On the first night, you may have some trouble keeping your dog in her bed. Just keep encouraging her during the first few weeks to sleep in it, and keep putting her back in the bed and praising her when she goes there herself. Make the bed a rewarding place to be and the bedtime ritual a routine. She'll soon love to curl up, right on schedule. In the meantime, here are some tips for establishing that routine right now:

- **Reach down and pet her.** A hand on her assures her you're nearby, so she doesn't worry quite so much. Just don't pick her up. Doing so teaches her that whining results in getting you to pick her up, and you want her to learn, instead, that whining results in nothing — neither good nor bad.
- **Cuddle her (only if she's already in bed with you).** Truth be told, if she's in bed with you, and you plan to let her sleep there indefinitely, you probably won't hear much whining.
- **Talk to her.** Reassure her with calming, quiet words. Let her know you're there and everything is just fine — but that she isn't coming out to play right now.

Eventually your Shih Tzu will give up her whining and go to sleep (maybe just out of sheer exhaustion). But that means she'll figure out that she *can* go to sleep in her new bed or den, and that everything will be just fine when she wakes up. After a night or two of this new routine, if you've stayed strong in your resolve to teach her how to sleep in her new home, she should be sleep quietly through the night — at least until she needs a potty break.

Potty breaks

When your Shih Tzu finally goes to sleep, the peacefulness may not last for long, because much like human infants, puppies need to pee. They can't hold it all night long, and they don't wear diapers. So during these first nights, if your puppy sleeps, then wakes up and whines, you need to take her to her potty spot, no matter the time. An adult dog may not need any potty breaks during the night, but young puppies will probably need at least two. For more detailed instructions on housetraining your puppy, see Chapter 16.

And remember — the more consistent your nighttime routines are from the very beginning, the faster you'll all enjoy peaceful slumber. Sweet dreams!

Chapter 8

Getting Through the First Few Days

In This Chapter

- Getting to know each other
- Establishing the all-important routine
- Laying down the rules with some family training

Although Shih Tzu tend to have better natural manners than *some* breeds (I won't name names, Mr. Labrador Retriever puppy!), no puppy should be expected to understand, without any information, a human's strange and unusual quirks and pet peeves.

Humans and dogs have fundamental differences in the way they see the world around them. That's why the first few days are so important. During this time you can introduce your dog to the ground rules, which can help him gain confidence, lose fear, and be an all-around happier fellow. And that's good for everyone.

And don't delay! Setting up the new routines, rules, and lifestyles must happen right away (in the first few days). The sooner your Shih Tzu learns what life's like now in the new house, with new people, the faster she can settle into her routines, resulting in a happy dog (and a happy you, of course!).

Making a Good First Impression

Consider how your new Shih Tzu must be adjusting to life with his brand new human. What's he supposed to make of you? And are you making the right first impression on *him?* Actually, because Shih Tzu have been bred for so many centuries to be close personal companions to humans, your Shih Tzu does have an inherent sense about who you are. She isn't some street dog who hasn't ever met a human. She knows what's what, and so far, you've been pretty nice.

And so have others, in the best of circumstances. Your Shih Tzu has probably already had loving care, gentle handling, and an idea that humans are safe and wonderful. Now that you're in charge, your new Shih Tzu expects you to take care of her, keep her safe, and give her a lot of attention. But if you don't fulfill those jobs right out of the gate, your Shih Tzu may begin to feel suspicious and distrustful.

Naturally trusting, your Shih Tzu will accept your direction and your leadership, if you provide it.

Setting Up a Daily Routine: Your Shih Tzu Day Planner

Dogs thrive on routines and routines keep dogs feeling calm and safe. If you like routine too, setting up a routine for your new dog will be easy. Just figure out how to incorporate your Shih Tzu's daily requirements — meals, potty breaks, naps, walks, training sessions, and so on — into your already-established routine.

If you're "routine-challenged" (like me), setting up and sticking to a routine may be more difficult. Even if *you* forget to eat, you still must feed your Shih Tzu at the same time every day. Consider it not only your responsibility but also one of the best ways to be kind to and care for your Shih Tzu.

Maintaining a routine doesn't mean you have to schedule every minute of your dog's day, but it does mean keeping up with a few important events. This section helps you plan your dog's daily activities.

Chow time

Most mammals have a deep instinctual attachment to food, and when they don't get it, or don't get it when they expect it, their bodies react negatively with hunger pangs and, in the case of some animals, even anxiety.

Small-breed puppies need to eat often, and rescued dogs in particular may feel stressed that they might not ever get fed again if feeding is irregular. Doing so keeps puppies comfortably fueled and assures rescue dogs that the new home is a place of abundance and bounty, instead of deprivation.

When planning your feeding schedule, remember that younger Shih Tzu (under 12 weeks old) need to eat three to four times a day. Puppies 12 to 24 months can eat two to three times a day. After 24 months, your Shih Tzu can eat twice a day (but feed the same amount of food — just divide it up into smaller portions). Some people feed adult dogs just once a day, but I think two meals are more satisfying — physically and emotionally — for all dogs. Keep the following in mind:

- **Choose two or three meal times every day, and stick to them.** These times are likely to be when you get up, midday, and when you eat your dinner.
- **Always feed your Shih Tzu at those times, in the same way, in the same bowl, in the same place.** If you have just one dog and that dog doesn't tend to overeat, you can leave food out during the day. If you have more than one dog, feed them in separate locations. Dogs have an instinct to guard their food from other dogs who may steal it. Feeding dogs in different places alleviates this anxiety.
- **If you can't get home during the middle of the day, someone should come by to feed and pay attention to the dog.** No Shih Tzu should be left alone all day — that's no way for a companion dog to live. Pet sitters, dog walkers, and doggy daycare centers are all good options. (For more on these options, see Chapter 14.)

Set a regular chow time for your dog to spare him these physical and emotional discomforts. This routine can help you in other ways:

- **Regular chow times mean regular bathroom times.** If you feed your dog on a schedule, she'll poop on a schedule, too, and that makes housetraining a lot easier.
- **When you control the food, it shows your dog who's boss.** Your dog looks to you as the benevolent giver of food, and that's a powerful person to be — somebody deserving of a Shih Tzu's worship. Your dog looks to you for direction in other areas, too, so training basic cues like Sit and Stay are easier.
- **Regular feeding means less stress.** Dogs get stressed out just like humans. Regular feeding is one of the most important things you can do to alleviate stress in your dog's life, which can make her healthier, calmer, and better behaved.

Housetraining on time

When it comes to housetraining, timing is everything and routines save the day (and the carpet). If you take your puppy outside on a leash and wait for him to do his business at the same times every day, he will learn *much more quickly* when and where to make those little puppy puddles and piles. Chapter 16 tells you a whole lot more about housetraining, too, and how to train your dog on a schedule.

The daily groom

You don't absolutely need to groom your Shih Tzu *every* day, but I recommend it. Daily grooming gives your dog something to look forward to and becomes part of the comfortable and reassuring routine. You get time together, and you'll have an easier job with coat care if you brush and comb through the coat every day. Grooming a Shih Tzu becomes a bonding ritual, too, and that's well worth those five little minutes in the morning or evening (or whenever you choose to groom).

Every day, at the same time, call your Shih Tzu, put her in a special spot such as on a table reserved just for grooming or on your lap in a chair on the deck. Then brush, comb, apply moisturizing eyedrops, wash her face, check her nails, and clip as necessary. Tell her how gorgeous and glamorous she is. Mission accomplished. (For more detailed info on grooming, see Chapter 10.)

Training and socializing

Every day reserve at least 15 minutes to spend totally focused on your dog, no matter how long you have had her. Work on fun training exercises, tricks, and games like fetch. Practice cues like Sit and Down (check out "Start Training, Without a Pro" later in this chapter), or just hang out together on the couch. Also schedule in time for socialization: walks through the neighborhood, a visit to a neighbor, a play date with a doggy friend, or even a trip in the car to an interesting new place (never leave your Shih Tzu in the car in warm weather, even for a few minutes — Shih Tzu are very susceptible to heatstroke).

Daily training and socialization quickly teach your Shih Tzu how to get along in the world, and these daily routines also help forge a strong bond between the two of you. (Check out Chapter 11 for more on socializing your Shih Tzu.) Remember, your Shih Tzu is your companion, and doing stuff together is the foundation for that relationship.

Exercise and play time

Shih Tzu don't need nearly the high-energy exercise some breeds do, but if they don't get exercise, they won't be as healthy or withstand the rigors of aging as well. Just like you, your Shih Tzu needs to keep in shape.

Make sure you spend time playing and exercising with your new dog every day. Some great games for a small dog include

- **Fetch:** Throw a ball or favorite toy, and encourage your Shih Tzu to bring it back to you. Hey, it could happen.
- **Hide and seek:** Hide somewhere, and then call your Shih Tzu to come and find you. Dogs *love* this game.
- **Tag:** Touch your Shih Tzu, and then run away. She'll probably chase you. Let her catch you, then chase her a short distance. Repeat. (Don't do this outside in hot weather — fortunately, Shih Tzu don't run too far so you can play this inside, too.)
- **Walking:** Stroll around the block and take in the sights. Fifteen to 30 minutes at a moderate pace is plenty. What are the neighbor dogs up to today?

Some exercises aren't appropriate for Shih Tzu. Keep these important warnings in mind to protect your Shih Tzu:

- **Shih Tzu get heatstroke very easily.** Their short noses and long coats aren't made for hot weather, so when the temperature and humidity rise, it's best to stay inside. Shih Tzu also aren't built to run very far or very fast, so keep that in mind. Don't throw the ball *too* far.
- **Shih Tzu can easily drown.** A Shih Tzu in a full coat shouldn't swim because the coat can pull him under! Watch your dog around water, especially a swimming pool where he may not be able to get back out if he falls in. Take the same precautions around water that you take with a small child. If your Shih Tzu likes water, however, you can put about two inches of water in a child's swimming pool and let her romp around. This is a great way for a dog to cool off in the heat (be sure her coat is brushed before it gets wet, or it *will* tangle).

Try to schedule exercise at around the same time every day, no matter what exercise you choose, just to reinforce, once again, the routine. If your Shih Tzu knows she gets to play tag every time you come home from work at 6, she'll look forward to it and feel safe and happy when the game starts on time.

Nighty-night

You may not go to bed at the same time every night, and Samson may wait for you to crawl under the covers before he hits the hay, but sometimes, dogs choose their own bedtimes and go to bed without you.

Even if bedtime doesn't always happen at 10 p.m. sharp (or whenever), follow the same bedtime ritual every day to keep your Shih Tzu feeling secure. Make sure you include these three parts:

- **Calm down:** Time to relax before bedtime. Stop playing with your Shih Tzu about 30 minutes before bed. Relaxing on the couch to read a book or watch television is fine.
- **Potty break:** Just before you put Samson down for the night, take him outside for one last pit stop. He may not always go, but if this is part of the routine, he'll be more likely to do it, and less likely to need to go out in the middle of the night.
- **Bedtime announcement:** Shih Tzu listen to what you say and learn to understand certain words. If you say "Time for bed," or something similar to that every night when it's time for bed, your Shih Tzu soon knows what that means, and she'll probably beat you to the bedroom.

Make sure your Shih Tzu can get to his bed or kennel whenever he needs to. If you can manage to go to bed and get up at about the same time on most nights, your Shih Tzu appreciates the regularity (and it's good for you too — studies show you'll get better sleep). Either way, just be sure your Shih Tzu has the option to go to bed if he wants to, and don't be surprised if he stands in front of you and gives you that look, as if to say, "Don't you realize it's bedtime now? Get off the computer already!"

Start Training, Without a Pro

Many people enjoy taking their Shih Tzu puppies (or adults) to a basic obedience or puppy socialization class. These classes can be a lot of fun and they give your Shih Tzu opportunities to meet other people and other dogs in a safe, structured environment. But whether or not you do this, you can start teaching your Shih Tzu some important cues and good manners, right from day one. Spend a little time every day working with your Shih Tzu on manners and training to help her know what you like and what you want her to do. Shih Tzu are smart — she'll pick it up quickly.

But how do you tell your Shih Tzu what you want her to do? Dog training is communication, so even spending time together makes you a better dog trainer. You can motivate your dog into position with a treat, then praise her and give her the treat when she does what you want. You can praise her when she does something good all on her own. And when she starts to do something wrong, you can distract her into a good behavior and reward that. Training isn't hard — you're simply rewarding the good stuff and convincing your dog that you're the source of all good things. Shih Tzu think that anyway unless you prove them wrong, so training a Shih Tzu is easy. You can start right now. This section helps you get started on the right paw, but for more detailed information about training, see Chapters 15, 16, and 17.

Remembering your Shih Tzu's primary directive: companionship

One very important thing to remember about training a Shih Tzu is that the Shih Tzu understands one thing ahead of all others: you. He wants to be with you, near you, on you, next to you. He's all about *you.* (And isn't that one of his best qualities?) When your Shih Tzu behaves or does something you like, reward him with time together, kind words, and affection. When your Shih Tzu does something you don't like, don't punish him physically, but ignore him for a few minutes. To a Shih Tzu, that sends a clear message: If he wants your attention, he has to behave in a certain way.

Because the Shih Tzu is so in-tune to you, harsher training methods can be physically and psychologically damaging. I argue that punishment, choke chains, yelling, nose flicking, and other such training methods aren't necessary for *any* breed, but a Toy breed least of all. The Toy breeds' size, sensitivity, and intuitive ability to bond with humans as a lap dog make him entirely ill-suited for these traditional training methods. Shih Tzu are intelligent and all they need to learn quickly is repetition. Show him something a few times, and Samson gets it.

The very best way to teach your Shih Tzu how to do something is to put him in a position where he's likely to do what you want, then reward him lavishly when he does it. That's a language your Shih Tzu understands. But if he doesn't do something that you want or like, think about why. If he had an accident in the house, did you take him out on time? If he nibbles your shoe, did you leave the shoe out where your pup could get it? Or didn't you provide him with something to chew on instead? If he growls, what has scared or threatened him? Don't ruin your good relationship by scolding. Foster it by helping your Shih Tzu succeed and earn your praise. (For more info on good methods to use for training your dog, see Chapter 15.)

Using positive reinforcement: What a good dog!

Whenever your Shih Tzu does something good, praise her. Praise can come in many forms, from verbal praise ("What a good girl!") to treats ("Who deserves a liver snap?"). Always have a reward ready to catch any and all good behavior. Pet owners often forget to reward the good because they're so busy shrieking "No!" Just make sure you don't *always* reward with a treat, or your Shih Tzu may take in too many calories. Besides, Lola would rather have your praise and affection.

Saying "No"

Sometimes, you have to say "No." However the main purpose in a loud sharp "No!" is that it distracts your Shih Tzu from the naughty thing she's doing and puts her attention on you, so you can then immediately redirect her to something you do like. Then, of course, comes the praise, the treats, and the reward.

When it comes to so-called bad behavior (or just plain doggy behavior), remember that dogs desire your attention. When your Shih Tzu does something you don't like that doesn't immediately threaten him or your possessions, ignore it, and make sure nobody else is accidentally rewarding his behavior. When your dog acts naughty to get your attention, she will hate being ignored and is likely to try something else to get you to turn around and look at her. When she does choose a good activity instead of a naughty one (like sitting down to look at you), start rewarding. (Check out Chapters 15 and 17 for more ways to implement these strategies.)

Kids can follow rules too

One problem many families encounter with training is that one person trains and everybody else ignores the rules. Doing so undermines training and your Shih Tzu won't understand the different directives. Everybody in the household must be in on the rules, what behavior to reward, and what behavior needs a "No!" and a quick redirect. Everyone should use the same cues (like the same word for Sit or Stay), and everyone should practice the same kinds of techniques. Even young children can help by doing things like totaling ignoring the dog when he jumps up on them but petting and playing with him when he sits nicely for attention. Don't count out the kids! Who knows, you may end up inspiring your child to become the next great dog handler!

The easiest way to start training with the family is to teach kids some easy ways to manage your Shih Tzu's behavior (everybody in the family should follow these strategies, not just kids):

- **Don't forget to reward a good dog.** Remind children that every time your Shih Tzu does something good, like sit nicely when asked, greet someone without jumping up on them, or act friendly to another dog, the child can say "Good dog!"
- **When the dog is naughty, ignore her.** Kids can learn to turn their backs, look away, or walk away when the dog misbehaves. Make sure they know what constitutes misbehavior: biting fingers and jumping up. Make sure your kids don't sneak extra food or treats to the Shih Tzu. They can accidentally reward behavior you don't want to reinforce.
- **If the dog gets into something she shouldn't, take it away.** Children should keep toys, socks, and other chewables off the floor, and if the dog gets them, or any other forbidden object, the child should take the item away calmly without yelling or scolding. Also teach kids to replace the item with an acceptable chew toy, instead of just taking something away from the dog and leaving the dog with nothing. If the dog gets something better in return for the forbidden object, he understands that the child is the source of good things and worthy of notice, and he also learns what's okay to chew and what isn't.

If you have a rescued dog that guards her possessions and can bite, have the child tell an adult if the dog has something she shouldn't have, instead of risk a bite. And seek professional training! Resource guarding is easy to fix under professional guidance. For more about how to address this problem, see Chapter 11.

- **Chill out.** Kids can get pretty excited, jumping around and shrieking and doing all the things active kids do, but this behavior also excites the dog. Kids often get frustrated with dogs that won't stop jumping up, barking, and nipping, without realizing they're causing the behavior. Teach kids to be calm around the dog. A calm child relaxes and reassures a dog, and when the child calms down, the dog will too . . . eventually.

Is this behavior a problem?

In the first few days when you bring your new dog home, he may need a few days to adjust to his new surroundings. However, a few behaviors are cause for concern and warrant a call to a vet and also to the breeder, just in case. If your Shih Tzu is a puppy, call your vet and your breeder if:

- Your Shih Tzu shows complete disinterest in you and the environment, acts depressed, or refuses to move.
- Your Shih Tzu hides and quivers for more than one whole day, runs away whenever you try to touch her, or yelps when you touch her.
- Your Shih Tzu growls and snaps constantly for no apparent reason.

If you adopted an older rescued Shih Tzu, you may also need to call a behaviorist to help you deal with aggression, which may not seem serious in a small dog, but which can be very dangerous for people, as well as for the dog. (For more on resolving behavior problems, see Chapter 11. For more on Shih Tzu health issues, see Chapter 13.)

Generally, the first few days with a new dog come with a few surprises — both pleasant and unpleasant. With a steady routine, plenty of supervision, and regular socialization and training, most problems probably iron themselves out.

Part III

Caring for Your Chinese Charmer

The 5th Wave   By Rich Tennant

"We're very careful about grooming. First I'll check his teeth and nails, then trim any excess hair from his ears, nose, and around the eyes. After checking for fleas and parasites, I'll let Roger go off to work so I can begin grooming the dog."

In this part . . .

Good health starts with good food. In Chapter 9, you discover how to feed your Shih Tzu a healthy diet that helps her thrive and avoid future health problems. You also discover the benefits of supplements and whether you should make a homemade diet for your dog.

Shih Tzu owners often ask about grooming, and Chapter 10 tells you everything you need to know about how to keep your Shih Tzu shiny, happy, and well-groomed, whether you do it all yourself or hire a professional groomer. Chapter 11 helps you as you socialize your Shih Tzu to the outside world, while Chapter 12 guides you in preventing health problems and following important health practices. Discover the common Shih Tzu health issues, deal with emergencies, and tackle parasites in Chapter 13. With info like this, your Shih Tzu is bound to be as healthy and pretty as she can possibly be. And don't forget traveling — Chapter 14 fills you in on how to travel safely with your Shih Tzu and what to do when you have to leave your pup at home.

Chapter 9

Feeding Your Shih Tzu Nutritious (and Yummy) Food

In This Chapter

- Deciding what to feed your Shih Tzu
- Understanding pet food labels and terms
- Planning your Shih Tzu's meals
- Providing treats and supplements
- Making sure your Shih Tzu maintains a healthy weight

Feeding a small dog can be a little tricky because small dogs have small stomachs and fast metabolisms. Not much food fits in a Shih Tzu at one time, so getting the right nutrition in every bite counts. If you fill your Shih Tzu with junk or feed him too much, you risk malnourishing and/or overfeeding him.

Today's pet owners are more educated about pet food than ever before, and dog food companies have responded by improving their formulas over the past few years. But you're standing in front of the shelves lined with so many different foods, and you aren't sure how to choose. Are they all the same? No. Does it matter which food you feed your Shih Tzu? Yes.

In this chapter, I cover some of the important basics of food: How to pick the right food, how much to feed your Shih Tzu, how to set a routine, and how to make sure your Shih Tzu is eating for optimum health. So dive into that kibble bag and take a look around.

What Your Shih Tzu Needs, Not What Your Shih Tzu Wants

Dogs are scavengers by nature, and if your Shih Tzu had her way, she would probably eat whatever she could find. Fortunately, however, you get to choose her food for her. You need to ensure that your Shih Tzu eats healthful foods, rather than cheap junky foods. A high-quality pet food includes the best combination of the following ingredients:

- **Proteins:** They build muscle, organs, and all the tissues in the body, plus they're necessary for proper growth, healing, and many necessary biochemical processes that go on inside every dog's (and every human's) body.
- **Fats:** They provide concentrated energy, more than protein or carbohydrates. They help build cells and help the body absorb certain vitamins. They also insulate the body and protect the internal organs.
- **Carbohydrates:** They provide energy and fiber to help keep your dog's system running smoothly.
- **Vitamins and minerals:** Vitamins make enzyme reactions in the body possible, and they also keep your dog's metabolism functioning properly. Minerals help build bones and teeth and regulate fluid balance in the body, plus they help with an efficient metabolism.
- **Water:** Your Shih Tzu is 60 to 70 percent water, and he needs water every single day to stay alive, not to mention healthy with well-lubricated joints. Water helps the entire body work better. No one can survive without it.

These nutritional components come in many forms — meats, organs, bone meal, grains, vegetables, and more. But having the right protein, fat, carbs, vitamins, minerals, and moisture ratio in a food isn't enough. Those components have to come from healthy, quality sources that your dog can absorb efficiently. Read the label (check out "Reading the label" later in this chapter about deciphering what's in the food) to get an idea of what's inside your dog's food. That's the first step to deciding which diet is best for *your* dog.

Different Diets for Different Dogs

Who is your Shih Tzu? Is she a roly-poly puppy? A glamorous grown-up? A sophisticated senior? Is she a little bit chubby? Does she have arthritis or allergies? All these considerations can affect what food you should choose for your Shih Tzu, and pet food manufacturers make foods to meet all these needs.

Before you choose any food, you need to know what category your Shih Tzu falls into:

- **Puppy:** Until your Shih Tzu is about a year old, a puppy formula is probably best, unless your vet advises otherwise. Puppy food is specifically formulated for growing dogs. Toy breed or small breed puppy foods are even more specifically made for dogs with tiny stomachs and quick metabolism who need to eat nutrient-dense food often to stay energized.
- **Adult:** Adult formulas, for Shih Tzu who are 1 to 10 years old (and even older, depending on your dog's health), meet the needs of active adult dogs of normal weight. Adult food isn't as high in calories as puppy food because the dog isn't growing anymore, but it provides everything your dog needs to maintain his body.
- **Senior:** Senior formulas may be lower in protein for dogs with kidney problems, or they may contain high protein to help keep aging muscles strong. Some contain fewer calories because many seniors slow down and use fewer calories, and these foods can prevent dogs from becoming overweight as they age. Many also contain added ingredients for digestion, healthy joints, and healthy skin and coat.

  However, many vets believe you shouldn't switch your dog to a senior formula unless she actually starts to show signs of aging, and then, her particular health issues determine which food is best. If she still acts healthy, pain-free, and active, stick with the adult food, unless your vet advises otherwise.
- **Breed-specific:** Manufacturers love a niche market and have created foods designed for specific breeds or groups of dogs. There may be a Shih Tzu food, although I haven't seen it. However, I have seen Toy and small breed foods, which are designed for dogs that need nutrient-dense food to provide their small stomachs and tiny bodies with adequate nutrition. Small breed kibble also has smaller pieces so it's easier to chew.
- **Weight control:** Shih Tzu getting a little tubby? A weight control formula may be the answer, although many people can control their pets' weight with a little exercise, smaller portions, and fewer treats. Because Shih Tzu are small, you only need small changes to help them lose weight. (For more on weight control, see the section "Monitoring Your Shih Tzu's Waistline," later in this chapter.)
- **Prescription diets:** You can't buy prescription diet food in the pet store, but your vet can prescribe a special diet if your Shih Tzu needs one for a medical condition, such as allergies, diabetes, digestive disorders, kidney disease, even cognitive decline with old age (similar to Alzheimer's disease in humans). If your Shih Tzu has a medical condition, talk to your vet to see if a prescription food can help.

Above all, if you question what food to feed your dog of any age or problem, consult your veterinarian.

Choosing the Right Food for Your Dog

What works to keep your dog healthy may not work as well to keep another dog healthy. You may choose a food based on your dog's age, breed, or health issues, or you may choose one based on your own preferences as well as what's best for your dog. As long as the food is high quality and nutritionally complete and your dog likes the food and does well on the food, that's great. This section helps you make the decision about which dog food to feed your Shih Tzu.

What your Shih Tzu used to eat

Your breeder, or whoever had your dog before you, was feeding your Shih Tzu something. Make sure you know what this food is, so you can decide if you want to keep feeding it or change to something else based on your dog's needs or your own preferences. Because a dog can experience some gastrointestinal distress if you switch a food too suddenly or drastically, be sure to transition from one food to another gradually, mixing in a little bit of the new food with the old food at first, and then increasing the amount of new food bit by bit over the course of a few days.

Many breeders even send you home with a small bag of your Shih Tzu's food so you can have something to feed your dog until you get to the store and something to use while transitioning to a different food if you decide to switch foods.

What your vet recommends

If you aren't sure what food to feed your Shih Tzu, your vet may have a great suggestion for you. Your vet may know that your Shih Tzu is prone to allergies and can recommend a food designed for Toy breeds that isn't likely to aggravate those allergies. Or she may prefer organic pet food or raw food for your Shih Tzu's individual needs because she believes these foods offer superior nutrition.

On the other hand, many vets stock certain food because they have contracts with particular pet food companies to carry that brand. In some cases, these foods are great. However, don't just assume you're getting the best food if you buy the food at the vet's office. Always read the food label. (For more information on reading the label, see the next section.)

Organic options

You may live a holistic lifestyle and want to feed an organic, homemade, or raw diet to your dog, too. These diets have become increasingly popular as people choose healthier diets for themselves. For more on dietary options, see the sidebar, "What about holistic, natural, and organic foods?" later in this chapter.

Reading the Label

Empowered pet food buyers read dog food labels to find out exactly what's in that food and whether it's not just adequate but truly healthful. (Check out Figure 9-1 for an example of a dog food label.)

You don't have to understand every single word on the label, but most of the words should make sense. The following sections cover what you do need to look for on labels.

AAFCO statement

The very first thing to look for on the pet food you're considering is the Association of American Feed Control Officials (AAFCO) statement. Dog foods that display this statement have been proven, through feeding trials to be complete and balanced nutrition for dogs of a certain stage, such as puppies or adult dogs. It's usually worded something like this:

> Feeding tests using the procedures established by the Association of American Feed Control Officials substantiate that this food provides complete and balanced nutrition for all life stages.

If a food doesn't have an AAFCO statement, it's probably meant to be a treat. Don't use it as your dog's primary diet. This statement doesn't state that the food is the best food out there, but the statement does mean that dogs can live on that food without any other supplementation, according to approved feeding tests.

Ingredients: Chicken, Corn Meal, Ground Whole Grain Sorghum, Chicken By-Product Meal, Ground Whole Grain Barley, Chicken Fat (preserved with Mixed Tocopherols, a source of Vitamin E, and Citric Acid), Fish Meal (source of fish oil), Chicken Meal, Dried Beet Pulp (sugar removed), Natural Chicken Flavor, Potassium Chloride, Dried Egg Product, Brewers Dried Yeast, Salt, Flax Meal, Sodium Hexametaphosphate, Vitamins [Vitamin E Supplement, Ascorbic Acid, Vitamin A Acetate, Calcium Pantothenate, Biotin, Thiamine Mononitrate (source of vitamin B1), Vitamin B12 Supplement, Niacin, Riboflavin Supplement (source of vitamin B2), Inositol, Pyridoxine Hydrochloride (source of vitamin B6), Vitamin D3 Supplement, Folic Acid], Choline Chloride, Minerals [Ferrous Sulfate, Zinc Oxide, Manganese Sulfate, Copper Sulfate, Manganous Oxide, Potassium Iodide, Cobalt Carbonate], Calcium Carbonate, DL-Methionine, Rosemary Extract.

Manufactured under U.S. Patent No. 5,616,569, 5,932,258, 6,093,418 and 6,238,708; other U.S. and foreign patents pending.

Guaranteed Analysis

Crude Protein not less than	26.0%
Crude Fat not less than	15.0%
Crude Fiber not more than	4.0%
Moisture not more than	10.0%
Omega-6 Fatty Acids not less than	2.5%
Omega-3 Fatty Acids not less than	0.25%*
Glucosamine not less than	350ppm*

*Not recognized as an essential nutrient by the AAFCO Dog Food Nutrient Profiles

Animal feeding tests using Association of American Feed Control Officials procedures substantiate that Iams MiniChunks provides complete and balanced nutrition for All Life Stages.

PET FOOD ONLY

Figure 9-1: A dog-food nutrition label.

Ingredients list

The ingredients list gives you the info that helps you make the best decision about what to feed your Shih Tzu. This list contains everything in the food, in order by weight. For instance, if the first ingredient is chicken, the food contains more chicken, by weight, than any other single ingredient. If the first ingredient is rice, the food contains more rice than any other single ingredient.

When you read the ingredients list, you may notice several ingredients that you don't understand. How do you know what you're putting in your dog's little body, and how do you know if the food is actually good for your dog? Some of the main ingredients you may see include the following:

- **By-products** are non-muscle-meat parts. Some people believe by-products are natural food for dogs who would eat the whole animal in the wild. Others suspect that by-products are the worst parts of the animal unfit for consumption and that these parts can lead to diseases like cancer and chronic conditions like allergies. I can't tell you for sure one way or the other — it's a controversial subject among pet food people. Talk to your vet, or avoid foods that contain by-products in the ingredients list, if they worry you.
- **Meal** in the form of meat or grain has the water removed so it's a more concentrated, more processed, source of protein or carbs.
- **Long chemical names** are often added vitamins, and the label should tell you this in parenthesis after the name. Pet food labels are getting better than they used to be about putting things in plain language or defining terms.

Knowing a good ingredient list when you see it

The ingredients list is informative but not necessarily straightforward. Dogs need digestible protein, and many books and magazine articles tell pet owners to look for meat protein listed first in the ingredients because studies prove dogs digest meat protein better than protein from vegetable sources like grains.

But here's the tricky part: Even though ingredients are listed in order according to how much of that ingredient is in the food, you have to look at the ingredients together to get a good idea of what's really going on.

For example, the beginning of your ingredients list may read as follows: "Chicken, chicken meal, brewers rice, chicken broth, whole oats, fish oil." This list has more meat sources and fewer grain sources in the first few ingredients. In other words, when you look at the first six, eight, or ten ingredients, you want to see more instances of meat than grain.

But what if the list starts out like this: "Corn, rice, chicken, corn meal, meat by-products, wheat . . . " This list has more grain sources in the first few ingredients, and probably isn't as good a source of concentrated nutrition, especially protein.

What about holistic, natural, and organic foods?

The biggest growing pet food segment today is the organic segment, and many pet food labels now contain buzzwords like *holistic, natural,* and *organic.*

The following list can help you decipher what these terms really mean when you see them on a dog food label.

- **Holistic:** If a food is holistic, it theoretically contains ingredients good for the whole animal, but this term isn't regulated. If a manufacturer says the food is holistic, that just means the manufacturer *says* the food is holistic. If you trust the manufacturer, you may choose to believe the food is a good one. However, the law doesn't have any official definition for the term holistic.
- **Natural:** This term is a regulated term. If a food says it's natural, then legally, the food can't contain any artificial ingredients, such as chemical preservatives. Some companies get around this by using the word in a way that allows them to use some artificial ingredients, such as by saying "with natural ingredients." That means *some* of the ingredients are natural.
- **Organic:** This term has been regulated by the USDA since October 2002 as it applies to human food. As of 2007, the term has a separate (but mostly the same) definition as it applies to pet food. In general, if a food says it's organic, it *must* contain at least 95 percent organic ingredients. That means those ingredients must have been grown in a system that promotes the natural ecological cycle and that are generally not polluted with chemicals like pesticides, herbicides, growth hormones, or antibiotics. Organic animals must be fed organic food and treated humanely. Organic products must come from USDA-certified producers. If a food says *made with organic ingredients,* the specific organic ingredients will be listed on the ingredients list, but the whole product wouldn't legally be organic.

Natural and organic foods are more expensive, but for many pet owners, it's an ethical choice, and the cost is well worth the health benefits they believe their animals will enjoy, as well as the environmental benefits to the world.

Some high-end foods contain no grain at all because some people (and some pet food companies) believe dogs shouldn't eat any grain. Also, dogs can have grain allergies. For a healthy dog, small amounts of grain are probably okay (talk to your vet if you aren't sure), but you don't want to feed your dog mostly grain.

Plus, not all grains are created equal. Some people believe that many dogs are allergic to corn and wheat, so these items are less desirable ingredients than rice or oatmeal, which tends to be less allergenic. The bottom line: Dogs aren't designed to live on corn.

They're designed to live on all the parts of small animals, from their bones and marrow, muscles and organs, to their half-digested stomach contents. Gross? Yes. True? Absolutely. The more a food ingredient list looks like the parts of a small animal, the better.

What else should be in there?

So far, you're looking for meat protein and a lot of it. You want to see chicken, lamb, turkey, fish, or other meat sources at the beginning of the list. What else do you want to see?

Many foods today contain vegetables and fruits, which add vitamins and fiber. Personally, I would rather see things like carrots, yogurt, blueberries, and salmon meal than long chemical names. Let common sense play a big part in your label scrutiny. If you can't pronounce it, do you really want your dog to eat it?

Considering Your Main Choices for Dog Food

Dog food comes in many different forms, and each form has its advantages and disadvantages. This section looks at your main options. You can buy your dog's food (store bought), make your own dog food (homemade), or even mix it up.

Store bought

Most pet owners buy their dog food in the store, which is easier, more convenient, faster, and less messy. Buying your dog's food can cost more than making it yourself, but you pay for the convenience, as well as the quality. If you've looked carefully at the dog food label and chosen a food based on healthy ingredients (see the previous section for more about reading the label), you probably notice that it costs more than foods with lesser ingredients (like more corn and wheat, less poultry and meat).

In most cases, premium brands are more expensive for good reason — the ingredients really are more digestible, less processed, and/or more humanely produced. And premium foods, to be quite frank, result in smaller, less stinky poop. The dog digests more of the ingredients so less comes out the other end, and that, for many pet owners, is worth the cost alone. But premium food from the store comes in several different forms — kibble, canned, and frozen raw. Which type you choose depends on you and your dog, but the next section give you some things to consider.

Kibble

Kibble is the most popular form of pet food. Kibble is so popular because of the many advantages of feeding it to your dog. To help you make a decision whether kibble is right for your dog, here are some pros and cons:

- Pros
  - **Kibble is convenient.** Feeding your dog doesn't take long. Just pour and measure.
  - **Kibble lasts longer without it spoiling.** It lasts up to three or four weeks.
  - **Kibble costs less than other kinds of food of equal quality.** Saving money is good, right?
  - **Most dogs like kibble.** It's crunchy, it's meaty . . . it's delicious!
  - **Kibble is good for your dog's teeth.** Some vets believe that kibble keeps teeth cleaner. Kibble can be particularly good for Shih Tzu, who can lose teeth early. Some breeders believe that along with yearly dental appointments, feeding kibble helps strengthen Shih Tzu's teeth so they don't fall out.
- Cons
  - **Some picky dogs don't like kibble.** It doesn't look or taste anything like meat.
  - **Some Shih Tzu have dental problems.** Chewing kibble is more difficult with sore or missing teeth.
  - **Kibble is highly processed.** People who want to feed a more natural diet may feel kibble is too processed.

If you choose kibble for your Shih Tzu, choose a premium brand made for small dogs, and don't buy more than your Shih Tzu can eat in three to four weeks, after which time the fats in the kibble can get rancid and the food can get stale. Keep kibble in an airtight container so it stays fresh longer.

You may have to try a few brands before you find one with an acceptable ingredients list and a taste your Shih Tzu likes. Don't buy the largest bag of food in the store. Instead buy a small bag of food to make sure your dog likes it first. Your dog may not like that super-healthy food with the picture-perfect ingredients list. A great food won't do your Shih Tzu any good if he isn't going to eat it.

Canned

Canned food costs more than kibble but tastes more like meat and many dogs prefer the taste of canned food. Choose a premium brand with quality meat sources in the first few ingredients and not too much grain. Also choose a brand without artificial colors, sweeteners, and chemical preservatives.

Canned food doesn't keep for more than a few days after you open the can (always store opened cans in the refrigerator), and you have to keep it covered. Premium brands contain good meat protein, but some vets think canned food can contribute to dental plaque (other vets don't agree with this). Too much canned food can also cause runny stools in some dogs.

Many people choose to put a spoonful of canned with a little kibble for their Shih Tzu, to get the benefits of both. For info on kibble and mixing it with canned food, see the "Mixing it up" section, a little later in this chapter.

Frozen raw

The *raw* food diet consists of feeding your dog raw meat, along with fresh fruits and vegetables (finely chopped) and in many cases, raw bones. Sometimes, this diet is called the BARF diet (an acronym for Biologically Appropriate Raw Food or Bones And Raw Food, depending on whom you ask). This diet is controversial because some vets insist dogs can get food poisoning from the pathogens in raw meat.

Raw meat from a store isn't as fresh or pathogen-free as raw meat from a freshly killed animal. Some pets have suffered food poisoning from raw food, although this is very rare. Handling raw meat isn't something humans are always keen to do, and preparation can be time consuming, plus it can be tricky getting the right nutritional balance with a raw meat because dogs can't live on meat alone. Feeding prepared raw diets you can buy in the pet store make this part easier.

But what about the upside? Many vets and pet owners swear that health problems clear up almost miraculously when they switch pets to a raw diet and that the dog's digestive system can handle it. Many dogs with skin allergies and other chronic conditions like arthritis, kidney disease, and diabetes improve on a raw food diet. Raw diets mimic what dogs eat in the wild, so they may be closer to what a dog's supposed to eat to be healthy. Very few wild dogs are overweight, while many pets are. Plus, heating kills many of the natural enzymes in food, but raw food leaves these enzymes intact.

Many canine nutritionists believe these enzymes are necessary for health and that even dogs on a manufactured food diet should get at least some raw food every day.

So, what am I saying? Are raw diets good or bad? The truth is probably that it depends on the individual dog. Because this diet is so controversial, talk to your vet before switching your Shih Tzu to a raw diet. Holistic vets are more likely to be open to the idea, and may have information to help guide you.

Homemade and delicious

What on earth did pet owners do before dog food was invented just a few decades ago? They fed their pets the food they were eating (or, the leftovers). Some people feel very strongly that dogs, as well as humans, aren't meant to eat processed food, but they should eat fresh natural foods, including meat, vegetables, fruits, and so on. Many of these people make foods for their pets at home, either giving them the leftovers from their own healthy meals (no junk food!) or preparing special meals just for their pets, such as boiled chicken and oatmeal with ground carrots and green beans, or ground beef with brown rice mixed with chopped leafy greens and yogurt.

Talk to your vet if you want to feed your dog a homemade diet. You have to make sure your dog has the right nutrients she needs — without them, your dog could suffer from malnutrition. However, if you discover what to do, feeding a nutritionally complete homemade diet isn't hard (although it can be time-consuming). If you have the inclination and the time, get solid advice from your vet, and go for it. Your Shih Tzu will probably love it.

A few human foods can be toxic to dogs. Check out "Avoiding not-so-healthy treats" later in this chapter for a list of foods to avoid.

Mixing it up

If you're like me, you may want the best of all possible worlds: The convenience of kibble, the nutritional benefits of natural foods, the palatability of canned and real fresh meat, and the benefits of certain raw foods. With the thumbs-up from your vet, you can combine these approaches.

One day, put a spoonful of canned food in with the kibble. Mix in some pot roast and mashed carrots or bits of chicken and brown rice the next day. Try some hardboiled eggs with oatmeal in the mornings, turkey with chopped collard greens and apples at night.

Or, feed kibble in the mornings and frozen raw food in the evenings. You may even throw your Shih Tzu the occasional raw bone (never cooked, which can splinter and injure the dog). With guidance from your vet and a little experimenting to see how your Shih Tzu responds, you'll hit on just the right diet for you and your dog.

Don't forget water

Your Shih Tzu must have a constant accessible supply of fresh water every day. Dogs who eat a diet of kibble are even more in need of water because kibble doesn't contain as much moisture as canned food and homemade food. Water keeps your Shih Tzu's body and organ systems functioning properly. Without it, your Shih Tzu can get sick.

Check the water bowl or bottle often throughout the day to make sure it's always full and clean. Don't just top it off — at least daily, dump the water, rinse the container, and refill. Wash the water bowl or bottle at least once a week with soap and hot water or in the dishwasher to make sure it stays clean and free of bacteria. If you don't use a water bowl, you may consider a water bottle. For more on choosing a water bowl or bottle, see Chapter 5.

Developing a Regular Meal Routine

Some Shih Tzu can be picky eaters. Others can be real chow hounds. Either way, a regular meal schedule can teach your Shih Tzu that she gets to eat at a certain time but not all the time. A schedule also helps picky eaters accept food more readily and keeps chow hounds from begging too much when it isn't time for dinner. (But don't be surprised if your Shih Tzu reminds you if you forget that it really is dinnertime!) Remember that dogs love routine (check out Chapter 8 for more on establishing a routine). They also love to eat. A regular meal routine combines two of your dog's favorite things into one happily daily ritual.

Your routine should include at least two and possibly even three daily meals, always at the same time. Small dogs do better if they eat more often, and once a day just isn't enough to keep a small dog's metabolism fired up properly, so they have energy and their bodies work efficiently. Plus, more meals mean more elements to that valuable routine. Just be sure to divide the same amount of food over the various meals so you don't feed your dog too much.

Some people free-feed their dogs, leaving food out all the time, but this only works if you have just one pet. Otherwise, your Shih Tzu may feel compelled to eat too often, just to protect her food.

Giving Treats

Look at that face. Those adorable pleading eyes. How can you not give your Shih Tzu just a little treat . . . and then maybe just one more? Treats are wonderful for special occasions and for training, but Shih Tzu can become overweight easily, so treats are best when doled out sparingly. This section helps you identify healthy treats and not-so-healthy treats.

Choosing healthy treats

Look for treats with healthy ingredients like fresh meat and whole grains, and read the label. You don't want artificial colors, salt, sweeteners such as corn syrup or other chemical ingredients like propylene glycol in your Shih Tzu's treats! Gourmet dog treats from a dog bakery can be delicious and healthy, but ask what's in the treat.

Some healthy treats can come right out of your refrigerator:

- Baby carrots
- Blueberries, strawberries, or any other berry you would eat
- Small broccoli florets
- Tiny bits of chicken, turkey, or fish
- A spoonful of plain, nonfat yogurt or lowfat cottage cheese

For training, use very tiny treats or pieces of treats. Also be sure the treats you feed your Shih Tzu are just as healthy as her regular diet. No matter how healthy the treat, always feed treats in moderation — no more than one or two each day.

Avoiding not-so-healthy treats

Those yummy-looking packaged treats in the grocery store are just about as healthy as the highly processed packaged treats kids beg their parents to buy. By that, I mean *not very healthy.* Dog treats are usually too big for a small dog and way too full of preservatives, sugar, and artificial ingredients. Some have even been linked to choking and other medical problems.

Some human foods aren't good for dogs. Watch out for the following items:

- **Liver and processed meat like lunch meat, hot dogs, and pepperoni:** Liver can cause loose stools in some dogs, although dogs love the taste. Also avoid too much processed meat, like hot dogs, bologna, and sausages. These contain too much salt and fat and too many preservatives for regular consumption, although some people like to give their pets tiny bits every now and then.
- **Junk food and processed food:** If you got it from a fast food restaurant, don't give it to your dog, with the exception of small bits of meat without the fried coating.
- **High-fat cheese:** Most dogs don't digest cheese very well, but some enjoy small bits of low-fat cheese like mozzarella or cottage cheese. High-fat cheese is too fattening for dogs, and too much cheese in general means too much salt.
- **Anything containing sugar and/or white flour:** Bad for you but *very* bad for a small dog.

Some foods are downright toxic. *Never* give your dog the following foods:

- **Onions:** They contain a toxic ingredient called *thiosulphate* that can cause hemolytic anemia. Symptoms include vomiting and diarrhea, weakness, bloody urine, and even death.
- **Grapes and raisins:** They can cause kidney failure.
- **Macadamia nuts:** They contain a toxin that causes neurological symptoms like weakness, tremors, and temporary paralysis, as well as pain.
- **Chocolate and cocoa powder:** They're very toxic to many dogs because of the stimulants: caffeine and the theobromine. The darker the chocolate, the more toxic it is.
- **Alcohol, coffee, coffee grounds, tea, tea bags, and tobacco products:** Alcohol and the stimulants in coffee, tea, and tobacco can have a toxic effect on a small dog. Even if you've seen big dogs lap up beer at parties, don't even think about doing this to your Shih Tzu. You can poison him.

Giving Your Dog Supplements

Many people take nutritional supplements to support good health or even to cure health problems. So does it work for pets, too?

If you feed your dog an excellent diet (see "Choosing the Right Food for Your Dog"), you probably don't need to feed her a multivitamin supplement. However, whole-food supplements can add important and beneficial dietary components to a processed pet food diet.

Pet supplements can't state on the label that they treat, prevent, or cure any disease, but you may hear stories of how these supplements did just that. Take these testimonials with a grain of salt, but don't entirely dismiss the potential benefit of supplements, either.

Scientific studies have shown that glucosamine and chondroitin, for example, really do minimize signs of pain in arthritic pets, but studies on other supplements are, so far, pretty minimal. Nevertheless, that doesn't mean supplements won't help or benefit your pet. Some of the most popular and most common include supplements to support joint function, healthy skin and coat, and digestive issues, and to put back live enzymes in the diet.

Some herbal and homeopathic formulas may also help with kidney and liver problems, diabetes, arthritis, allergies, and stress and anxiety, even if they can't say this in so many words. Many people use these supplements in conjunction with conventional therapy (always tell your vet if you give your pet any supplements). Talk to your vet if you're curious about supplements, and always buy supplements formulated for pets, not people, to avoid giving the wrong dosage.

Monitoring Your Shih Tzu's Waistline

Is your Shih Tzu just a little too chubby? Even a two-pound weight gain in a small dog is a lot of weight on a ten-pound dog. That's like a 150-pound person gaining 30 pounds! Extra weight puts strain on internal organs like the heart and lungs, stresses joints making them more prone to arthritis, and contributes to a host of chronic diseases as your dog gets older. Some Shih Tzu can also be underweight, although this issue is less common. These dogs can be underweight because of a health issue or just because they're extra finicky, and they may not be getting the proper nutrition to stay healthy.

This section addresses overweight and underweight dogs and helps you identify if your dog has a weight problem.

Portion size

Portion size matters, especially for small dogs, who can gain too much weight if they eat even a little bit too much. Every dog's different, and the amount you feed your dog depends on your dog's individual metabolism and activity level. Dog food bags and cans often recommend more than dogs should really eat unless they're extremely active (which most Shih Tzu aren't).

A good place to start is on the very low end of the recommended portion on the dog food label. If this amount keeps your Shih Tzu at a healthy weight (which is 9 to 16 pounds), you're on the right track. If your Shih Tzu gets too thin, increase the amount by just a tablespoon. If your Shih Tzu gets too heavy, decrease the amount by a tablespoon, even if it's less than the lower limit the dog food label suggests.

Watching for signs of obesity

According to many vets, being overweight is the number one most common health problem among companion animals today. But your Shih Tzu doesn't have to suffer that fate, as long as you monitor what he eats and make sure he gets enough exercise. The Shih Tzu breed standard states a Shih Tzu between 9 and 10½ inches at the shoulder should weigh between 9 and 16 pounds. However, despite what the scale says, your Shih Tzu may be overweight for her build.

Determining whether your Shih Tzu is becoming overweight under that fluffy coat can be difficult, so to monitor your Shih Tzu's waistline, you need to use your hands. Feel your Shih Tzu's ribs. If you can't feel them at all, and if you can feel no discernible waist curving in from your Shih Tzu's ribcage, your pup is probably overweight.

Talk to your vet to confirm your findings and then ask about the best way to get your pet back to a healthy weight. If your Shih Tzu gained weight suddenly, he could have a medical problem, so be sure to mention this to your vet.

Looking out for signs of an underweight Shih Tzu

If your Shih Tzu weighs less than 9 pounds and you can easily feel her ribs, and if she has a dramatic tuck-in below the rib cage, she may be underweight. A sudden weight loss can also indicate a medical condition. If you think your Shih Tzu is underweight, talk to your vet about it. She may recommend a special food or high-calorie supplementation to get your Shih Tzu back on the right track.

Chapter 10

Making Your Baby Beautiful: Time to Groom

In This Chapter

- Grooming puppies from day one
- Choosing a hairstyle for your Shih Tzu
- Picking a professional groomer or going it alone
- Collecting the proper grooming tools and making a schedule
- Getting into grooming: Daily and monthly chores

If you line up all dog breeds, a Shih Tzu starts to look like a pretty easy breed to own . . . that is, until you remember how much grooming work you have to do. That long hair requires maintenance, if not extensive primping. Otherwise, your dog will be pretty unhappy and possibly (gasp!) unattractive. Even if you keep your Shih Tzu in a short haircut, you still need to do regular grooming maintenance. It's an essential chore.

Many breeds don't require daily grooming, but a Shih Tzu will be happier and healthier if you groom him daily. You don't have to spend a long time doing it, but a daily grooming is important in even more ways than keeping your Shih Tzu clean and presentable. A daily grooming session provides you with an opportunity to monitor your Shih Tzu's physical well being more closely than if you were just mindlessly petting your Shih Tzu or carrying her around in your handbag. This chapter helps you navigate through the hardest and most labor-intensive part of owning a Shih Tzu.

Teaching Puppies to Love Grooming Now

Just try grooming an adult dog who's never been groomed before and you can see why teaching very young puppies about the grooming routine is important. Adult dogs can be scared of grooming equipment, resistant to paw and ear touching, and won't sit still when you try to tease out the tangles. The grooming routine is one of the most important routines to get your dog used to while she's still young. If a puppy learns that grooming is part of her regular day, she even looks forward to the love and attention. She'll also love how great she feels when she's smooth, clean, and spiffy.

Puppies lose their puppy coats and grow into their adult coats between six months and one year, but before that happens, start grooming. During the coat transition time, you'll need to brush out the shedding hair every day to keep it from tangling, and if your puppy isn't used to this yet, it won't be easy for anyone. Your puppy may not actually *need* much grooming before this difficult stage, but the point is to get her used to the routine — the time, the place, the tools, and the feel of grooming. You can begin grooming the very first day you bring your puppy home, and I recommend this because it immediately sets the standard for her life in your home.

A puppy doesn't need an all-out grooming session just yet, so for now, spend just five or ten minutes every day following these steps, talking gently and encouragingly throughout the process:

1. **Feel all over your Shih Tzu's body, giving him a gentle massage.**

   This procedure loosens dead hair and skin and also alerts you to any skin or body changes. It also relaxes your Shih Tzu.

2. **Very gently brush your puppy's coat with a soft natural-bristle brush.**
3. **Gently comb your puppy's coat with a steel comb.**
4. **Wash your puppy's face with a soft washcloth, and wipe gently under her eyes.**

   At this step, apply moisturizing eyedrops if your breeder and/or vet recommend them.

5. **Touch each toe with the nail clippers designed just for small dogs, and clip off just the very tip of one nail per day.**
6. **Touch each paw and press gently on each paw pad.**
7. **Check Lola's rear end to be sure it's clean.**

   Carefully clip away any hair getting in the way of your Shih Tzu's rear (use a blunt-tipped grooming scissors), and wipe her rear clean with a disposable, hypoallergenic baby wipe if it looks soiled.

How can you say no to a cuddly and adorable Shih Tzu puppy? Experienced hobby breeders are the best source for healthy Shih Tzu puppies. Check out Chapter 3.

Although your Shih Tzu may enjoy going outside with you, remember that he's an indoor dog. His thick coat and short nose make heat stroke a real risk. See Chapter 13.

With a Shih Tzu's long hair, you can experiment a bit and have some fun giving your dog a new look. See Chapter 10.

Being your companion and looking this adorable is definitely hard work! See Chapter 2.

© Isabelle Francais

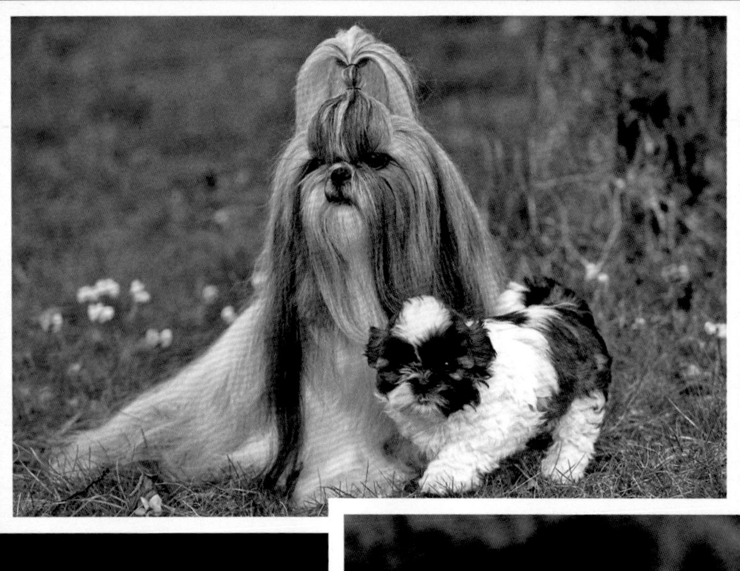

A Shih Tzu requires grooming to keep his coat healthy and beautiful. How you style your Shih Tzu depends on your personal taste. See Chapter 10.

Shih Tzu come in all sizes and colors with all different types of hair styles. Ask your breeder which type is the easiest to maintain. See Chapter 3.

© Isabelle Francais

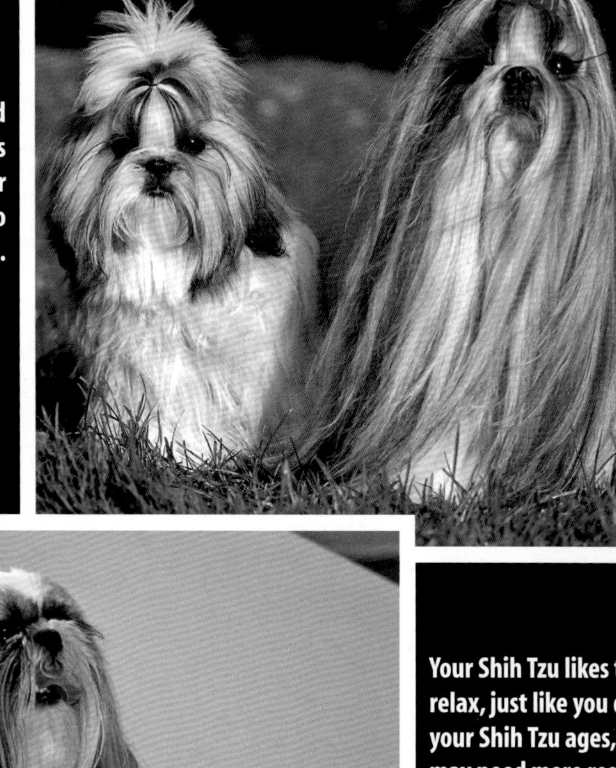

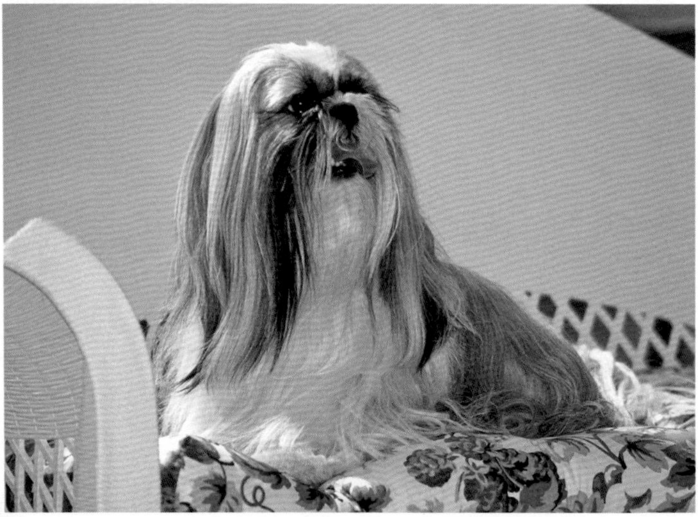

© Jean M. Fogle

Your Shih Tzu likes to relax, just like you do. As your Shih Tzu ages, she may need more rest and relaxation time. See Chapter 12.

No matter your age, a Shih Tzu makes a great companion. Check out Chapter 2.

Shih Tzu puppies are cuddly and cute, but they do require your time and dedication. Make sure you're prepared when you bring your Shih Tzu puppy home. See Chapter 6.

A Shih Tzu is a great dog for responsible children. He's cuddly and devoted, but remember that your Shih Tzu is a small dog and should never be left alone with small children. See Chapter 7.

Although Shih Tzu aren't overly athletic dogs, they still need and enjoy exercise to keep them in good shape. See Chapter 8.

Are you eager to adopt a new Shih Tzu puppy (or two)? They're cute and cuddly, but make sure you know what to look for before you make a decision. See Chapter 4.

A Shih Tzu is a loyal dog who enjoys spending time with you. Whether he's sitting on your lap or following you around the house, he'll always be your companion. See Chapter 2.

A top knot keeps your Shih Tzu's hair out of her face. You can do it yourself or hire a professional groomer. See Chapter 10.

Have some fun with your Shih Tzu. Take him outside regularly to play his favorite game. See Chapter 8.

In order to keep your Shih Tzu's beautiful coat healthy, you need to regularly brush and groom her. Grooming time is great for bonding with your Shih Tzu. See Chapter 10.

© Jean M. Fogle

Training your dog with important cues, such as Sit and Stay, is a great way to bond with your dog and give him the guidance and direction he craves. See Chapter 17.

© Jean M. Fogle

Always a favorite breed at dog shows, Shih Tzu charm the judges with their beauty and friendly personalities. See Chapter 17.

© Isabelle Francais

Your Shih Tzu is a curious, playful dog who enjoys playing and socializing with you. Make sure you spend time with him. See Chapter 11.

© Jean M. Fogle

Are you feeling a tad blue today? Your Shih Tzu can cheer you up. Pick him up and he'll show you unconditional love. See Chapter 1.

Your Shih Tzu will look to you for guidance. She'll feel safe and confident knowing that you're in charge. See Chapter 15.

© Cathi Winkles

8. **Fix her topknot so her ribbon, barrette, or band looks straight and pretty, and tell her how beautiful she is.**

9. **Repeat daily.**

   Wasn't that fun? Your Shih Tzu will think so if you do this every day. Pretty soon, she'll look forward to these fun times together . . . and so will you. (Check out Figure 10-1.)

© Jean M. Fogle

Figure 10-1: Brushing your dog is a great way to build camaraderie.

Considering Your Style Options

Your Shih Tzu puppy may not have a lot of hair yet, but before long, he will, and you have to decide what you want to do with it. Do you want to keep it show-dog long or maintain that cute puppy look with a short puppy cut? This section considers the pros and cons of longer and shorter styles.

Long and lovely

Something about a Shih Tzu in a full-length coat is just so glamorous. The long coat feels and looks gorgeous, and your dog will certainly get noticed. Show dogs have long coats and aren't supposed to be trimmed very much, except to straighten the ends and trim around the feet and the rear end for neatness. But, a long coat takes a *lot* of work because the Shih Tzu has a *double coat* — a downy undercoat with a longer, smoother layer on top. This kind of coat can tangle easily when the undercoat sheds and gets caught in the outer coat.

You need to bathe and blow dry your Shih Tzu about every three weeks, and spend quality time brushing and combing every day. If you don't have the time, you need to take your dog to a professional groomer for these chores every month. Also consider that coat quality is genetic. Some dogs have coats that tangle much faster than others. The more you groom your own dog, the more you get to know his coat and how often you need to brush it.

Short and sassy

Shih Tzu puppies in their fluffy, furry coats look so adorable that many people want to maintain that puppy cut even when their Shih Tzu grow up. (Check out "Styling the short coat" later in this chapter for more info.) A monthly trip to the groomer is all it takes: snip, clip, and you have one cute little Shih Tzu. Or, you can learn to clip your dog's hair yourself, to save a few bucks.

A Shih Tzu in a short coat takes a lot less daily grooming time than a Shih Tzu in full coat, even though you still need to brush and comb through the coat on most days. If you like the idea of a low-maintenance do, then short and sassy is probably the "do" for you (I mean for your dog).

Doing the Grooming Yourself or Hiring a Professional

Some people just love to do things themselves: home improvement, home-cooked meals, home-groomed dogs. Grooming a Shih Tzu can be time consuming, but it isn't necessarily difficult. If you keep up daily grooming, then you can do a more extensive grooming session once a month.

Hiring a pro costs money, of course, but you also get to drop off a scruffy dog and pick up a freshly washed and coiffed beauty. Mobile groomers even come to your house. Whether you keep your dog's coat long or want it cut short, you may prefer to have a professional handle the more extensive grooming tasks. Many Shih Tzu owners feel that the cost of professional grooming is well worth the time saved and are happy to pay for a good groomer's expertise. (Costs vary quite a bit depending on the groomer and where you live. Call first to get an idea of price.)

The decision is, obviously, up to you — what are you willing to do yourself, and what are you willing to pay for? This section helps you make those decisions.

Going it alone

If you decide to be your Shih Tzu's groomer, you can start shampooing, snipping, or clipping to your heart's content. Or, you can get some professional input about which products work best and the smart way to cut a dog's hair short (if that's what you want to do). Pros can also give you tips on removing mats, keeping eyes clean, poofing the topknot in show-dog style, and other Shih Tzu tips. Talk to your dog's breeder, breeders and handlers at dog shows, or even a professional groomer willing to show you some tricks of the trade. You can't substitute a professional's advice.

Grooming a Shih Tzu is a learning process. Your first attempt at a puppy clip may not look so cute, but fortunately, Shih Tzu hair keeps growing and your mistakes soon grow out, giving you the opportunity to try again . . . and again, until you finally hit on the perfect grooming products, routines, and haircut for your Shih Tzu. Different products work best for different dogs, too, so you may need to try a few different shampoos, conditioners, tear stain removers, and other products before you find the one you like. (For a complete list of products you need, check out "Grooming Tools and Products: A Primer" later in this chapter.)

Seeking out a groomer

A professional groomer (see Figure 10-2) bathes, shampoos, conditions, and blow-dries your dog, styling the coat and doing up the topknot (if your dog's hair is long on his head). The groomer also trims hair around the rear and paws, neatens up the coat, and trims your dog's nails, if necessary. Or, if you like a short cut, the groomer uses scissors and, in many cases, an electric clipper to give your dog his "do."

If you decide to have your Shih Tzu professionally groomed, you should take him to the groomer about every month if he has a long coat or every six to eight weeks for a short cut. Some groomers work out of pet shops, while others have their own facilities. To find a good groomer, ask friends with long-coated dogs which groomer they recommend, or talk to your dog's breeder or veterinarian. You can also find groomers listed in the phone book.

Figure 10-2: A professional groomer can treat your Shih Tzu like royalty.

Many groomers go to school to study professional grooming and some have certificates or registrations as professional groomers, but these licensures aren't regulated and groomers aren't required to have a license, so recommendations from clients can be more significant than a certificate from a grooming school. Even if your groomer comes highly recommended by a friend, ask to see the license, or see if the groomer has a portfolio of clips he's done.

Your goal is to find an experienced groomer you like and trust, and that your dog likes and trusts, too. He also has to do a good job (of course) grooming your dog. If you don't like the results after your first visit, talk to the groomer. A good groomer should be willing to change what he does so you're happy. If you feel you can't communicate well with the groomer, look for someone else. You aren't obligated to continue working with a groomer who isn't working with you. Fortunately, most cities and even small towns have several groomers to choose from.

Grooming Tools and Products: A Primer

Whether or not you decide on a professional groomer, you need grooming tools for grooming at home. You can find all these tools at a pet store or online. If you're having trouble finding something, talk to local groomers or your breeder, or ask your pet store if they can order it for you.

Here's what you need to have on hand at home:

- **Spray conditioner:** Long-coated dogs can suffer hair breakage with rough brushing and combing. A spray conditioner helps smooth out hair and ease out tangles. Use spray conditioner before brushing and combing, and the job will be much easier.
- **Natural bristle brush:** Use a natural bristle brush for puppies. This brush has softer bristles made of animal hair (usually from a boar) or plant fiber; a synthetic brush made of nylon or plastic is coarser and can hurt or break hair. This book's technical editor and Shih Tzu breeder and exhibitor Victor Joris recommends the Mason-Pearson natural bristle brush with the rubber base. For more info go to `www.masonpearson.com`.
- **Pin brush:** This brush has metal pins instead of bristles and is better to use on adult Shih Tzu. The pins have rounded ends so they aren't sharp, and they get through tangles and thick hair better than a natural bristle brush, which is more likely to smooth just the top layer of hair. Some brushes have pins on one side and natural bristles on the other, giving you both options.
- **Slicker brush:** These brushes have a lot of tiny metal bristles that are perfect for pulling out your Shih Tzu's undercoat when he sheds. You can get rid of a lot of dead hair this way, rather than having it fall out and get tangled in the outer coat. Use a slicker brush carefully and never around the dog's eyes; slicker brushes are sharp. Use a steel comb for your Shih Tzu's face.
- **Steel comb:** A steel comb is the best way to get at those tiny tangles forming right at the skin that you can't see until they snag in your comb. After brushing, comb through the coat all the way down to the skin. You can also use a comb to work out tangles by pulling tiny pieces of hair from the tangle a little at a time. With patience, even stubborn mats can come out this way.
- **Toothbrush and toothpaste:** How long would you go without brushing your own teeth? Dogs are prone to dental plaque, gum disease, and other health problems related to dirty teeth, just like humans. Brush your dog's teeth every day or at least once a week with a soft-bristled toothbrush and toothpaste made for dogs. (Check out the "Toothy grin" section later for how to brush your dog's teeth.)

- **Moisturizing eyedrops:** Some Shih Tzu are prone to a condition called *dry eye,* which leaves their eyes lacking in tear production. Although dry eye is irritating and painful, it's easily remedied with the regular application of over-the-counter moisturizing eyedrops (and in some cases, prescription medication). Ask your vet if your Shih Tzu needs eyedrops.
- **Clippers:** A pair of clippers, like the kind you use to buzz off a person's hair, is most necessary for grooming your Shih Tzu yourself and keeping him in a short cut. However, you can also use a clipper around your Shih Tzu's rear end. When purchasing clippers, look for one designed for dog grooming, so you get the right blades and attachments for your needs. Good clippers can be costly (they can range from $50 to more than $200). Clippers must be kept very clean and carefully maintained, or they can break down. Protect your investment.
- **Toenail accessories:** Healthy feet have short, well-groomed nails, and regular nail trimming is easier on you and your dog than trying to chop off too-long nails every few months. Buy a good-quality nail clipper made for small dogs. Some people use electric grinders instead of nail clippers, but these aren't safe for Shih Tzu because the rotating mechanism can catch in the Shih Tzu's long coat. Regular, old-fashioned nail clippers are the best choice.
- **Grooming scissors:** A sharp pair of grooming scissors with rounded tips (pointed tips are too dangerous) can be a valuable tool for trimming the rear end, trimming extra hair on your Shih Tzu's paws (particularly in the winter or if she goes outside a lot), and even neatening body and facial hair. Scissors can also cut through a mat (see the sidebar "What's a mat?" for more information). If you have your Shih Tzu professionally groomed, you probably don't absolutely need grooming scissors, but these can be nice to have around. Always use scissors with caution so you don't injure your dog.
- **Tear-stain remover:** The Shih Tzu's sensitive eyes can tear, and these tears can cause stains that are particularly visible on light-coated dogs. Mild tear stains don't hurt your dog (although built-up gook under the eyes can cause bacterial infection). However, tearstains can make your Shih Tzu's face look messy, so tear stain remover removes unsightly stains and keeps your dog fresh faced.
- **Dog shampoo and coat conditioner:** If you have your dog professionally groomed, the groomer typically shampoos and conditions your dog's coat. But if your Shih Tzu rolls in the

mud and doesn't have a grooming appointment for another week, you should have shampoo and coat conditioner handy, just in case. If you groom your Shih Tzu yourself, you need these products for the monthly bath. Always choose a shampoo and conditioner formulated for dogs. Human shampoo has the wrong pH for dogs.

Dog spa products are everywhere these days, so you have plenty of shampoos and conditioners to choose from:

- Choose a shampoo and coat conditioner or crème rinse for long-coated dogs that need extra moisture to keep coats from breaking or getting frizzy.
- If your Shih Tzu has a white or black coat, you can also get a shampoo to enhance those colors.
- If your Shih Tzu has sensitive skin, choose a hypo-allergenic shampoo.
- If you have flea problems in your area, a shampoo with natural botanicals that repel fleas is good.

- **Blow-dryer:** Long-coated dogs need to have their hair blown-out to keep it smooth and tangle-free. Without blow-drying, the coat can get tangled and messy as it dries. A freshly washed and blown-dry Shih Tzu is a joy to hug and cuddle, but buy a dryer with a low or cool setting. Small dogs are sensitive and if the blow-dryer is too hot, the heat can actually burn your dog. Even if your Shih Tzu has a short coat, blow-drying can dry him faster and make him look fluffier, but it isn't absolutely necessary.
- **Bows, barrettes, and other doggy hair accessories:** A small rubber band made for dog grooming keeps your Shih Tzu's topknot in place, but you can also decorate with ribbons, bows, or barrettes. A professional groomer can bedeck your dog with these optional accessories, but you may want to change your Shih Tzu's look for special occasions between professional grooming sessions.

Grooming on a Schedule

Incorporating grooming into your regular routine is essential to keep your Shih Tzu looking fabulous. However, how regularly do you need to groom? It depends. For example, you do some tasks, such as brushing and teeth cleaning daily, while you do others, such as nail trimming, less often. Table 15-1 shows you a grooming schedule.

Table 15-1 Your Shih Tzu's Grooming Schedule

Task	*Frequency*
Bathing	Monthly
Brushing and combing	Daily
Checking the body	Daily
Cleaning the teeth	Daily or weekly
Clipping the nails	Every two to four weeks
Maintaining the rear end	Monthly
Washing the eyes	Daily
Washing the face	Daily

Taking Care of Your Dog's Coat

If you've decided to handle coat care yourself from start to finish, this section is your guide. From brushing and combing to bathing, blow-drying, and styling, you get everything you need to know to keep your Shih Tzu's coat healthy and beautiful. Remember, practice makes perfect! It's really pretty fun to play beauty shop.

Brushing and combing the coat

Without regular brushing and combing, any Shih Tzu's coat will form tangles and mats, which feel uncomfortable for your dog, but even worse, they can trap dirt and moisture, providing bacteria with the perfect place to thrive. To keep your Shih Tzu's coat clean, healthy, and tangle-free, brush and comb through it once each day.

Follow these steps, whether your dog has a long or a short coat:

1. **Spray with coat conditioner.**

   Never brush a dry coat! Always start with a good dousing of coat conditioner before you brush. To avoid breaking the hair, spray down the coat every time you brush with coat conditioner. This process protects the hair shaft and keeps the hair lubricated and soft.

2. **Brush from the bottom.**

   Brush down your Shih Tzu's legs and work through hair from the end upward.

3. **Brush the rear end by lifting the tail.**

4. **Remove the tangles from the tail from the end upward, working tangles out from the bottom up.**

   Work from head to toe with a pin brush or slicker brush.

5. **Brush along the back and around the mane (the neck area).**
6. **Brush the head and ears.**
7. **Comb through.**

   Switch to your steel comb and comb through the entire coat, head to toe, combing all the way down to the skin and working out any tangles that didn't come out with the brush.

Bathing your baby

The Shih Tzu's coat requires a bath about every month or so to wash out any dirt that can cause tangles and to keep it hydrated and gorgeous. If you do this process yourself, make some decisions first about location and products.

You have a few options about where to bathe your Shih Tzu:

- **The bathroom or kitchen sink:** Because your dog is small, you may decide to bathe her in the sink. The sink is a convenient height, and you don't have to stoop down to bathe her (like you would with the bathtub).
- **The bathtub:** If you don't mind bending over, the bathtub can be a convenient place for bathing.
- **A basin, indoors or out:** A basin is portable so you can wash your Shih Tzu wherever it's convenient.
- **An infant bathing tub:** This tub is ideal for small dogs because they usually come with a nonskid surface in the bottom, so little Lola won't slip and slide.

If the surface you choose for bathing is slick, get a bath mat or other small nonslip mat for the sink or tub, so your Shih Tzu doesn't feel insecure, sliding around on the slick surface. Now it's time to bathe! Just follow these simple steps:

1. **Before you start running the bath water, gather all your grooming supplies:**
   - Nylon collar and leash, to keep your dog from jumping out in the middle of the shampoo
   - Brush and comb
   - Spray conditioner

- Cotton balls for your dog's ears
- Petroleum jelly for her eyes
- Shampoo
- Crème rinse
- A sprayer attachment or big cup for rinsing
- A big fluffy towel
- Blow-dryer with cool setting

Keep all your grooming items in a big basket so you can easily grab the basket and take it right to the bathroom.

2. **Brush and comb your Shih Tzu's coat thoroughly.**

   Tangles tighten when wet, so you want your dog's coat to be completely tangle-free before you bathe her. (Check out the "Brushing and combing the coat" section earlier in this chapter.)

3. **Put a nylon collar or harness and leash on your Shih Tzu if she tends to try to run away when wet.**

   Some Shih Tzu don't mind bathing at all or wouldn't think to jump out and run away, but if you have a runner, this equipment helps you keep hold of her. Just loop the leash over the faucet or your wrist. Or, if you bathe her in the bathroom, just shut the door. Whether you use a leash or not, never leave her unattended, even for a minute. She can drown or jump off the sink and choke herself.

4. **Plug her ears and protect her eyes.**

   Put a small piece of cotton in each ear to keep the ear canal dry. Because Shih Tzu ears are dropped, moisture can get trapped inside and cause infection and smelly ears. Put a small dab of petroleum jelly in the corner of each eye, to keep water and soap from irritating the Shih Tzu's sensitive eyes.

5. **Run lukewarm water into the bathing container.**

   Depending on what kind of bathing container you use, you can start running the water at this point and use the running water to help get your Shih Tzu wet, or you can run the water into the tub as the first step, and then get your dog ready. Be sure the temperature of the water isn't too hot or too cold (about body temperature is fine). If it feels comfortable when you run the water over the inside of your wrist, it should be fine for your Shih Tzu.

6. **Put your Shih Tzu into the bath.**

   Make this step fun and reassuring by talking to her gently and telling her how much fun this will be. After she's used to bathing, putting her in the water won't be a big deal, but you may need to reassure her quite a bit the first few times.

7. **Wet her coat with a sprayer or by filling a cup with water and pouring it over her coat.**

   Thick coats take awhile to get really wet, so make sure the coat is wet all the way down to the skin.

8. **Put about a quarter-sized dollop of shampoo into your hands and rub them together; rub the shampoo into your dog's coat.**

   Apply the shampoo carefully so you don't get any into your dog's eyes. Scrub the shampoo all over, including paws, tail, tummy, and rear end.

9. **Rinse the shampoo thoroughly.**

   Rinsing takes a long time (especially for long coats), so when you think you have all the shampoo out, keep rinsing. Periodically squeeze or press on the coat to get the water out. Rinse, rinse, rinse! Soap residue can cause nasty tangles and skin irritations.

10. **Apply conditioner or crème rinse so your dog's coat is smooth and manageable.**

    Rinse again. And again.

11. **When you're sure your Shih Tzu is squeaky clean, take her out of the bathing container and wrap her in the big fluffy towel.**

    Dry the coat gently so you don't break off hair — blotting, pressing, and squeezing the coat. *Don't rub it.* After you dry her, she'll shake and get out even more water than you thought possible, which will probably get you wet, so be ready. Praise her for being such a good girl!

12. **Blow-dry.**

    After towel-drying, use your steel comb to make a long part from the crown of your Shih Tzu's head all the way to the tail. Now, blow-dry the hair on low or cool setting, gently brushing the coat out as you dry it so it hangs down nicely on both sides of the part. Some dryers come with stands so you can use both your hands to hold the dog and the brush. If your dog has a short coat, you don't need to part it. Just blow-dry and brush until it's soft and fluffy.

What's a mat?

A *mat* is a hair tangle that has turned into a thick mass, either because the tangle wasn't combed out or because foreign matter got caught in the hair and the hair tangled around it. You can't just comb out a mat without a lot of work. You may need to tease it out or even cut it in strips and tease out each section. Severe mats may need to be cut out of the coat entirely. Regular brushing and combing prevents tangles from becoming mats.

A mat splitter makes it easy to slice mats into smaller pieces so you can work them out more easily without cutting out the mat entirely. A mat splitter is an optional tool, and if you keep your Shih Tzu well combed, you probably won't ever need it. For more info on other grooming tools, see "Grooming Tools and Products: A Primer" earlier in this chapter.

Styling the "do"

If your Shih Tzu has a long coat, you have just a little bit of styling to do after your dog is freshly washed and blown dry. Styling a long coat is easy. Short coats require a little more work during trimming but are much easier to maintain every day.

Long coat styling

Follow these steps to style your Shih Tzu's long coat:

1. **Make a long straight part, using your steel comb, from the crown of your Shih Tzu's head all the way to the base of his tail.**
2. **Comb the hair down both sides.**
3. **Take a look at the bottom edge of the dog's long coat.**

   Using a scissors, trim the edges so they're straight, like cutting someone's bangs.
4. **Look at each foot and trim any stray or long hair from between paw pads.**

   Be careful with the scissors so you don't cut and injure the dog.
5. **Trim any long hair from inside your dog's ears.**

   Some people prefer to have a vet or groomer pluck out the ear hair.
6. **Now, tie up the topknot (check out Figure 10-3).**

© Isabelle Francais

Figure 10-3: A topknot keeps your Shih Tzu's long hair out of his eyes.

1. **With a comb, make a part from ear to ear.**
2. **Gather up all the hair in front of the part into a ponytail.**
3. **Secure the hair with an elastic band made for dog hair.**
4. **Add a bow or barrette, if you want.**
5. **For show-dog flair, tease the hair before tying it in the topknot, so it poofs out.**

   You can also make two topknots or any other fun variation. Tug gently on the hair after you tie it, pulling it out a little to make it poofier. Some exhibitors even curl the ends of the ponytail with a curling iron into ringlets. If you do this, be careful not to burn your dog.

Be careful with the scissors and clippers! These tools work better sharp, but that also makes them dangerous. Don't ever let children use these tools on a dog, and pay close attention to what you're doing when *you* use them. Don't watch TV or talk to other people during the part of grooming when you're using these tools. You don't want to nick, cut, or clip your Shih Tzu's skin or injure an ear, an eye, a tail, or any other precious part!

Styling the short coat

If you keep your Shih Tzu in a short coat, you can keep it trimmed yourself, although many pet owners prefer a pro to do it. If you want to try it, you can trim down your Shih Tzu in a variety of ways. You have several different options for a styling a short coat. You can also check out `stfsc.bizland.com/grooming3.htm` for more options.

To style the most popular puppy cut (see Figure 10-4), just do the following:

Figure 10-4: The puppy cut is easy to maintain.

1. **Use scissors and cut all the hair on your Shih Tzu's body to about 1 to 2 inches all over.**

   Leave the tail, ears, and beard a little bit longer.

2. **After you cut the hair, fluff it up with a slicker brush and even out any places that stick out.**

3. **Cut the ear, tail, and beard hair so they're neat along the bottom edge.**

4. **Shape the head.**

   To shape the head, you can

   1. **Clip the hair on the skull short (where the topknot would be), but leave the ears and beard longer.**

2. **Cut the beard and ears in a reverse bowl shape, so that a line from the bottom of one ear dips down under the beard and rises up again at the opposite ear, when you look at your dog from the front.**

Another option for the head is

1. **Shape the Shih Tzu's head by leaving the hair on the skull long.**
2. **Cut the ear and beard hair so they form a straight line along their bottom edge, parallel to the ground, leaving the hair on the top.**
3. **Always trim hair around paw pads so excess hair doesn't get tangled around your Shih Tzu's feet.**

Handling Other Grooming Tasks

Just because your Shih Tzu's coat looks fabulous doesn't mean you're finished. Grooming includes nail care, eye care, ear care, dental care, and more. Don't neglect these tasks. This section goes more in-depth.

Body check

A daily once-over with your hands alerts you to any changes, such as rashes, lumps, bumps, rough patches, sore weepy areas called *hot spots* (these can form beneath hair tangles), or painful areas in your Shih Tzu's skin and body. If you do this body check every day, you just can catch problems before they get too serious.

Start out this process by giving your Shih Tzu a massage. Rub her skin from head to toe, to loosen dead hair and slough off dead skin, stimulate oil production, and feel for any skin changes. If you notice a lump, a sore, or a painful area (your Shih Tzu may yelp or shy away from you), give your vet a call to have the issue checked out.

Face up

Using a soft, moist washcloth, wash your Shih Tzu's face. Gently wipe under her eyes, up her muzzle, and under her chin. Don't forget the beard! Because a Shih Tzu often gets food and water in his beard and can get runny eyes and tear stains, this daily facial cleansing keeps her feeling and looking clean.

Teary-eyed

The Shih Tzu's naturally sensitive eyes can get runny, dirty, or so dry they become painful. Apply moisturizing eyedrops if your vet recommends them, and tear stain remover if your dog needs it. Eyedrops made for moisturizing human eyes work fine, but check with your vet to be sure. Most pet stores and grooming shops stock tear stain remover.

Toothy grin

Dirty teeth can contribute to dental plaque, gum disease, and early tooth loss, all of which can lead to decreased immunity and even early death, according to recent research, because oral bacteria can travel straight to the heart. You brush your own teeth every day (or at least I hope you do) to prevent tartar buildup and cavities, so give the same courtesy to your dog. Give your dog's teeth a good inspection during brushing.

If you get a young dog used to tooth brushing, he'll soon accept the ritual as part of the regular grooming routine. For older dogs who won't accept tooth cleaning (although most Shih Tzu don't mind too much), you can add an oral rinse product made for dogs into his water, to help eliminate dental bacteria. Chew toys can help, too.

If your dog resists tooth brushing, start slow. Let him lick some dog toothpaste off your finger the first few times and just touch his teeth. Do a little more each day. Work up to these easy steps:

1. **Put a little dog-formulated toothpaste on a soft-bristled toothbrush.**

   Brush the teeth with a toothbrush and toothpaste made for dogs — human toothpaste can be toxic to a dog if he swallows it, and your dog probably won't like the taste, either.

   You can use a child's soft toothbrush, a toothbrush for dogs, or other tooth cleaners made for dogs, including "brushes" that fit over your finger so you can just massage your dog's teeth with your finger. If you don't have access to a dog's toothbrush, at the very least, wrap a soft cloth around your finger and wipe the teeth.

2. **Brush Samson's teeth the same way you would brush your own, gently scrubbing all surfaces.**

3. **Brush gums or massage with your finger, to keep circulation going for healthier gums.**

If you notice plaque build-up, talk to your vet about a professional cleaning. Older dogs often require a professional cleaning about once a year.

Paws for a moment

Without grooming, your Shih Tzu's nails can also become too long and damage his foot or make walking difficult. Get your dog used to having just one or two nails clipped every few days, or clip off the very tips every two or three weeks, instead of clipping a lot of the nail every few months. Frequent clipping keeps the *quick* — the vein running down the nail — from growing toward the end of the nail. When this happens, and you accidentally clip the quick, the nail bleeds and your dog feels pain, so frequent clippings are safer.

To clip nails (refer to Figure 10-5), follow these steps:

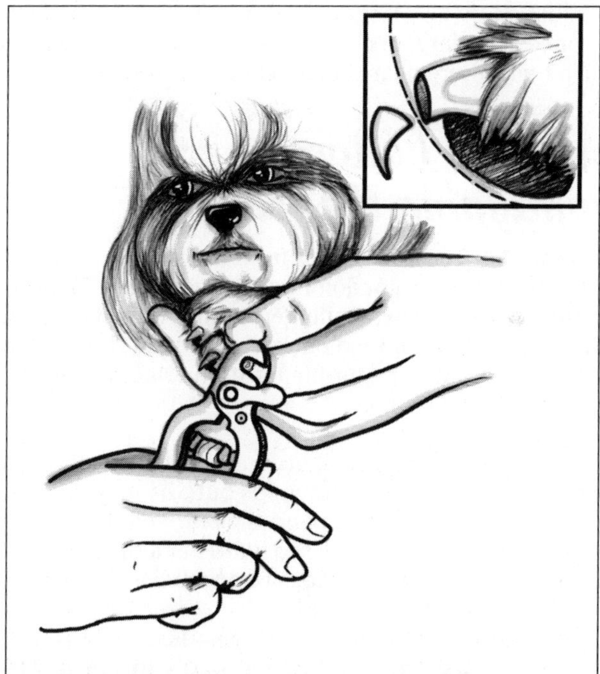

Figure 10-5: Hold your dog's paw and carefully clip the nail.

1. **Take your Shih Tzu's paw in your hand and position the nail clipper to clip off just the very end.**

2. **Clip the nail using a quick motion with the clipper.**

   Don't move the paw or jerk the dog. With practice, this step becomes easier.

3. **After clipping, smooth the rough edges of each nail with an emery board.**

You don't ever want to clip the quick in your dog's nail, but just in case you do (it happens), keep a little styptic or coagulating powder nearby (your pet store stocks this product). A dab will stop any bleeding. Even more importantly, get back on that horse and clip the very next day with plenty of treats in hand, so your dog doesn't associate nail clipping with this one bad experience.

In dogs with light nails, you can see the quick, which looks like a dark line inside the nail. The quick doesn't go all the way to the end of the nail, so find where the quick begins and clip just before it. In dogs with dark nails, you have to guess, which is why it's best to clip just a tiny bit off the end more often, instead of clipping a lot at once. Regular nail clipping tends to force the quick to recede so it isn't anywhere near the tip where you're cutting.

Get to the bottom of it: Maintaining the rear

Sure, your Shih Tzu looks cuter from the front than from the rear. (Most of us do!) Even so, don't neglect your Shih Tzu's rear view. Wipe the area with a hypo-allergenic baby wipe if the area seems dirty, and keep hair clipped back from around the anus so your Shih Tzu won't have any problem with hair getting in the way when he goes to the bathroom.

If your Shih Tzu starts licking his rear a lot or scoots around on the carpet like he's trying to scratch his butt, he may have impacted anal glands. These glands around the rear end fill up with a stinky substance that's usually released a little at a time naturally when your Shih Tzu poops. Small dogs often have a problem in this area.

Some groomers can empty the anal glands for you, but most people entrust the dirty job to a vet, who's specifically trained. If you don't want to pay the vet, have her show you how to do it. But personally, I think this task is difficult, and really, frankly, quite disgusting. You have to use paper towels and squeeze around and under the anus until the substance comes out. You may not enjoy it, but if your dog's prone to this problem, doing this step yourself saves you money. Good luck!

Chapter 11

Socializing and Shaping Your Shih Tzu's Behavior

In This Chapter

- Introducing your Shih Tzu to the world (and vice versa)
- Spending time with your Shih Tzu to improve behavior
- Solving common behavior problems
- Seeking professional help for your Shih Tzu's behavior

Every day, you discover something new about your dog, and the better you know him, the more you can see his own unique and individual personality emerging. Maybe he's a little reserved or the most loving and sociable dog. Maybe he loves kids or cats but seems fearful of tall men with beards or the two big dogs next door.

Your Shih Tzu has certain inborn qualities, but on the other hand, you can shape much of her behavior. How you behave toward her and what you do with her all affect how she grows up to behave. The more people, other dogs, and new situations your Shih Tzu experience, the better she'll understand the world. The more you guide her, the safer she'll feel. This chapter helps guide you toward shaping your Shih Tzu's behavior to be the best that it can be, within the limits of her own unique personality.

Drum Roll, Please: Presenting Your Shih Tzu

Routines and a lot of interaction with you socialize your Shih Tzu to life in your house, but socialization is a much broader and important concept to understand. *Socialization* is the process of introducing your dog to a variety of people, animals, and new situations. This process should, ideally, start the day a new puppy is born. The puppy should be handled several times a day, gently, or even more often so that when he first opens his eyes, he's already accustomed to people. You hope the breeder did this (this is one sign of a good breeder — for more, see Chapter 3). But even if your Shih Tzu is already an adult, you can still do a lot to socialize her.

What will your Shih Tzu discover as you introduce her to the world? If Lola's new experiences are positive, safe, and fun, she'll understand to enjoy new experiences. If Samson's experiences are frightening, dangerous, painful, or just generally mind-numbingly dull (like sitting in a crate for eight hours), he quickly figures out that new experiences aren't something that he's going to be interested in — they'll be too highly stimulating and stressful.

This section looks at some strategies for socializing your Shih Tzu with the outside world. Remember that Shih Tzu puppies need to experience the human world because they live in it, and you can make those experiences positive so your Shih Tzu grows up to be happy, confident, and well-adjusted.

Starting your dog's socialization

You can socialize your Shih Tzu in many different ways. When you introduce her to someone or something new, you're socializing her, and whatever impression she gets influence her future perception.

Try to take your Shih Tzu somewhere new or introduce her to a new person at least a few times every week. Here are some ideas:

- **Take a walk to a busy park.** Let your Shih Tzu interact with friendly people and dogs.
- **Visit extended family and friends.** Let them hold and pet your dog, one at a time.
- **Throw a puppy shower.** (See the "Party on: Throw a puppy shower" section for more info.) If your Shih Tzu gets used to people coming over, he won't feel threatened every time the doorbell rings.
- **Take her with you when you run errands.** Doing so lets your Shih Tzu get used to traveling in the car, so she doesn't associate the car with vet visits only. Many places allow small dogs in carriers. Whenever possible, take your Shih Tzu. She'll love to be at your side, exploring the world, if she's used to doing it. Remember to *never* leave your Shih Tzu alone in a car on a warm day. Shih Tzu are prone to heatstroke.
- **Organize play dates with other dogs.** Find other small or larger but gentle, friendly dogs your Shih Tzu likes, and get together regularly for playtime.

Meeting (and greeting) other people

Humans tend to get a bit over exuberant when they see cute, little dogs, but you must remember that those little pups can easily get frightened by loud noise and rough physical contact. Remember that a Shih Tzu sees you and everyone else at ankle level when he's on the ground. Ankles aren't the most welcoming parts of people. Shih Tzu need to meet people, so how do you make sure these experiences are pleasant? Simple. You have to be in charge and protect your Shih Tzu from getting overwhelmed.

Every dog is different, and you don't know how your Shih Tzu will react to socialization until you try. Keep these things in mind:

- **If your dog gets overly excited, limit social activities to five or ten minutes at first.** Then give your dog some down time to rest in her crate or on your lap at home.
- **If your dog seems afraid of someone or something, transform the interaction into a positive one.** For example, if your dog seems to fear children, pick a few gentle kids, arm them with doggy treats, and let them greet your Shih Tzu, offer a treat, and then go away. Your Shih Tzu will soon discover that the child (or whomever else she fears) is okay.

  Introduce your Shih Tzu to many different kinds of people: Men, women, kids, seniors, people of different sizes and ethnicities, and people in wheelchairs. The first time your Shih Tzu meets anyone new, that meeting forms a strong impression.
- **If your Shih Tzu fears loud noises, you can desensitize her by occasionally making a loud noise at home (dropping something or turning on the vacuum cleaner), and then reassuring her everything is fine.** Don't get in the habit of picking her up every time she gets scared of a loud noise, or she'll figure out that she really does have a reason to be afraid and only you can protect her. Let her figure out that loud noises don't cause bad things to happen, and loud noises don't scare *you.*

Whenever you introduce anyone to your Shih Tzu, tell that person (even your own family members) that you're working on socializing your dog and you need them to help you. Whenever your Shih Tzu has the opportunity to meet friends, neighbors, even passersby who stop to *kitchy-kitchy-koo* your puppy, give the person a small treat and tell her to approach slowly, speak softly, and gently extend her hand for a sniff, offer a treat, and then very slowly pet the dog on the back or under the chin with a soft touch.

Meeting other strange animals

Your Shih Tzu is bound to meet other animals at some point in her life. Do you want her to think that other animals are scary and dangerous, or do you want her to be able to have other dog and cat buddies to play with and keep her company when you aren't around?

To expose your Shih Tzu to other people's animals, you can

- **Hold a play date with other dogs.** The Shih Tzu is naturally friendly and loves to have animal friends if introductions occur safely and in a fun environment. If everyone involved can manage their pets and someone has a good space in his home or a safely fenced yard, doggy play groups and play dates can be fun. For more info on introductions, see Chapter 7.

  In most cases, because Shih Tzu aren't threatening, other dogs and cats will make friends or at least accept your dog. But never stop supervising. Keeping interactions positive is easier than having to undo the damage of a traumatic interaction.

- **Drop in on friends who have animals.** Visit friends with your dog in tow so your Shih Tzu can meet your friend's cat or bird.

  Shih Tzu even learn to get along well with small animals, but some exceptions exist, so never leave your pet hamster, guinea pig, ferret, bunny, or any other small animal alone with any dog, even the docile Shih Tzu. Just remember, supervise, supervise, supervise, and keep it friendly.

- **Enroll your Shih Tzu in a puppy or dog socialization class.** These classes focus less on training and more on safe, friendly interactions, so puppies and dogs can learn to get along with each other in a fun, nonthreatening, and organized environment. (Check out the "Puppy classes" section later in this chapter.)

If your Shih Tzu fears other dogs, let her interact, one on one, with dogs you know are gentle and friendly for short periods until she begins to trust other dogs. During all interactions, you and someone else should each have control over each dog to prevent any kind of negative interaction. Don't take her to dog parks or other places with a lot of big dogs that can overwhelm her.

Before your Shih Tzu is fully vaccinated, avoid areas with a lot of dogs, like dog parks and obedience classes with a lot of dogs, so your Shih Tzu isn't at risk for contracting a contagious disease. However, you can still socialize your Shih Tzu in your own neighborhood, in your own home, and in small puppy socialization classes where all the dogs are healthy, until he's fully vaccinated.

Making the puppy shower happen

Love the idea of a puppy shower? You aren't the only one and that's why many forward-thinkers have designed puppy shower products sure to make your puppy shower *the* event of the season:

- Buy invitations: www.doodlebugpress.com/puppy_announcement.html
- Register for gifts: www.barkavenuepetboutique.com/puppy_showers.html
- Looking for the perfect puppy shower gift?: www.funstufffordogs.com/Qstore/Qstore.cgi?CMD=011&PROD=1153445001
- Buy party supplies at two different spots:
    - www.funstufffordogs.com/Qstore/Qstore.cgi?CMD=009&DEPT=1151864534&BACK=A0011A1E01153445001E1
    - www.birthdayinabox.com/lobby.asp-page-theme-dept_id-168
- Get or make puppy cake and pastries that dogs can really eat:
    - www.kooldogkafe.com
    - www.party-photo-favors.com/dog_birthday_cake_recipes.htm
- Get party ideas: www.dog-birthday-parties.com/puppy-shower.html

Party on: Throw a puppy shower

A good way to teach your Shih Tzu about people is to have a few friends over to your home, where your puppy already feels safe. As long as you don't let everyone mob your puppy, a puppy shower can be fun. Keep it small, serve good food and a few cool doggy treats, and party on — but always supervise all interactions between your Shih Tzu and your guests. (Check out the nearby sidebar, "Making the puppy shower happen" for more tidbits.)

Here are some tips to make your party successful:

- Invite people and their gentle dogs and children.
- Let people approach one at a time, instead of in a big mob.

- Provide food for both people and dogs. (But no food that's bad for dogs, just in case people can't resist sharing. See Chapter 9 for info on avoiding the not-so-healthy treats for dogs.)
- Remind party guests to speak softly, move slowly, and handle the puppy gently.
- Play, offer treats, introduce the puppy to other dogs (as long as everybody's fully vaccinated), and have fun!

Your puppy won't believe what a great new posse she's scored! But she may get a little grumpy or tired, so let her take a rest in her bed or crate away from the crowd if she starts to act scared, growl, or she looks tired and starts to snooze. She can always come back out after a nap, and besides, it's her party. She can nap if she wants to!

Hanging with Your Shih Tzu

Before you can modify your Shih Tzu's behavior (if it's a problem), you must first understand his natural tendencies, and you can't really know your Shih Tzu unless you spend time with him. Of course, you'll be doing this anyway — that's why you chose a companion breed, right? But you can discover a lot more if you pay attention when you're together.

Watch how your Shih Tzu reacts to his environment. Most Shih Tzu are friendly and trusting, but these qualities can come with many variations. Ask yourself the following questions. If you see a potential problem, check out the next section to resolve it.

- Is Samson quick to rush in, or does he tend to hang back?
- Does Lola hide behind your legs or stand bravely in front of you like a guard dog?
- Does Samson prefer to stay in your arms or in that cushy Sherpa bag?
- Is Lola a barker or less likely to voice her opinion?
- Does Samson express fear with a growl, a nip, or by cowering and hiding?
- Is Lola seemingly without fear?
- Is Samson a social butterfly or a wallflower?

Companion dogs thrive on human interaction. Just as you're learning about your dog when you hang out, your dog's learning about you and about human behavior in general. Just watching television together on the couch or playing a game of fetch or tug-of-war helps your Shih Tzu feel that he's doing his job. The more time you spend together, interacting or just relaxing, the stronger your bond and the happier your Shih Tzu will be.

Nipping Potential Behavior Problems

Even the sweetest, nicest dogs tend to do some things people don't like, such as barking a lot, chewing things, or guarding their toys and food. These doggy behaviors are natural, but they don't work well in human society. Even if your new Shih Tzu doesn't have any behaviors you don't like just yet, being prepared can give you the tools to deal with any behaviors that arise later.

Before I get into specifics, don't forget to reward the *good* behavior! People forget, but rewarding the good behavior is important. (Check Chapter 17 for more on rewarding.) In these moments of good behavior give your pup a kind word or a tiny treat — the dog equivalent of the thumbs-up. Positive reinforcement works much faster than punishment for shaping the behavior you want, because although a punishment may hint to your dog about what you don't like, it still doesn't give him any info about what you do like.

This section looks at some potential behavior problems your Shih Tzu may exhibit and what you can do to nip them in the bud before they drive you and everyone else crazy.

Shhhh!: Keeping your Shih Tzu quiet

Yip yip. Yip yip yip. Yip yip yip yip yip yip . . . Enough already! Dogs bark, but does your Shih Tzu have to keep making that noise every time a sparrow hops across the lawn? How can such a small animal make that much noise?

Some Shih Tzu don't bark often, but others do. Just like people, some Shih Tzu are more talkative than others, and some are also more protective of their homes and want to be sure you know about anything suspicious. (Remember, part of the Shih Tzu's ancestry was to guard the Buddhist temples in Tibet.) But you can keep your Shih Tzu from barking excessively with a few simple strategies. Before you can get him to stop, you need to determine his barking triggers. For example, does he sit on the couch and bark at every moving thing he sees out the window? Does he only bark when the doorbell rings? Does something else cause him to bark?

After you determine what triggers your dog's barking, you can take action to get him to stop. The following hints can keep him quiet:

- **To stop the barking when he sees someone or something outside, close the curtains.** "But Lola just loves to watch!" you protest. If you don't mind the barking, let her watch. If you do, close the curtains and let her find something else to do. Or open the curtains only when you leave, so you don't have to listen to her (if you live in an apartment complex, the neighbors may not appreciate this as much).
- **To stop the barking when the doorbell rings, convince your pup that the sound of the doorbell means he gets a treat, but only if he doesn't bark.** Barking can be helpful — it alerts you that someone is coming. However, if your Shih Tzu is just a little *too* exuberant an alarm system, train your Shih Tzu not to bark by following these easy steps:

  1. **Grab a pocketful of your Shih Tzu's favorite treats and enlist a friend's help.**

     Have your friend go outside.

  2. **Stand in front of the door with your Shih Tzu and her favorite treat.**

     This process works best when your dog is hungry, so try this trick before a meal and not after.

  3. **Show your Shih Tzu the treat and then have your friend ring the doorbell.**

     When your Shih Tzu barks, say "No" and turn away.

  4. **Open the door, greet your friend, and then close the door.**

     Show your Shih Tzu the treat again.

  5. **Have your friend ring the doorbell again.**

     If your dog barks again, again say, "No," open the door, greet your friend, and close it. Keep doing this until your Shih Tzu finally gets so interested in the treat, and so bored with that doorbell, that she doesn't bark. As soon as the bell rings and she doesn't bark, give her the treat and praise her.

     Repeat this process every day at least a few times, for a few days. And always keep treats nearby. The food-motivated Shih Tzu will quickly figure out that a ringing doorbell means treats, but only if she doesn't bark. She may still bark once in awhile, especially if the sound of the doorbell surprises her, but this exercise should correct any problems.

The above technique works to stop your Shih Tzu from any undesirable behavior linked to a sound. Try it if she jumps on people or nips at people when they come in the door, but this time, say, "Sit" before letting anyone in the door. She only gets the treat if she stays seated. For more info on how to teach your Shih Tzu to sit, see Chapter 17.

Tackling biting problems

Your furry little pup would never bite the hand that feeds her, but some Shih Tzu tend to get nippy, particularly if they start to figure out that nipping works. If children harass the dog, the dog has few ways of defending herself other than with her teeth. If people approach a shy dog too forwardly, the dog may bite out of fear. If biting makes the child or threatening adult go away, or if you pick up your Shih Tzu and cuddle her when she nips, the behavior has been reinforced, and the dog is likely to keep doing it.

As a responsible pet owner, make sure that your dog doesn't bite people. Only you know whether your Shih Tzu has a tendency to bite, but if you know this fact to be true, you need to get the problem under control ASAP.

Dealing with biting puppies

Fortunately, biting problems are usually easy to fix with puppies, if they haven't gone on for long. Never let puppies bite human skin! To teach a puppy not to bite, pull away and say a sharp, loud "No!" *every* time your puppy nips you. He'll soon realize that human skin isn't for chewing. This realization results in what trainers call *bite inhibition.* The dog learns to control his urge to bite.

Are *you* the problem?

If you constantly reward your Shih Tzu by picking her up or soothing and petting her whenever she "defends" you by growling and nipping at anyone who comes near you, you may be causing the problem. You're rewarding her bad behavior, even if your intention was only to calm her down. On the other hand, if you react harshly or hit the dog when she behaves badly, you're teaching her to fear you but not to behave better.

Remember, every reaction you have to your companion dog's behavior either reinforces or discourages that behavior, and all your interactions determine how your Shih Tzu sees your relationship, so be careful how you react to the behaviors you don't like. Ignoring bad behavior or separating yourself from the dog works best.

Handling biting older dogs

Teaching older dogs bite inhibition can be more difficult. Some dogs have lived much of their lives as biters. Plenty of small dogs, Shih Tzu included, can develop a biting habit. Sometimes, a dog bites because he feels threatened and thinks he has no other options.

Most importantly, don't ignore any kind of aggression, even though your dog is small. Ignoring it won't make it better, and for everyone's safety (including the dog's, who could end up in a shelter or worse if he keeps biting), address the problem now. With some dogs, biting is a habit. They never learned bite inhibition as puppies (see the previous section), or they were taught earlier in life that biting works or is a necessary defense mechanism.

If your older Shih Tzu bites — not just out of extreme self-defense but as a regular way of dealing with certain situations like meeting new people or having someone touch his toy — consult a professional behaviorist or trainer specializing in aggression, for an evaluation. (See the section "Identifying When You Need Help [and Who Can Help]" later in this chapter to find a professional to help you with behavioral issues.)

Guarding their goods

Resource guarding is an aggressive reaction dogs sometimes display when they feel that their food, toys, or even their turf (and that can include you) may be stolen. For example, a dog who growls and snaps if you come near him while he's chewing his favorite rawhide or who bites anyone who tries to get near you when he's on your lap is guarding his resources. Many Shih Tzu would never think of growling when you approach the food bowl or a favorite toy, but others feel very threatened about their possessions. This issue is much more common in rescued dogs that may have been mistreated, dogs that have lived in multiple-pet households and always felt they had to guard their food against other dogs, or dogs that have frequently had food, space, toys, or favorite people taken away from them.

Some people think you should constantly take things away from resource guarders to teach them that they don't get to own anything. Doing so may work with some dogs, but in my opinion, it isn't an effective strategy with a Shih Tzu. The dog gets frustrated, and it teaches her not to trust you because you keep taking away her stuff. How would you like it if someone kept taking your dinner away from you before you were finished eating? Okay, you probably wouldn't bite that person's hand, but you might wish you could.

Instead, you need to teach your Shih Tzu that she has plenty of everything and she doesn't need to guard it. You can do a lot of things to resolve resource guarding. Here are some ideas:

- **Let her eat alone and in peace.** Many dogs, especially those who live or have lived with other dogs, feel very threatened when they eat. This reaction is instinctual and natural, but you can teach your dog that she never has to feel anxiety when she eats at *your* house. Always feed her away from other dogs, children, or even you, in a closed room if necessary, and always at the same time each day. Soon she'll relax and realize that nobody is around to threaten her food.
- **Don't give your dog things she tends to guard.** Some dogs only guard particular things. She may not guard a stuffed toy, but she may guard a pig ear or a rawhide with ferocity. If so, don't give her those trigger items.
- **Shower her with abundance.** If your dog guards everything, she's afraid her resources will disappear. Teach her that in your home, resources are so abundant that she never needs to guard them. Feed her ten times each day (but the same amount as you did before, so she doesn't become overweight — just a few pieces of kibble per serving will work). If she guards toys, put toys everywhere. She can't possibly guard them all.
- **If your dog guards a place or a person, you must also refuse to let her have possession over that place or person.** If your dog growls at people when you're holding her, put her down immediately. If she growls while sitting on the bed when someone approaches, don't allow her to sit on the bed. The very moment she displays territorial guarding reaction remove her from the territory. You don't want her to lose her territory; you just want her to understand that her reaction won't result in what she wants. Pick her up again, and praise her if she lets someone approach *without* growling. But if she guards you again, put her down. She'll soon discover that guarding means she doesn't get what she wants.

When guarding truly becomes an aggression problem, you may need to consult a professional. See "Identifying When You Need Help (and Who Can Help)" later in this chapter to find a pro.

Overcoming extreme shyness

Shyness in dogs may be partially genetic, but in many cases, it's based on experience. A sensitive dog that gets over-stimulated, frightened, or even hurt tends to back off from the unfamiliar just to keep safe. Shy dogs need extra patience and sensitivity, and for these fearful fellows, safe and frequent socialization is even more important than for other dogs. There isn't anything wrong with having a slightly more cautious personality. But when shyness compromises your dog's quality of life, you need to act.

You can help your Shih Tzu overcome his shyness by trying these do's and don'ts:

- **Do take your shy dog on a walk *every* day.** Doing so can help him gradually feel more confident because he's getting out of the house, seeing new sights, and meeting people and other dogs but always on a routine. Your walks don't have to be long; even a ten-minute walk can help.
- **Do introduce him to new people or situations in the same way every time.** Make intros regularly and make sure that you supervise all interactions so your dog never feels like anyone or anything has crossed the line and poses a threat to him. After a while, he'll get used to other people.
- **Don't keep him isolated.** Make sure you let other people and animals near your dog. If he never gets out or meets anybody, he'll never overcome his fear. Sure, you want to protect your sensitive Shih Tzu, but the best way to do that is to help him build up his owner inner confidence.

Some Shih Tzu have physical or serious emotional problems that make shyness issues too difficult for the average pet owner to manage. These dogs require professional intervention. Check out "Identifying When You Need Help (and Who Can Help)" later in this chapter for info on help with behavioral issues.

Separation issues

Because companion dogs not only want but also *need* to be with people, some get very distressed when their people go away, resulting in *separation anxiety.* Even though you may be flattered by your godlike status in your dog's life, separation anxiety isn't good for your Shih Tzu. The stress can compromise his immune system and his quality of life, and he can even injure himself if he goes into a panic because of your absence. He can also bark excessively, disturb neighbors, and damage property.

Of course, your Shih Tzu *can* live without you, at least for short periods of time. He should look to you for guidance and care, but you want him to have enough confidence and independence that he can hang out by himself once in awhile. Here are some things to do to help your pet deal with your absence in a healthy way:

- **Train your Shih Tzu to spend some time alone in his crate every day.** If at first he cries, speak reassuringly to him but not with emotion in your voice. Be calm. Leave the room frequently but not for long. When he sees you keep coming back, he'll stop crying and relax. Keep at it and be patient, making a routine, which turns into a comfort for your dog. Just don't leave him in there for *too* long. For the purposes of teaching your Shih Tzu independence, 15 to 30 minutes at a time is plenty.
- **Don't make a big deal about leaving or coming back.** Tell your Shih Tzu that you're leaving, but don't act emotional about it. When you return, don't greet her right away or make a big deal about that, either. Greet her lightly, "Hi Lola," and then do something else. Dote on her later when she isn't dealing with the stressful transition of your comings and goings.
- **If you put your Shih Tzu in his crate when you leave, put him in about ten minutes before you leave.** Don't let him out until a few minutes after you get back. Open the mail, put away your coat, check your messages, and then let the dog out. This process eases him into the transition.
- **Pretend to leave frequently throughout the day.** Practice not making a big deal about it, but go out the door, walk around the yard for a few minutes, and then come back in. Go back out, get in the car, drive around the block, and then come back. Do these activities several times daily, leaving for a bit longer each time.
- **If you have to leave your dog for more than a few hours, hire a pet sitter or take your dog to a doggy daycare center.** Pet sitters spend time visiting and walking dogs whose owners have to work all day, and your dog gets some social interaction during that long stretch of time when you're away. Doggy daycare centers are a great experience for dogs that need help overcoming separation issues. To find places to care for your dog when you're away, see Chapter 14.

Separation anxiety can also be a pathological condition requiring medication and more serious professional intervention when it interferes with your Shih Tzu's life and well-being. If you can't manage separation anxiety issues by yourself, consult a professional (see "Identifying When You Need Help [and Who Can Help]" later in this chapter).

Delusions of grandeur

Some Shih Tzu have an amusing and all-encompassing sense of entitlement that adds to their charm. However, when that power-happy personality starts nipping, excessively barking, or becoming a serious nuisance to your life, you have a problem.

To cure your over-confident pooch can be tricky. You don't want to discourage her, frighten her, or destroy her self-confidence. But the following actions send the clear message that you're in charge:

- **Ask her to do things before you give her any treats.** Don't just give her treats for anything. Have her sit first, lie down, come to you, or look at you.
- **Don't reward him for bad behavior.** If he growls, take away his toy. If he nips, give him a timeout. If he barks rudely to get your attention, ignore him.
- **Make sure she knows who's in charge (that would be you).** If she tries to dominate you, ignore her. Don't cave in to her demands. You're the human with the bigger brain.
- **Don't forget to reward him when he *is* a good dog and isn't acting like a dictator.** Whenever he listens to you, looks at you with adoration, lets others pet him, plays nicely with another pet, or sits quietly in your lap, reward him. The reward doesn't always have to be a treat. Your attention is all your dog wants.

Identifying When You Need Help (and Who Can Help)

When a regular routine, plenty of attention, and smart training don't do the trick, who ya gonna call? Doggy professionals! Sometimes behavioral problems are too big or too serious for a pet owner to handle without some professional help. These problems most often occur in dogs who've suffered abuse, neglect, abandonment, poor breeding, or those dogs who didn't receive early socialization from the breeder or training from their previous owners. Behavioral problems may also come from physical problems. (A dog's response to pain, for example, can look like aggression.)

When your dog really does have a problem, don't ignore it. Just because your dog is little doesn't mean his problems can't be big or put others or himself in danger. This section is your guide to pet pros who understand dog behavior problems.

Your veterinarian

If your Shih Tzu's behavior changes suddenly, he becomes aggressive for no apparent reason, or he suddenly becomes shy and withdrawn and you don't know why, the problem may be physical. Pain and illness can cause dogs to behave differently. Whenever your dog has a behavior problem, consult your vet first just to rule out a physical illness or injury. (Check out Chapter 13 for more.)

Puppy classes

Puppy classes are perfect for young Shih Tzu who need experience with other people and other dogs in a safe, structured setting. Puppy class instructors can help you with basic behavioral management, such as housetraining, eliminating barking, puppy mouthing (when puppies chew on your fingers or playfully nip at you), and general manners training. Problems you think you can't handle may be easy to fix with your puppy instructor's help.

To find a good puppy class in your area, check out these options:

- Ask your veterinarian for a recommendation.
- Search the Association of Pet Dog Trainers' Web site (`www.apdt.com`) by zip code for trainers near you.
- Ask your local dog obedience club about classes.
- Look in the phonebook under *dog training.*

Obedience classes

Obedience classes, or dog training classes, are for puppies that have had all their vaccinations, as well as for adolescent or adult dogs. You can start your Shih Tzu at the beginner level for basic cues like Sit, Stay, Come, and Lie down. You can also ask the teacher all about dealing with basic behavioral issues.

Some instructors specialize in particular areas like aggression problems or shy dogs, and some also teach classes that train you and your dog to compete in competitive obedience, agility, or the show ring (check out Chapter 17 for more). Obedience classes can work wonders for dogs with behavioral problems because the classes and instruction teach *you* how to train your dog and communicate better.

To find a good obedience instructor, I recommend the following:

- Get a recommendation from your vet.
- Ask your breeder or rescue group for good local trainers.
- Search the Association of Pet Dog Trainers' Web site at `www.apdt.com`.

Before you sign up your Shih Tzu, be sure to visit a class first. Talk to the instructor to ensure that she advocates reward-based training and has experience with small dogs. Also express any concerns about bringing a Shih Tzu to a class with large dogs who could potentially be aggressive toward small dogs. If you find someone you feel comfortable with, go for it. Dog training classes are fun!

Some people say that Shih Tzu don't need obedience classes, and it's true . . . some of them don't! It all depends on what you want from your relationship. You may be able to teach your little Lola everything she needs to know, right there at home. But if you do want to take your relationship to the next level, get involved in competition or just have fun together with other dogs and people.

Animal behaviorists

Why does your Shih Tzu *do* that? *Animal behaviorists,* also referred to as *pet psychologists,* know. They have an advanced degree in animal behavior and can help you understand and correct behavior problems. Some behaviorists are also vets. Many specialize in pet behaviors and can help solve seemingly unsolvable problems related to severe separation anxiety or biting (see previous sections in the chapter relating to these issues).

Many animal behaviorists tell me that they wish people would come to see them *before* problems became serious because prevention is easier than fixing serious and advanced problems. Animal behaviorists may be able to give you an entirely new and helpful insight into your dog's problem, and they help you with concrete tools for solving those issues. Many of them have helped pet owners who thought their pets were beyond saving. Get recommendations from your vet and other dog owners before consulting these pros.

Animal behavior consultants

Animal behavior consultants may also be able to help you. These folks don't have to have any particular training or an advanced degree to call themselves behavior consultants, but they're often dog trainers who've had a lot of experience in the field dealing with certain issues like aggression or fear. Many behavior consultants do excellent work, and others may not have much experience or employ techniques you don't like, so get recommendations and check references before working with an animal behavior consultant.

Chapter 12

Keeping Your Shih Tzu Healthy and Safe

In This Chapter

- Hunting down a good veterinarian
- Vaccinating your Shih Tzu against dangerous diseases
- Arming your Shih Tzu with the proper identification
- Spaying or neutering your Shih Tzu
- Looking at different health options
- Caring for a senior Shih Tzu

A fluffy, bouncy puppy may look like the picture of health, but dogs don't always stay healthy without the right care. Preventive care helps keep your Shih Tzu at her best. Any vet will tell you that preventing health problems is easier than curing them, and curing health problems that have just started is much easier than curing them in their advanced stages. Don't wait until your Shih Tzu develops a health problem to adopt the strategies in this chapter. They really will make a difference *right now.*

In this chapter, you discover how to find a good vet and what to expect when you go there. You also find out easy care strategies that make a huge difference in how healthy your dog can be.

Finding the Right Vet

After you first buy or adopt a new dog, you need to take your dog to a veterinarian within the first 36 to 48 hours. This timeframe is very important — and often specifically required in the purchase or *adoption contract* (the agreement you signed when you purchased or adopted your dog; see Chapter 4). Many pet owners already have a vet they like, but if you don't, find one *before* you bring home your Shih Tzu. That way, you can have an appointment already made and feel good about the vet you've chosen.

Most cities and even small towns have at least a few vets, so visit more than one before choosing the one who'll be your Shih Tzu's healthcare provider. When comparing vets and narrowing down your search, you want a vet

- **That you like:** You should feel comfortable with the vet and be able to communicate well with her. She should explain things clearly and be willing to listen, not rush you through a visit.
- **Who understands small dogs — yours in particular:** Not all vets specialize in or treat very many small dogs, but small dogs have unique care needs. Ask your vet if she has a lot of small dog clients, and any other Shih Tzu clients in particular.
- **Who shares your beliefs about health:** For instance, if you like to try natural or holistic methods before resorting to medication or surgery, you may prefer a vet with training in, or at least an open mind about, holistic health. Maybe you like the idea of a vet fresh out of veterinary school and current on the latest developments in veterinary research, or you may feel more comfortable with someone who's been a practicing veterinarian for many years and has a wealth of experience.

Location, pricing, and atmosphere in the vet's office all matter, too, not to mention the vet's bedside manner. Consider your own preferences and priorities when choosing your vet. Keep looking until you find one you really like and who makes you and your Shih Tzu feel comfortable. During the first year with a new puppy, you and the vet spend a lot of time together. Better make it a positive relationship from the start.

Knowing What to Expect at the Vet's Office

Dogs don't always love going to the vet if it means they have to get a shot or a lot of poking and prodding, but veterinary visits are important for maintaining your new dog's good health, and quickly resolving any health problems that may occur. If you choose a vet you feel comfortable with, vet visits should be pleasant (mostly!) and a great chance to ask questions and get advice.

Most vets have different recommendations for the number of visits, depending on the age of your dog:

- **Puppies (through the first year):** Make four to six vet visits in your puppy's first year of life.

- **Adults (1 to 8 years):** Annual vet visits throughout adulthood allow your vet to keep a close eye on your dog's health.
- **Seniors (starting at 8 to 10 years):** Visit the vet twice a year, to nip any problems of aging before they get too advanced.

If your Shih Tzu stays healthy, you probably won't need to see the vet more than these recommendations, but these regular visits can make a big difference in your Shih Tzu's future health. But what happens during these visits? The next section sheds some light.

The first vet visit

During the first visit, you meet the vet (if you haven't already), and the vet meets your new Shih Tzu. Typically, the vet gives your dog a physical exam, which consists of looking at the dog; examining her ears (check out Figure 12-1), eyes (see Figure 12-2), mouth, and the way she walks; and feeling all over his body for any physical abnormalities that may not be evident because of the dog's coat.

If the vet detects any serious problems during the initial visit, you may need to contact your breeder, rescue group, or pet store to discuss your options. More often, the vet may notice more minor problems that can be easily resolved. Vets are trained to detect subtle signs of illness you may not notice, and if the vet suspects a problem, she may order some tests, such as blood tests or tests of urine or feces. She may prescribe medication, such as a deworming product, skin cream, or a flea control product. Or, she may suggest that you return in a few days or weeks for a follow-up exam.

Chances are pretty good that your Shih Tzu will get a clean bill of health at the first vet visit — and if he does, congratulations! But your job is far from over. If your vet advises you return at a certain time, make an appointment and keep it. *Keeping* your Shih Tzu healthy is all up to you.

Your puppy's first visit

For puppies, the first vet visit also sometimes includes a round of puppy vaccinations, depending on how recently she has had her last round from the breeder or rescue group. (Check out "Puppy shots" later in this chapter for more info.) Vaccinating your puppy is an important safeguard against disease.

Your adult dog's first visit

Adult dogs may need a booster vaccine, or they may just need a physical exam. The vet specifically checks older dogs for arthritis, dental plaque, and other signs of aging.

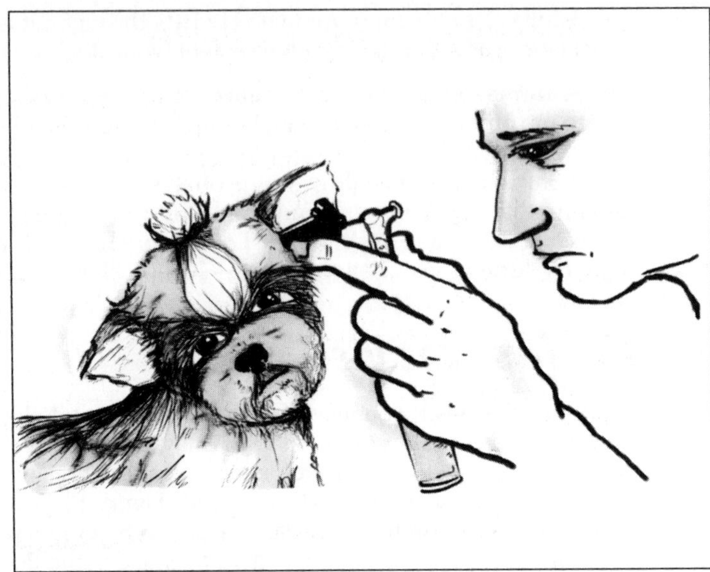

Figure 12-1: Your vet examines your dog's ears for signs of bacterial infection and ear disease.

Figure 12-2: Your vet examines your dog's eyes, looking for any signs of eye problems, like cloudiness, redness, or dryness.

Subsequent puppy visits

The first vet visit with a new puppy is super important, but you need to bring your puppy back according to your vet's recommended schedule a few more times in that first year. Your puppy needs several rounds of vaccinations to be sure she gets the full immunity as she grows and establishes her own immune system.

Also, puppies can sometimes develop health problems you may not notice, and your vet needs to make sure your puppy is growing and thriving. Just as human babies need a visit to the pediatrician every few months to monitor growth and development, your Shih Tzu needs that regular monitoring, too. The visits usually only take a few minutes — time for a shot, a general check, and the chance to ask any questions.

Regular check-ups for your adult dog

Your Shih Tzu can't just tell you in plain English when he isn't feeling well. Regular vet visits may be the only chance to catch a health problem you may not have noticed. Healthy adult dogs need a regular check-up once a year, for booster shots, weight check, and a general physical exam. Your vet will also probably give your dog an annual heartworm test and a new prescription for heartworm medication, as well as a prescription flea control product, if you're using one (for more on fleas and other pests, see Chapter 13).

When your dog becomes older, he needs more regular vet visits. Check out the "When Your Shih Tzu Slows Down: Senior Care" section later in this chapter for more info.

Doing your part

Sure, the vet is the health professional, but you see your Shih Tzu every single day. You're most likely to notice when she starts limping or won't eat or starts drinking more water than usual or suddenly doesn't want to play. *You* are your dog's first line of defense against health problems, so keep a close watch on her. When anything changes from the norm — what she does, how she acts, how her skin feels, how her coat looks, how much she eats and drinks, even what her poop looks like — give your vet a call. You may just be the one to save her life by alerting your vet to a problem in the early stages.

Getting the Right Vaccinations at the Right Time

Long ago, thousands of pet dogs died from diseases like distemper and rabies. Today, because of vaccinations, these diseases are rare, which is great news for your pets. Different vets have different vaccination protocols depending on what they feel is best and what particular diseases are common in your area. Some cities have specific laws about vaccinations, and some facilities like doggy daycare centers and boarding kennels also have rules about which vaccinations are required to participate. If you travel with your Shih Tzu, you may also need proof of vaccinations.

Some breeders and pet owners like to administer vaccinations themselves, but some states require that a vet administer vaccinations such as rabies. Check with your state to see what is required. If in doubt, however, let a vet do the job and you'll have the official paperwork to prove your pet is vaccinated.

This section identifies the types of shots your new puppy needs to protect him, and it also names the many common vaccinations that your vet may suggest your dog gets. Although vaccinations are important, occasionally your dog may have a bad reaction to one. This section also helps you deal with adverse reactions.

Puppy shots

Puppies still nursing from their mothers obviously don't get out much, so they aren't exposed to many germs. They also get a lot of natural immunity from their mother's milk, but as soon as a puppy is weaned, that immunity begins to decline. When the puppy goes home with a new owner and goes outside on walks, to puppy classes, and all the places that you take him for socialization, vaccinations protect the puppy from bacteria and viruses in the environment, until his immune system is mature and fully functioning.

Depending on the area in which you live, the shots given to your pup vary. Your vet can best advise you which shots are best for your dog. (The most common vaccinations are covered in the next section.) Holistic vets may be less inclined to include a lot of different vaccinations, while conventionally trained vets may be more likely to administer a combination vaccine.

Most puppies will have received at least one set of shots, typically at about six weeks, before the breeder allows the puppy to go home with anyone. The rest of the shots are up to you, and you need to schedule them every three months until the puppy has received three sets of shots. Some vets recommend four sets, so check with your vet on his schedule recommendation.

Common vaccinations

Understanding what the common diseases are and what they could potentially do to your puppy can help you recognize the importance of vaccinations and can also help you decide, along with your vet, which vaccinations are necessary for your dog. The following sections contain brief descriptions of some of the diseases your vet may suggest you vaccinate your puppy against depending on the prevalence of the disease in your area, your dog's individual needs, and state laws.

Rabies

Rabies is a dangerous, highly contagious, and fatal disease that occurs in wild animals. Whether or not you want to vaccinate your puppy against rabies, you'll probably be required to do so, by law. Humans can catch rabies, too, which is probably the main reason for the legal requirement. In most cases, vets give dogs the rabies vaccine at about six months of age.

Canine distemper

Once the number-one killer of pet dogs, *distemper* is no longer running wild, but this virus is still considered among the most serious viral diseases a pet can catch. Infected dogs stop eating and have major intestinal and respiratory distress, inflammation, coughing, vomiting, diarrhea, and fever. Don't neglect this one!

Parvovirus

Parvovirus is an intestinal virus that causes serious and acute vomiting and bloody diarrhea. Parvovirus is also one of the reasons why many vets and breeders recommend keeping your puppy indoors and away from foot traffic and other dogs (such as in a dog park or puppy socialization class) until he's received at least a couple of sets of the vaccine. The disease is often fatal in young puppies and because it's so prevalent in the environment and so contagious, you absolutely must vaccinate your puppy against it.

Adenovirus

Canine *adenovirus* is a respiratory virus that can cause bronchitis, pneumonia, and other respiratory problems in dogs. It can also cause infectious canine hepatitis, so the adenovirus vaccine is considered protection against this very contagious form of hepatitis in dogs. Dogs can pick up the adenovirus easily in boarding kennels and doggy daycare situations where a lot of dogs are breathing, barking, and coughing in the same room. This one's important.

Leptospirosis

Leptospirosis, a serious bacterial infection, can result in *jaundice* (a yellowing of the skin) and liver problems, kidney damage, vomiting, excessive urination, dehydration, fever, and other problems. Leptospirosis isn't as common as it used to be, and it's one of the vaccines that's more likely than others to cause a vaccination reaction (see "Keeping an eye open for vaccine reactions" later in this chapter), so not all vets recommend vaccinating against it. However, some areas of the country have recently had a resurgence of leptospirosis, so your vet may recommend this vaccination, depending on where you live.

Parainfluenza

Nobody likes getting the flu, and *parainfluenza,* a canine version of the flu, is highly contagious and can cause serious upper respiratory problems in your dog. Symptoms include coughing and trouble breathing. If a dog gets parainfluenza, he'll often recover on his own, just like you do when you have the flu. However, some dogs (like some humans) develop serious respiratory complications, so most vets still recommend vaccinating against this one.

Coronavirus

Coronavirus, an intestinal virus, can cause bloody vomit and severe diarrhea. Some vets don't automatically give this vaccine unless you plan to board your dog in a kennel (where viruses are often passed around) or unless the disease has recently occurred in your area.

Bordatella

The *bordatella* bacteria can contribute to a respiratory condition generally known as *kennel cough* (several viruses can also cause this general condition), which is a dry hacking cough and a runny nose. Although this condition isn't life-threatening, bordatella is contagious and dogs in or around other dogs in a boarding or daycare situation should be vaccinated against bordatella so they don't contract the disease, which is like passing around the common cold. Because Shih Tzu have flat faces, they can have breathing difficulties and bordatella can be very uncomfortable for them, so vaccinate against this one.

Lyme disease

Lyme disease is a serious, debilitating disease that dogs and humans can both catch from certain kinds of infected ticks. If you don't live in a tick-infested area known for Lyme disease risk or you never take your dog into areas that harbor ticks, you probably don't need to worry about this vaccination. Just ask your vet what he thinks; ticks aren't just in forests — they can even be in your backyard.

Are you overvaccinating?

Once upon a time, dog owners vaccinated their dogs every year, or at least, that's what vets told everyone to do. Today, however, many vets, breeders, and pet owners suspect that annual vaccinations are too frequent, and too much vaccinating can compromise the immune system and even cause dangerous reactions and diseases. This controversial issue has been the subject of much debate in recent years, so talk to your vet about how often your adult Shih Tzu needs a vaccination or a booster shot. Some vets recommend *titer tests,* which are tests that measure antibodies to various diseases. The results tell your vet exactly which vaccinations your dog does and doesn't need. These tests cost extra, but they can keep you from overvaccinating your Shih Tzu.

Don't skimp on puppy vaccinations, however, and follow your vet's recommendations. Most vets still agree that three or four sets of combination vaccines in the first year of life can prevent the most common dangerous diseases in puppies.

Adult or booster shots

When your puppy reaches the one-year mark, she's technically considered an adult dog (even if she still frolics like a puppy). For adult dogs, vaccinations are still important, but your Shih Tzu won't need them as often. Enter the booster shot!

A *booster shot* is another dose of the combination vaccine and any other relevant vaccinations that is given to your dog about once every one to two years starting at one year of age. At 18 months, your dog needs another rabies vaccination, and then again every two to three years after that, depending on the law in your area. Your vet may also recommend other vaccinations for your adult Shih Tzu, depending on the situation. So check with your vet.

Keeping an eye open for vaccine reactions

Most dogs handle vaccinations just fine, but some are particularly sensitive and can suffer from vaccine reactions, ranging from mild to severe. Think about how shots affect you —sometimes you don't feel so great for a day or two. Shih Tzu can feel sore or a little bit under the weather after a vaccination, too. The rabies shots are given deep in the hip area, and that can hurt!

Toy breeds like Shih Tzu are sometimes more likely to experience a low-grade fever, muscle aches, depressed appetite, and fatigue for one or two days following a vaccination. Sometimes, the dog will get irritation around the injection site, too. These side effects aren't usually anything to worry about, unless your dog refuses to eat anything for more than a day, seems unusually depressed, or has inflammation around the injection site. If you have any concerns about reactions, call your vet.

In more severe reactions, dogs can suffer breathing problems, severe allergic reactions, or even go into shock in response to a vaccination, with a drop in heart rate and blood pressure. The mouth and tongue may look white or gray and the dog could collapse. These situations are emergencies that require immediate veterinary care! If your dog has sudden breathing problems or stops moving or responding after a vaccination, don't wait to see what happens. Call your vet or emergency veterinary facility right away.

This info may sound startling, but in most cases, dogs have no reaction at all, and the risks to an unvaccinated puppy far outweigh the risks of vaccination. Even so, keep a close eye on your dog for a few days after any shot. If your Shih Tzu does have a reaction to the vaccination, you're more likely to notice and get your dog to the veterinarian right away, where she can be treated.

IDing Your Dog

One of the most important things you can do to keep your Shih Tzu safe and healthy is to keep identification tags on her at all times. Unlike some breeds that can run for miles if they happen to escape, chances are, your Shih Tzu will sit on the front stoop and whine to be let back in if she does get out. However, sometimes a Shih Tzu will find a reason to wander, even if it is just to dash across the street to greet your neighbor. If your Shih Tzu does end up beyond your yard's perimeter, proper ID can spell the difference between a fast and safe return and a permanently lost dog.

A proper ID can't save your Shih Tzu from cars, large dogs, or other dangers that exist beyond your home's safety, so take all precautions to ensure that your Shih Tzu *doesn't* end up wandering the neighborhood. However, mistakes happen and a proper ID can turn a potential disaster into a happy reunion.

Your ID options include the following:

- **Tags:** Your first line of defense in IDing your dog is a simple collar tag. Put an identification tag on your Shih Tzu the moment you bring him home, and never take it off. The tag should list your contact info: your phone number and/or address.

You can also add your dog's name and your name, but these items aren't as important because anyone who finds your dog won't need this information to contact you. Just make sure the tag gives the info needed to bring your Shih Tzu home.

- **Microchip:** A *microchip* is an identifying mechanism that's placed under the skin of your dog, usually in the back of the neck. The chips are about the size of a large grain of rice and hold your contact info. A vet or shelter can scan the chip with special equipment and get the dog's identifying information.

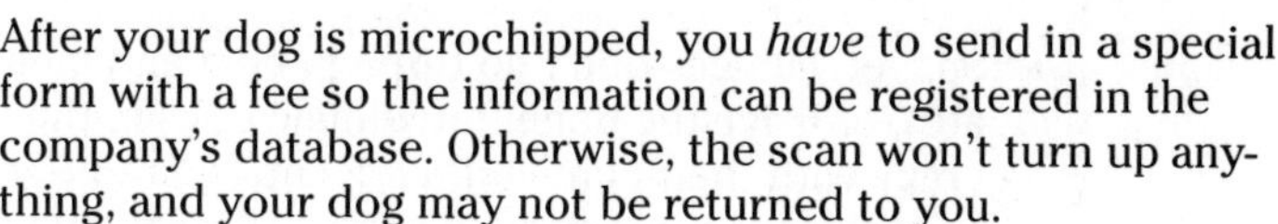

After your dog is microchipped, you *have* to send in a special form with a fee so the information can be registered in the company's database. Otherwise, the scan won't turn up anything, and your dog may not be returned to you.

Most shelter and rescue groups, and an increasing number of breeders and pet stores, require or strongly suggest that you have your pet microchipped with identifying information. Microchips can also serve as an important and life-saving backup if your dog ever does get out without his collar, or loses his collar on his adventure away from home. Even with a microchip, however, your dog should always wear her collar with ID tags. Someone who finds your dog may not think to take the dog in to have her scanned for a microchip.

- **Tattoo:** Some breeders advocate tattooing instead of, or in addition to, microchipping. The dog is typically tattooed with his purebred registration number or some other number, usually something chosen by the breeder. This same number should be on all your paperwork when you purchased the dog. If someone finds your dog and sees a tattoo, they may take the dog to a shelter or vet to see who can use that info to locate you. However, a lot of people wouldn't think to look for a tattoo, and these aren't easy to see on a Shih Tzu because of all that hair. A microchip is usually more reliable. Also, always keep that collar and ID tag on your dog, even if she has a tattoo.

Spaying or Neutering Your Shih Tzu: Yes or No?

Chances are your purchase contract states that you agree to spay (in the case of female dogs) or neuter (in the case of male dogs) your Shih Tzu. If you purchased a show dog, you won't spay or neuter your pet because show dogs can't be spayed/neutered. In most cases, however, your pet will be better off.

Even though the breeder may never know whether you got around to it, there are serious, compelling health reasons why you *should* spay or neuter your Shih Tzu.

- Your dog can't contribute to the serious problem of pet overpopulation, and your female won't have to endure the serious health risks of pregnancy and birthing.
- Your dog will be less likely to have behavior problems, may master housetraining more quickly, and will make a better, friendlier pet.
- Spayed females don't go through heat and bleed (menstruate), or drive the unneutered male dogs in the neighborhood crazy with their come-hither scent. Neutered males don't try to escape or wander off in search of a willing partner.
- Your dog will be far less likely to suffer from certain cancers of the reproductive organs, like mammary tumors (common in unsprayed females).

Most vets recommend having a pet spayed or neutered at about six months to one year, but some shelters and rescue groups require the spay or neuter surgery at an even younger age, which doesn't seem to have any negative effect on the dog. You may have heard that spayed or neutered dogs get fatter, but this isn't true. Spayed and neutered pets tend to be more affectionate but just as active and in most cases, healthier.

Finally, consider that the world is filled with unwanted pets. Do you really want to create more of them just because you can? Some breeders, pet stores, and rescue groups even provide you with discount vouchers to make spaying or neutering as easy and inexpensive as possible. Dog breeding really is something to leave to the experts.

Considering Holistic Health Options

One of the fastest-growing categories in the pet industry today is holistic health. You can find holistic products, from nutritional supplements and flower essences to pet massage DVDs and organic pet foods, in many pet stores, and more and more pet stores have devoted themselves solely to the holistic lifestyle. Holistic services abound, too, from canine chiropractic care to specialists in veterinary homeopathy, acupuncture, herbal medicine, or Chinese medicine, all for pets.

This section defines holistic health medicine and helps you locate a holistic vet if you're interested in exploring these options for your Shih Tzu.

What is holistic health?

Holistic health is a method of health maintenance and disease prevention that advocates balancing and nurturing all the elements of an animal's (or person's) life for optimal health. Keep the *whole* animal healthy — the heart of the holistic method. Practicing good holistic health is really about common sense eating a healthy natural diet, getting moderate exercise, reducing stress, interacting with others, and using natural substances for healing, when necessary.

Holistic health practices can also address pain, disease, and dysfunction, which the holistic method sees as a deep inner imbalance. Holistic healing methods don't just mask symptoms. They seek to tap the body's own healing potential by bringing all elements of the body, mind, and spirit into balance in ways conventional medical techniques can't necessarily measure but which holistic health practitioners believe is significant. This approach helps the body heal itself. Holistic health practitioners believe that symptoms signal an imbalance, and you must treat the underlying imbalance instead of simply covering up or superficially relieving the symptoms.

Holistic health healing therapies work for chronic issues like arthritis, dry skin, allergies, and even cancer. For acute health problems like emergency situations — broken bones, trauma, car accidents, severe rashes, animal attacks, and so on — conventional care can save your Shih Tzu's life. Many practitioners like to call holistic health methods *complementary medicine* because holistic and conventional care complete each other in many ways.

Holistic methods include such things as:

- **Nutritional therapy:** Improving the diet in targeted ways to address health problems, such as switching to a raw food diet (for more on raw diets, see Chapter 9).
- **Herbal remedies:** Supplements in pill, capsule, or liquid form include such natural plant substances as echinacea for building the immune system, glucosamine and chondroitin for arthritis and other joint problems, hawthorn berry to strengthen the heart, and milk thistle for liver problems.

- **Acupuncture:** This Chinese healing therapy involves inserting wire-thin needles into certain energy points to relieve pain and improve energy circulation. Many pet owners report dramatic improvement in pets that undergo acupuncture.
- **Pet massage:** Relaxing therapy for muscles and pain relief, pet massage increases circulation, reduces stress, and can help increase mobility in stiff, arthritic pets. Many massage therapists have added pets to their clientele.
- **Homeopathy:** These remedies, made from plants and other natural substances, are highly diluted but made with a special process that can boost healing for certain specific conditions. Homeopathic remedies are very safe but will be most effective under the guidance of a trained homeopathic veterinarian.

In general, holistic therapies are safe with few if any side effects, but ask your holistic vet about any therapies you want to try, first, for your pet's safety. Always tell your veterinarian if you're giving your dog any kind of holistic health treatment, even if you think he won't approve. Your vet must have this information so he can accurately prescribe treatments for any problems.

Locating a holistic health vet

If you choose a holistic lifestyle for yourself, you're probably interested in exploring some of these options for your pet. The best way to begin is to find a vet who's trained in holistic medicine. Ask your breeder and friends for referrals, or check out the American Holistic Veterinary Medical Association's Web site (`www.ahvma.org`) to find holistically oriented vets in your area.

As you look into holistic care, be aware that a lot of information you can find on holistic therapies is very helpful, and some of it isn't. If a so-called cure sounds too good to be true, it probably is. No pill in a bottle, even if it is made with natural ingredients, can cure cancer or banish chronic pain entirely.

Instead, look for holistic health practitioners with good reputations and training. Get recommendations and check references. Also take everything you read with a grain of salt. Holistic health practices bring the body into a state of optimal health, slowly and gently, so internal healing processes can work their best. With some professional guidance, you may just find the holistic way to be an incredibly satisfying path to vibrant health for your Shih Tzu (and even for yourself!).

When Your Shih Tzu Slows Down: Senior Care

Nobody likes growing old, but of course, everyone does. Small dogs typically have longer life spans than large dogs, but starting at about 8 to 10 years old, your Shih Tzu can safely be considered a senior. Many dogs may act just the same as they did when they were younger, but know that your Shih Tzu *is* experiencing the aging process. This aging process may include achier joints, drier skin and coat, and less efficient digestion. It can also include problems with the major organs — heart, kidney, liver, and pancreas.

However, aging doesn't necessarily mean your Shih Tzu will have to experience health problems, especially if you practice good preventive care. The most important things you can do to keep your senior Shih Tzu healthy long into her golden years are

- **Increase the annual visits to every six months, starting at age 8.** As dogs age, diseases like cancer, diabetes, cataracts, kidney and liver disease, and chronic conditions like dry skin and excess dental plaque become more likely. Many Shih Tzu contract mouth cancer, so your vet should pay particular attention to your dog's teeth, mouth, and gums (and so should you; don't forget to brush your dog's teeth! See Chapter 10 for more info.). More frequent check-ups provide your vet with the opportunity to catch and treat these diseases early.
- **Keep your Shih Tzu at a healthy weight.** Regularly feel your Shih Tzu's ribs; she should have a moderate tuck-in below her rib cage. Her body shouldn't be shaped like a sausage! Excess weight puts a strain on aging joints and internal organs. If your Shih Tzu slows down and starts to gain weight, adjust her diet accordingly. Being overweight will just make aging more difficult and uncomfortable.

  Ask your vet what your dog's weight should be, and then seek to keep it there with regular exercise and a sensible diet, which can include dog food made especially for seniors or overweight dogs. Aging is no excuse to let your dog become fat. (For more info on the right way to feed your Shih Tzu, see Chapter 9.)
- **Keep up the good grooming, and consider a short cut.** As your Shih Tzu ages, an easy-care coat may feel more comfortable for her, and aging dogs with arthritis or dry skin may not enjoy all the brushing, combing, and bathing the way they once did. But don't neglect grooming! Short nails, clean eyes, clean teeth, and a well-groomed coat can help aging dogs feel and look better. (Check Chapter 10 for more info.)

- **Keep exercising.** Exercise helps older Shih Tzu age more comfortably and can make arthritic dogs feel better. It increases circulation, reduces stiffness, and lessens pain, as well as helps to keep your dog at a healthy weight. (Refer to Chapter 8 for good ways to exercise your Shih Tzu.)
- **Consider supplements.** Talk to your vet before giving your Shih Tzu any supplements, especially if your dog is also on any other medications. This discussion ensures that drug interactions won't be a problem. If you get the go-ahead, here are some great supplements to consider:
  - Glucosamine and chondroitin supplements have been shown to decrease pain and increase mobility associated with arthritis.
  - Fatty acid supplements can help keep aging skin and coat supple and shiny, and may even minimize skin allergy symptoms. Look for formulas labeled for "healthy skin and coat."
  - Probiotics like acidophilus (found in plain, nonfat yogurt or in probiotic supplements) can help ease digestive woes.
- **Pay attention to changes in your Shih Tzu's behavior.** Sudden growling or snapping can indicate pain. So can a refusal to move. Changes in eating and drinking can be early signs of health problems. Dogs can even develop a cognitive dysfunction similar to Alzheimer's disease in humans. Signs include confusion and getting lost in a familiar room or stuck behind a chair or in a corner. Report any behavioral changes to your vet.
- **Be patient.** Senior dogs need a lot of love, care, and attention. Think about all your dog has done for you and return that kindness by making her golden years some of the very best. As your dog slows down, she'll focus even more on you.

Unfortunately, dogs don't live for nearly as long as humans, which means that most Shih Tzu owners will eventually have to deal with the loss of a beloved pet and family member. But with good preventive care, your senior Shih Tzu has the best chance at a long, healthy, happy life with you. She's lucky to have such a caring and conscientious friend.

Chapter 13

Handling Important Shih Tzu Health Issues

In This Chapter

- Banishing fleas, ticks, and worms
- Handling emergency situations
- Managing common Shih Tzu health issues

You don't want to think about your beloved little Shih Tzu ever getting hurt or sick. That's why you practice preventive care, good health habits, and regular grooming. Unfortunately, even with the best care, sometimes dogs get sick, injured, or infested with fleas.

A responsible pet owner not only pays attention to the signs of health problems but also knows what to do when they strike, and that's exactly where this chapter comes in. I share how to banish parasites, what to do in case of an emergency, and how to manage some of the common health problems your Shih Tzu can develop.

Of course, if you ever have any questions about your dog's health or worry about what to do to prevent or manage a problem, always consult your vet first. She's your number-one ally in keeping your dog healthy. This chapter is simply a guide to help you spot problems and deal with them in addition to your vet's direction.

The Attack of the Parasites (And How to Avoid Them)

Be afraid . . . be very afraid! Like tiny vampires, fleas, ticks, mites, and other parasites want to prey on your pet, sucking blood, transmitting diseases, even invading your pet's internal organs. Some of them can even infect you, too!

Parasites are a serious concern for any pet owner, and if you keep your Shih Tzu's coat long, they can be difficult to see and catch in the early stages of an infestation. Arm yourself with knowledge. A string of garlic won't keep these vampires away, but fortunately, other products and practices really work. This section can help.

External parasites

External parasites like fleas and ticks latch onto your dog or hitch a ride on his coat and feed off his blood. Not only can external parasites cause uncomfortable itching and skin allergies, but they also can transmit serious diseases like tapeworms and bubonic plague, and they can even hop off the dog and onto *you.* Eek!

The following sections look at the different external parasite risks for your Shih Tzu and discuss the best ways for you to protect him.

Fleas

Fleas lay eggs that can lie dormant in your carpet, your dog's bedding, and *your* bedding, long after you thought your flea infestation was resolved. Obviously, if you can avoid ever getting fleas, you should, right? But wait. Before you start dousing your little pet in chemicals, consider whether your dog is even at risk. You can hardly avoid fleas in warm climates, such as in the southeastern or southwestern United States. Fleas thrive all year round because the weather rarely gets cold enough to kill them. In these climates, you want to take preventive measures. In colder climates, however, such as in the upper Midwest, northeast, or northwest, you may not ever see a flea. Then again, if the neighbor dog has them, you may have a problem.

If you do wind up with a flea problem, follow these tips:

- **Vacuum the entire house thoroughly, especially carpets and furniture where the dog has been.** Throw away the bag immediately. Some people like to cut a flea collar into pieces and put that into the vacuum bag first. If you do, wash your hands *thoroughly* after touching it because of the pesticide residue. (I don't recommend ever using a flea collar on the dog or in the house because of the toxicity of the pesticide.)
- **Wash and dry all bedding in the house, especially your dog's bedding.** Do so every two to three days until the problem is under control to eliminate any eggs waiting to hatch.
- **Brush your pet daily and then work through her entire coat with a steel comb, manually eliminating any fleas.** If you see any, pluck them off and drop them into a small cup of alcohol to kill them before dumping them down the drain. Fleas have

tough shells and you usually can't kill them just by crushing. They can also hop away, so hang on.

- **Bathe her every week, too, until the problem is under control.** You can use a shampoo with natural botanicals that repels fleas, but avoid shampoos with harsh chemical pesticides, unless your vet recommends them. In most cases, simply bathing the coat thoroughly with lots of rinsing will drown the fleas and wash them down the drain, without having to resort to chemical intervention. (Check out Chapter 10 for more info on how to give your dog a bath.)

The best preventive flea products are the monthly spot-on flea control products. These medications really have revolutionized the pest control industry for dog and cat owners, making messy sprays and dips unnecessary. Visit your vet to get a prescription for these effective products, and always follow package directions. Following package directions, apply the medicine between your dog's shoulder blades once a month, and fleas (and ticks) don't have a chance.

You can also try over-the-counter spot-on remedies from the pet store, for less severe flea problems or as a preventive. Always read package directions and follow them exactly. If you don't want to use chemicals, a careful daily comb-through to manually eliminate fleas, and a good bath in a botanical flea-repellant dip containing products like citrus oils can keep mild cases of fleas at bay.

Ticks

Ticks can bite everyone in your family and transmit Lyme disease, Rocky Mountain Spotted Fever, and other nasty infections. They attach to the dog and suck blood. A tick can swell from the size of a small pea to the size of a large marble after a blood meal. Then, the tick drops off and digests, before starting the whole cycle again. However, unless your Shih Tzu is the outdoorsy type (most aren't), you probably don't have to worry about ticks. Unless your dog is exposed to ticks — maybe you walk her every day in a wooded area — you probably don't need to apply any tick protection.

Whenever she goes outside in a wooded area, into a park with trees, or even if she goes out into your yard if you live in a tick-infested region (ask your vet if this applies to you), check her all over with your hands, feeling for any bumps. If you feel something, take a close look. If you see a tick attached to her skin (or crawling around looking for a place to attach), remove it right away. Most tick-borne diseases won't be transmitted if you remove the tick right away. For example, a tick needs to be attached to your dog for at least five and up to 20 hours before it can transmit Lyme disease.

To remove a tick, follow these steps:

1. **Put on rubber gloves or use a paper towel.**

   Tick bacteria can infect you too, if the tick pops when removing it.

2. **Pull the tick straight out, in a direction perpendicular to your dog's skin.**

   Pull slowly and carefully so the tick doesn't break apart and leave mouth parts under the skin.

3. **Dab a little antibiotic ointment (the kind you put on yourself that you can buy in the pharmacy) on the spot.**

4. **Watch the spot for a few days.**

   If it starts to look infected, some parts of the tick may still be under the skin. Give your vet a call, so she can help cure the infection.

Mites

These tiny little spider-like parasites can cause *mange* (a red, scaly skin infection) and other serious skin problems and can also invade your dog's ears causing severe itching and discomfort. *Mites* are most common in puppies who haven't built up a strong immune system yet. Mites can also cause other skin diseases to develop, and they can even jump onto you!

The best way to prevent mites is to avoid contact with a mite-infested animal, but of course, you can't always know that another animal has mites, so look for the signs:

- Head shaking and ear scratching
- Odor from the ears
- Inflamed, swollen ears or an oozy rash
- Severe scratching and chewing
- Small red bumps on the skin
- Patchy hair loss (in severe cases)
- Big crusty sores (in severe cases)

See a vet who can treat mites with a thorough cleaning and medication. Treatment may involve weekly baths (for about a month) with a medicated rinse, an antiparasite drug, a topical ointment, or a combination. If the skin is infected, your dog may also need an antibiotic. Make sure to vacuum your house thoroughly and wash all dog bedding regularly to prevent a reinfestation.

Maggots

When a long-coated dog hasn't been groomed for a long time and spends time outside in that long dirty coat, flies can find him and lay their eggs in his coat. The result? *Maggots.*

If you ever had a good reason to keep your dog clean and well groomed, the very thought of maggots may just do the trick! Shih Tzu shouldn't spend too much time outside in the heat anyway because they're prone to heatstroke (see "The very real danger of heatstroke" later in the chapter for more info), but if your Shih Tzu just loves the outdoors, don't neglect that daily grooming session! Keep the coat clean and preferably short so you can watch for parasites of all kinds. If you do find a maggot in your Shih Tzu's coat — they look like tiny white worms — pluck it out, flush it, and take the hint. A good brush-out, comb-out, and bath are overdue.

Ringworm

Contrary to the name, *ringworm* isn't a worm but a fungus that forms a ring-shaped rash with hair loss over the infected area. Ringworm is easily passed from dog to dog or from dog to human. Young dogs, unhealthy dogs, and dogs that already have skin problems are most likely to pick up a ringworm infection.

The only way to prevent ringworm is to keep your Shih Tzu from other humans or animals with ringworm and to keep your Shih Tzu healthy by feeding him a healthy diet and giving him plenty of exercise. A healthy dog has a strong immune system and will be less vulnerable to the fungus. If your Shih Tzu develops ringworm, your vet can prescribe oral and/or topical medication.

Internal parasites

Some parasites aren't so easy to spot, and their effects can be dangerous because you don't know your pet is sick or infected until the infection becomes advanced. Internal parasites, such as worms and protozoa, can invade your Shih Tzu through a flea or mosquito bite, contact with infected animal waste or food, or the mother during pregnancy or nursing. Many pups are born with worms, and a vet typically deworms them during the initial exam.

Internal parasites can cause diarrhea, intestinal blockage, heart failure, or even death. For this reason, all pets should be protected against internal parasites, both through deworming at the vet and worm prevention medication.

Heartworms

One of the most dangerous and potentially fatal internal parasites is the *heartworm.* Mosquitoes transmit heartworm larvae by biting an infected dog and then biting an unaffected dog and passing along the tiny worms. The worms then grow inside the dog and, in their adult form, live in the pulmonary artery of the heart.

Although heartworm is hard to detect because usually dogs don't show any signs until the infection is advanced, fortunately preventing it is easy. Every year, your Shih Tzu should get a heartworm test from the vet and should be on monthly heartworm medication, during mosquito season or all year long (ask your vet which method is better for your dog and your climate). If your dog does develop heartworm, your vet can treat the disease with medication, and your dog must not exercise vigorously for about four weeks so the body can break down and eliminate the worms without too much cardiovascular activity to get in the way.

In warm climates, give the monthly medication year round. Heartworm pills are easy to administer and are tasty (like a treat). If you keep your dog on heartworm preventive, you don't need to worry about your Shih Tzu getting heartworm.

Hookworms

Hookworms are internal blood suckers often transmitted from mother to puppies during pregnancy or nursing, but infection can even occur through the skin. Older or sick dogs can also be prone to hookworm infection. Most pets acquire hookworms before they go home with their owners, but keep your home and yard clean to prevent hookworms in your own environment. Hygiene matters. Hookworms can cause anemia, gastrointestinal conditions like diarrhea and vomiting, loss of appetite, weakness, and weight loss.

Responsible breeders deworm puppies during nursing and keep puppy areas clean to prevent the presence of hookworms. If your vet determines that your Shih Tzu has hookworms (by doing a *fecal test,* testing the dog's poop), she'll prescribe a deworming medication.

Roundworms

Dogs catch *roundworms* by eating the eggs, which could be in soil or feces, while in the womb or by nursing from an infected dog, or by catching an infected animal and eating it. Good breeders typically deworm puppies to guard against roundworms (and other worms), but if your Shih Tzu has roundworms, you'll have to take care of it. Your vet can detect roundworms through a fecal test.

You don't want these critters or their eggs in your home or yard. Not only can the worms infect dogs, but also they can infect humans, especially people who are gardening or otherwise in contact with the soil (children are most frequently affected, although infections in humans are rare and more common in densely populated hot climates with poor sanitation). Symptoms include gastrointestinal distress, such as vomiting or vomiting including the actual worms, which can be startlingly large, and an inflated belly and even intestinal obstruction. If your vet determines your dog has roundworms, she'll prescribe a deworming medication.

Tapeworms

Tapeworms come from flea infestation. When your dogs has fleas and licks and bites at his skin, he may swallow an infected flea, which starts the tapeworm infection. These worms attach to the small intestine wall and can grow to eight inches long! Sometimes, parts of the tapeworm break off and dogs pass them. When this happens, sometimes you can see the squirmy pieces around your dog's anus. They look like little moving pieces of rice. (*Ewwww!*)

The best prevention of tapeworms is prevention of fleas (see the "Fleas" section earlier). If your dog acts sick, and you know fleas are present in your area or if your dog has had flea problems, it may be tapeworm. Symptoms of tapeworms include severe weight loss, anal irritation, vomiting, and weakness. If you suspect tapeworms, your vet can do a fecal exam and prescribe medication.

Whipworms

Whipworms live in the dog's small intestine. Dogs usually get these whip-shaped worms by drinking water or eating food that contains whipworm eggs, which live in the soil where animals can easily pick them up. Whipworm can cause intestinal inflammation, diarrhea, weight loss, hemorrhaging, and anemia.

As with many other worms, your vet can diagnose whipworms through a fecal exam, and your vet can prescribe a deworming medication. Prevent whipworms by having new puppies dewormed and keeping your dog in a clean environment.

Protozoal infections

Usually harmless, *protozoa* are one-celled organisms all over our environment. But a few types of this infection can cause serious gastrointestinal distress, which includes diarrhea, vomiting, and consequentially, dehydration, weight loss, and weakness.

Some common protozoa include giardia and coccidian. If your dog has unexplained gastrointestinal distress, see your vet, who can

How to take your Shih Tzu's temperature

Sometimes, your vet will want to know if your dog has a fever. Dogs have a higher body temperature than humans, with a normal temperature of about 100 to 102.5 rectally, but you can't just feel a dog's forehead to guess if he has a fever. Instead, you need to insert a thermometer into his rectum.

Believe me, the dog doesn't like it any more than you do, but that doesn't mean you can skip this often important task. To take your dog's temperature, follow these steps:

1. **Use a mercury or digital rectal or oral thermometer and reset it or shake it down.**
2. **Coat the thermometer with petroleum jelly to lubricate it.**
3. **Holding the dog still, lift up his tail and slowly and gently insert the thermometer about one inch into the rectum, just under the tail.**

   Be prepared to hold him steady.
4. **Hold the thermometer and the dog still for about two minutes for the mercury thermometer or until the digital thermometer beeps.**
5. **Remove the thermometer and read the results.**

   If your dog's temperature is below 100 degrees or over 104, call your veterinarian immediately.

test for protozoal infections and give you a prescription medication to kill the nasty little invaders.

Emergency, Emergency! What to Do ASAP

If emergency strikes — and sometimes, despite everyone's best intentions, it does — your Shih Tzu has the best chance of recovery if you act fast and appropriately. Of course, you need to know first what constitutes an emergency and where you need to take your Shih Tzu if you do face an emergency.

You can't dash off to the emergency veterinary clinic if you don't know where it is. Ask your vet what you should do if you ever have an emergency situation. Should you call or go to the office or is there an emergency or after-hours clinic you should know about? If the emergency vet clinic is in a separate location from your vet, pay them a visit once, so you're sure you know how to get there.

Someday you may be very glad you did. Everyone else in your household should know where the emergency clinic is, too.

To prepare yourself and your family for an emergency, post this and other important emergency information in a visible place, such as on the refrigerator or on the inside door of the medicine cabinet:

- The emergency veterinary clinic's name, phone number, address, and directions, just in case someone other than you needs to know
- Your regular vet's name, phone number, address, and office hours
- The number of the Animal Poison Control Center Hotline: **888-426-4435** (Have your credit card ready, too — a $55 consultation fee may apply.)

The next section gives you a better idea whether certain situations really are emergencies, so you know what to look for and how to respond *before* an actual emergency happens. This section also identifies some common Shih Tzu emergencies.

Recognizing emergencies

You may not always be sure whether you should call the vet or rush your dog straight to the emergency vet clinic. Knowing which action to take can save your dog's life!

In general, go immediately to the emergency vet clinic if your Shih Tzu experiences any of the following:

- Trauma, such as a fall, fight with an animal, getting shut in a door, or hit by a car
- Signs of a seizure (see the "Seizures and other neurological problems" section later in this chapter)
- Any evidence of a broken bone, head trauma, or a bleeding wound
- Severe gagging or getting something stuck in his throat
- Extreme vomiting or diarrhea that won't stop
- Any sudden, extreme behavioral change
- Refusal to move or a sudden yelp after jumping off furniture or coming downstairs and then reluctance to move
- Limp rear legs, dragging the rear legs, or any other sign of paralysis

- Abnormal discharge from the nose, eyes, or other body openings
- Non-responsiveness, lethargy, loss of consciousness, or collapse

Sometimes, you should call the vet but don't necessarily need to rush into the office. Give the vet a call if your Shih Tzu experiences any of the following:

- Occasional vomiting or diarrhea for more than one day
- Loss of appetite
- Noticeable increase in thirst and/or urination
- Poop that looks different than normal
- Restlessness or unusual hyperactivity
- Any sign of moderate pain, such as yelping when you touch her
- Signs of parasites like fleas or ticks
- Skin rash, hair loss, or itching

Giving pet CPR

If your Shih Tzu collapses and stops breathing, you have no time to lose. You can perform CPR on your Shih Tzu, preferably while someone else transports you both to the emergency vet clinic.

Ask your vet to show you how to perform CPR on a small dog during your next vet visit, *before* you ever need to do it (and I hope you never will!). If you haven't had any instruction and find yourself in a position where you need to perform pet CPR, here are the basic directions:

1. **Put your Shih Tzu on his side, being careful not to overextend his neck.**
2. **Check for foreign objects in his throat, swiping with a hooked finger to remove anything blocking his airway.**
3. **Gently pull your Shih Tzu's tongue forward so it's even with his teeth (to prevent the tongue from slipping back into his throat) and close the dog's mouth.**
4. **Exhale gently into the dog's nostrils, hard enough that you can see his chest expanding.**

   Doing so makes his chest inflate.

5. **Take your mouth off the dog and let him exhale naturally.**
6. **Repeat, giving one breath about every two seconds, checking for breathing after every four to five breaths.**

   If your dog starts breathing, stop breathing for him. If your dog's heart isn't beating (you can't hear a heartbeat when you put your ear to his chest), begin chest compressions as follows:

   1. **Place the dog on a firm flat surface on his right side.**
   2. **Cup your hands and put them on both sides of the rib cage at the level of the dog's elbows (above the heart.)**

      If the dog is a puppy or a very small dog (less than ten pounds), use your thumbs instead of your hands).
   3. **Squeeze on both sides of the chest and then release.**

      A squeeze and release should take about one second.

If your Shih Tzu isn't breathing and doesn't have a heartbeat, you can do artificial breathing and chest compressions at the same time. Give one breath for every three to five chest squeezes.

Identifying common Shih Tzu emergencies

When an emergency strikes, it can be pretty scary. If you aren't prepared, you may panic. This section gives you some preparation, so if an emergency does happen, you'll be ready. (I hope you never need to use this info, but if you do, you'll be glad you have it.)

Accidents and injuries: Watch where you step!

Some of the most common kinds of emergency situations involving small dogs are accidents and injuries. If you step on or drop a small puppy, he can break a bone! Because the Shih Tzu doesn't have very strong front legs, a common accident is a broken jaw — the dog jumps down off a high surface or someone drops him, and he lands on his chin. Small dogs can also be injured by being struck by a door, or by jumping off a piece of furniture that's too high.

To prevent accidents and injuries, remember these rules:

- **Never let small children carry around or play roughly with a Shih Tzu.** (Check out Chapter 7 for more info.)

- **Try not to let a Shih Tzu jump off high furniture, and never drop a Shih Tzu or let him jump from your arms.** Remember a Shih Tzu is a small dog and a long drop can hurt him.
- **Always watch where you step, especially when you step backwards.** Shih Tzu like to follow their people around and are often standing behind you.
- **Look before you shut the door, recline the recliner, or turn on the dryer.** Make sure your Shih Tzu isn't in the way!
- **Keep your Shih Tzu away from traffic.** A no-brainer.
- **Keep your Shih Tzu protected from dogs that might attack.** Keep him on a leash and away from strange dogs unless both dogs are on leash and under control by a responsible adult.

If your dog has an accident, like a fall off a bed or a scuffle with another dog, but seems fine, call the vet anyway. The vet may want to see your dog or may tell what to watch out for. If, after an accident, your Shih Tzu acts hurt, yelps in pain, limps, has a visible wound, stops eating and hangs his tongue out of his mouth (a sign of a painful jaw), or acts strange in any way — fearful, non-responsive, aggressive, or any other uncharacteristic behavior — go to the vet or emergency vet clinic immediately.

Poison

If your Shih Tzu gets into something poisonous, from deadly antifreeze to spoiled food to chocolate to household chemicals or human medications, you need to act fast. If you know or suspect what your Shih Tzu ingested, call your vet or the ASPCA Animal Poison Control Center hotline (888-426-4435).

Many other health problems can cause the same symptoms, but according to what the poison is, signs of poisoning can include collapse, diarrhea, distress, lethargy, seizure, and vomiting. If your dog vomits or has diarrhea, give your vet a call and keep an eye on your dog. If she experiences other marked behavioral changes, seems extremely anxious, or becomes non-responsive, has a seizure, or collapses, go immediately to the vet or emergency clinic. If you think you know what poison she has ingested, take it with you.

In some cases, the vet or poison control center may advise you to induce vomiting using ipecac syrup or hydrogen peroxide, both of which you should have in your first aid kit (see the list for what your first aid kit should contain, in the sidebar "Your Shih Tzu first aid kit"). In other cases, vomiting can make the problem worse, so *never* induce vomiting unless a qualified pro tells you to do so.

Your Shih Tzu first aid kit

In the case of an accident, injury, poisoning, or any other emergency, having a well-stocked first-aid kit can provide you with the supplies you need, right when you need them. Don't ever give your dog any medicine without a vet's or poison control center's advice first, and make a note of all dosages appropriate for your dogs to keep with all medicine in the first aid kit. Keep your first-aid kit in an easily accessible place, and if you use up any supplies in the kit, replace them right away. Your canine first aid kit should contain the following items:

- ❑ Antibiotic ointment — to prevent infection
- ❑ Bandage scissors
- ❑ Benadryl tablets — for allergic reactions and stings
- ❑ Blanket — to keep the dog warm or still
- ❑ Buffered aspirin — for fever and pain
- ❑ Copies of all vet records
- ❑ Cotton balls — to clean small wounds or apply medication
- ❑ Ear wash — to help clear debris from ears
- ❑ Elastic athletic bandage — the kind that sticks to itself so you don't have to tie or clip it
- ❑ Eye wash — to help clear debris from eyes
- ❑ Gauze bandages — to wrap wounds
- ❑ Gauze pads — to help stop bleeding
- ❑ Hydrocortisone crème — for rashes and allergic reactions
- ❑ Hydrogen peroxide — for sterilization and wound cleaning or to induce vomiting
- ❑ Ipecac syrup — to induce vomiting in case of poisoning
- ❑ Phone number for the Animal Poison Control Center hotline: **888-426-4435**
- ❑ Rubbing alcohol — for sterilization
- ❑ Small splint — to stabilize broken or injured limbs
- ❑ Stomach distress tablets
- ❑ Thermometer — digital or mercury
- ❑ Veterinary and emergency clinic contact information and driving directions
- ❑ Water-soluble lubricant — to insert thermometers

The very real danger of heatstroke

Shih Tzu can't stand the hot weather because

- **Their short noses and squished-in faces make them less efficient at self-cooling.** Dogs cool the air they breathe as it moves through their muzzles, but because the Shih Tzu's muzzle is so short and not particularly efficient, the air doesn't cool down very much before it enters the lungs.
- **Their long coats act as insulation.** A long coat can be great when Lola has to go outside in the winter, but this coat is entirely unsuited for hot humid weather. Puppies, overweight Shih Tzu, and dehydrated dogs are at even greater risk for heatstroke. (Many pet owners shave their Shih Tzu's body coat during the summer to keep them cooler — a comfortable and sensible option for pets.)

Signs of heatstroke include bright red gums, labored breathing and panting, weakness, nonresponsiveness, and collapse. You can take the following precautions to ensure that your Shih Tzu doesn't suffer from heatstroke:

- **Keep your Shih Tzu inside in a cool environment when the weather gets hot or humid.** Taking your Shih Tzu out for short bathroom breaks and brief play sessions are okay. Just make sure that you supervise your Shih Tzu at all times.
- **Always be sure your Shih Tzu has plenty of fresh water.** A dehydrated dog overheats much more quickly, and dogs get dehydrated more easily in the hot weather.
- **Never leave a Shih Tzu in a parked car!** Even if the temperature outside isn't all that hot, the car acts like a greenhouse when the sun shines on it, and the temperature inside the car can quickly skyrocket far above the temperature outside. When the day is warm and sunny, take your Shih Tzu with you in a carrier when you leave the car or leave her home.

If you suspect your Shih Tzu has heatstroke, take steps to cool your dog immediately — put him in front of a fan or in cool water. And then call the vet or emergency vet clinic. Take Samson's temperature rectally, and if it is more than 105 degrees, call the vet. (Check out the sidebar, "How to take your Shih Tzu's temperature" earlier in this chapter for more info.)

If your dog has collapsed, go to the vet immediately. If your dog's temperature is above 105 degrees, your vet will probably give intravenous fluids to hydrate your dog and may give other medication appropriate to any symptoms. The vet may also immerse your dog in cool water or even give oxygen therapy.

Choking, coughing, wheezing, and gagging

Short-faced breeds like Shih Tzu tend to snore and snuffle a lot, and those with the flattest faces tend to do it more. However, sometimes choking, coughing, wheezing, and gagging can be a sign of more serious conditions. These conditions include choking, heart disease, internal injury, kennel cough, respiratory obstruction or infection, an allergic reaction, or a side effect from some other serious disease.

If your Shih Tzu starts choking, drooling, gagging, and having trouble breathing, if he starts vomiting or acts very distressed and paws at his mouth, he probably does have something in his throat. Take these steps to help your dog.

1. **Immediately remove your Shih Tzu's collar.**
2. **If you can see the object in the throat, carefully hook your finger and swipe inside his mouth.**

   Be careful not to push anything that may be stuck in his throat.
3. **If Step 2 doesn't work, carefully hold your Shih Tzu by the hind legs, head down, to see if gravity can help dislodge the object.**

   If you can't get the object out, go to your vet or emergency vet clinic immediately. Choking is an emergency. Even if you do remove the object, call the vet and schedule an appointment to be sure your dog doesn't have any kind of throat injury.

If you don't see anything, chances are, your Shih Tzu is having an issue with his trachea, which is common in small dogs and can be aggravated by pulling on a collar. Collapsing trachea can be a serious condition in Toy breeds, so if your Shih Tzu gags and coughs a lot, have the vet check it out.

Shih Tzu also have a condition called reverse-sneezing, a strange but common thing many dogs do in which they start rapidly inhaling through the nose while standing still. The dog may make gasping or snorting sounds and his eyes may look like they're bulging. Reverse sneezing looks scary, but it's perfectly harmless and usually only lasts for a few seconds or up to a minute or two. You can easily stop a reverse sneeze by gently pressing your dog's nostrils together for a few seconds, until normal breathing resumes.

Finally, never ever leave your dog tied out on a leash unsupervised. The dog can choke and gag pulling on the leash and damage his trachea. Also, many dogs accidentally hang themselves over the edges of decks or porches or get tangled up and strangled, and if a wandering dog attacks, the dog can't get away.

Gastrointestinal distress: Did that just come out of my dog?

Many dogs suffer from short-term gastrointestinal distress if they eat something they aren't used to, but parasites or other health problems can also cause gastrointestinal problems like vomiting, diarrhea, constipation, bloating, and general tummy pain. Gastrointestinal problems can be signs of many different issues that any gastrointestinal distress lasting more than one day is worth asking you vet about. Give your vet a call and describe the symptoms. She can tell you whether you need to bring your dog in.

If you have a young puppy, vomiting and diarrhea is more urgent. Shih Tzu puppies are small and can quickly become dehydrated and malnourished, so call your vet right away if your young puppy has more than one or two episodes of vomiting or diarrhea.

Seizures and other neurological problems

Shaking, stiffness, collapsing, sudden unexplained aggression, a vacant stare, or failing to respond to your voice or touch can be signs of a seizure. Other neurological signs include confusion, stumbling, stiffness, bumping into things, seeming to get lost in a familiar place, and biting or growling for no reason. If you think your dog is exhibiting any symptoms, call the vet immediately. Your Shih Tzu may have epilepsy or another serious problem.

Understanding Common Shih Tzu Health Issues

Every dog has the potential to develop a serious health problem, and any dog can get any disease. With mixed breeds, you never know what you're getting, but with purebred dogs, you have a better idea which diseases — particularly, genetic diseases — your breed is prone to develop.

Like all other breeds, Shih Tzu have a few genetic vulnerabilities. The following section covers some of the more common genetic diseases Shih Tzu can sometimes get. You also find out what to watch for and what to do if your dog is diagnosed with one.

Dental problems

Shih Tzu, like most other Toy breeds, are prone to crooked teeth, missing teeth, tooth decay, gum disease, and early tooth loss. They don't have much space in their mouths, so sometimes teeth get overcrowded and crooked. Tooth pain and loss can result in the inability to eat, and gum disease can cause early death because dental bacteria can get into the bloodstream and into the heart.

Keep your Shih Tzu's teeth clean and have your vet check your dog's teeth at every vet visit. Many Shih Tzu need annual dental cleanings, which require a general anesthetic. The risk of the anesthesia is less, in most cases, than the risk of serious problems related to tooth decay and gum disease.

Allergies and other skin problems

Allergies may or may not be genetic. Many people suspect they're environmental. However, if your Shih Tzu develops skin problems, such as a rash, hives, or weepy itchy sores, then he may be allergic to a food, something in the air, flea bites, or even to poor grooming. Some dogs can develop an allergy to a household product, such as a carpet cleaner or deodorizers.

Good grooming and a good diet go a long way toward keeping your Shih Tzu's skin and coat strong and healthy. Good health equals a strong immune system, and that can help to keep allergies and many other health problems at bay. Poor grooming can also cause skin problems. A mat left untangled can trap bacteria and moisture, and a *hot spot* (a red, weepy, extremely painful wound) can form.

See your vet to diagnose any skin irritation or conditions. Your vet may advise changing your Shih Tzu's food and may prescribe steroids or other medications.

Breathing problems

Because Shih Tzu have flat faces and short noses, their nasal passages are squished compared to some other breeds. They have less space for cooling the air they breathe before it reaches the lungs and breathing passages that don't always work very well.

Many Shih Tzu are prone to snoring, snorting, and snuffling, not to mention wheezing, coughing, and overheating. To help your Shih Tzu breathe as well as he can, practice these general care tips:

- Always keep your Shih Tzu cool and well hydrated.
- Avoid hot humid weather and always give him fresh clean water.
- If your dog tends to wheeze and cough when he pulls on a leash, use a harness instead of a collar.
- If your dog wheezes or coughs when he gets over-excited, calm him down with soothing words.

- Recognize that snorting and snoring are all part of a Shih Tzu's charm, but if your Shih Tzu ever seems to be having a real problem breathing, call the vet immediately.

Eye problems

Many dogs suffer from genetic eye diseases, and the Shih Tzu is no exception. Your dog may suffer from any of the following:

- **Cherry eye:** If you notice a large swollen red lump on your dog's eye, don't be alarmed. He probably has *cherry eye,* a problem in which a tear gland comes loose and bulges out from under the eyelid. Call your vet, who can perform a simple corrective surgery to reposition the tear gland and secure it.
- **Dry eye:** Many Shih Tzu have insufficient tear production resulting in a problem called *dry eye,* or *keratoconjunctivitis sicca.* The result: Dry, painful eyes and irritated corneas, plus thick sticky eye discharge. Dry eyes are also more prone to infection and even ulceration, resulting in blindness. Fortunately, applying moisturizing eyedrops every day can keep your Shih Tzu's dry eyes more comfortable. Your vet can also prescribe medication for severe cases. In most cases, treatment for dry eye must continue throughout your Shih Tzu's life, but adding eyedrops to your dog's normal grooming regimen isn't too inconvenient (refer to Chapter 10 for more).
- **Progressive retinal atrophy (PRA):** PRA is of the most common eye diseases. This degenerative eye disease results in eventual blindness and usually affects older dogs. This condition is genetic; dogs with this condition shouldn't be bred.
- **Juvenile cataracts:** They occur in young dogs and also result in blindness. This condition is genetic and dogs with this disease should never be bred.

Responsible breeders have the eyes on their breeding dogs checked and certified as disease-free by a veterinary ophthalmologist. If your Shih Tzu develops PRA or juvenile cataracts, she'll probably eventually go blind, but talk to your vet. And, by the way, blind dogs can live happy and successful lives, so these diseases aren't a death sentence.

Other eye diseases that sometimes occur in Shih Tzu are related to the Shih Tzu's short face, which leaves less room for eye development. Some of these problems are

- **Logaphthalmos:** A structural problem in which the dog can't close his eyes all the way
- **Keratitus:** Inflamed cornea

- **Distichiasis:** Abnormally formed eyelashes that can scratch and scar the cornea
- **Ectopia cilia:** Eyelashes grow out of the wrong place causing pain and scarring

Joint (and back) problems

Some Shih Tzu develop joint (and back) problems, particularly as they get older and gain more weight. Three common problems in Shih Tzu include

- **Luxating patellas:** Also called *slipping kneecaps.* If your Shih Tzu suddenly yelps and then refuses to walk on one leg, hopping around or stretching it out, chances are good that his kneecap has slipped out of place. Many dogs have a mild case of this and figure how to pop their kneecaps back in by stretching, but if your dog has a severe case, a simple surgery can correct the problem. Your vet can determine how severe the luxation is by feeling the kneecap.
- **Hip dysplasia:** This is a degenerative condition in which the hip bone doesn't sit tightly in the socket. As the dog ages, the friction from this improper fit can cause arthritis and pain. In mild cases, vets typically prescribe pain medication. Many vets also recommend glucosamine and chondroitin supplements to keep joints functioning well and reduce pain. In severe cases, hip replacement surgery can correct the problem.
- **Spinal disk ruptures:** Many dogs with long backs are also prone to this problem. This isn't as common in Shih Tzu as in some other breeds like Dachshunds, but it can happen. If your dog suddenly yelps, especially after jumping down from a high spot, and then refuses to move, call the vet immediately. A disk rupture is an emergency, and without immediate treatment, the dog can become paralyzed.

Juvenile renal dysplasia

One of the better known genetic problems some Shih Tzu have is *juvenile renal dysplasia,* a serious kidney disease. Dogs with juvenile renal dysplasia are born with immature kidneys that fail to mature normally and result in reduced kidney function and eventual death from kidney failure.

Signs of juvenile renal dysplasia in puppies and young dogs include the following excessive thirst and urination — urine is often almost clear, rather than a normal yellow color (you may notice this if your dog is paper trained) — as well as slow growth, weight loss, fatigue, loss of appetite, vomiting, dehydration, and weakness. Some dogs show no symptoms and can pass on the disease. Fortunately, a genetic test is now available that can detect both of the two genetic mutations involved in juvenile renal dysplasia. These tests are 100 percent accurate and non-invasive. Breeders swab the dogs' cheeks and send in the cheek swab for analysis. Your breeder should have this test done on the parents of the litter, so they know the puppies won't have this disease.

If your Shih Tzu puppy starts drinking large amounts of water, ask your vet about the possibility of juvenile renal dysplasia. Treatment includes dietary changes and easing uncomfortable symptoms.

Liver disease

Shih Tzu sometimes develop liver disease in the form of chronic hepatitis. Symptoms can include energy loss, weight loss, jaundice, and even death. Some dogs show no symptoms. A vet can examine a Shih Tzu's liver via ultrasound and can advise you on treatment.

Another liver condition Shih Tzu can develop is called *canine portal caval shunt,* or liver shunt disease. This disease results in an inadequate processing of ammonia. Blood is diverted around the liver and doesn't get detoxified in the body. Symptoms can include weight loss, poor growth, fatigue, depression, diarrhea, vomiting, drooling, excessive thirst and urination, and behavioral changes. In severe cases, the dog can lapse into a coma or even show signs of dementia. If your Shih Tzu develops liver shunt disease, your vet may advise treating the disease with medicine and/or surgery.

Give a dog a pill

Some dogs gobble up pills if you sneak them into something really yummy like a small piece of meat or bit of peanut butter, but others aren't so easily fooled. If your Shih Tzu manages to spit out the pill every time, you'll need to give her that medication a little more efficiently. Here's how:

1. **Hold your Shih Tzu's head and gently slip your fingers inside the sides of her mouth, coaxing her mouth open.**
2. **Put the pill in your other hand, and place it as far back on her tongue as you can, pushing it down in.**

   Try not to make her gag.
3. **Close her mouth and hold it closed while rubbing her nose, which makes her swallow.**
4. **Afterwards, tell her she's a *very* good dog and give her a little treat.**

Chapter 14

Traveling (Or Not Traveling) Safely with Your Shih Tzu

In This Chapter

- Planning the best way to bring your Shih Tzu along
- Leaving your Shih Tzu with friends, family, or a pet sitter
- Finding your Shih Tzu a temporary home away from home when you travel

Everybody needs to get away now and then. But when you travel, whether you go away for a day or a month, you have to decide whether you can, or should, bring your Shih Tzu along with you. Shih Tzu usually travel well, and most of the time, Lola and Samson would rather be with you anyway. However, you can't always take a dog where you're going, and being the responsible dog owner that you are, you want to think of all your options.

This chapter tells you everything you need to know about traveling with your Shih Tzu, as well as leaving him home or at a doggy day-care or boarding kennel when you travel. You'll feel much better prepared to make the right decision when you have all the information, so you can feel comfortable knowing that Lola really is better off at home with that nice pet sitter, or Samson really is happier resting in his little box beneath your seat on the airplane.

Taking Your Shih Tzu with You

Traveling with dogs can be fun. They keep you company, they get to see new places and meet new people, and you have new experiences together. But traveling with your dog can be difficult. You have to remember to bring everything your dog needs, and you have to watch her to make sure she doesn't get lost, stolen, or injured.

Most Shih Tzu travel well because they're small and relatively adaptable, especially if they're well trained and socialized. But are you going to a place your Shih Tzu can go? Think about the following when deciding whether to take your Shih Tzu:

- **Are you staying at a pet-friendly hotel or with friends who don't mind a dog visitor?** Check with hotels first. Some have fees for pets and some don't allow them.
- **If you fly, does the airline allow pets?** Will the airline let you take your Shih Tzu in the cabin in the proper kind of enclosure? How much does flying with your Shih Tzu cost? Check with the airline before you make your reservation.
- **If you drive, can you stop every few hours for potty breaks and exercise?** Remember, most dogs have to pee every few hours, and puppies may need to have a potty break even more often. Furthermore, do you have a dog seatbelt or crate that can strap into the car with a seatbelt so your Shih Tzu is safe in an accident or even a sudden stop? (Check out Chapter 6 for more on finding the right dog seatbelt.)
- **When you arrive at your destination, will your schedule include activities that your Shih Tzu can do, too?** Is the place safe for dogs? Are dogs allowed? Or does she have to stay in the hotel room for many hours, while you're in a conference for 12 hours? If so, think again about bringing her.

If you decide that you really do want to travel with your Shih Tzu, and that doing so will be better and more fun for both of you, read on for more info about how to manage the trips.

Riding in cars with dogs

You and Samson are flying down the highway, wind in your hair, heads hanging out the window, tongues wagging . . . but wait one minute! Apply the brakes.

This picture of freedom may sound fantastic, but in reality, the dog shouldn't be loose in the car. He can easily jump on you and distract you from the road or get tossed around in a sudden stop, or even worse, Samson can get seriously injured or injure the driver or passengers in a car accident. Plus, if he sees something out the window, he may want to jump out the car. No matter how fun having your little dog wandering around or curling up on your lap while you drive sounds, it just isn't safe.

The bottom line: You want to keep your dog safe. But that doesn't mean he can't have fun while you ride down the highway. Some dog seatbelts allow freedom of movement so the dog can look out the window, if not hang his head out there in the wind. If you decide to

Across the pond

If you travel overseas with your dog, check before making your travel plans about what documentation you must have before leaving the country. Some countries require dogs to stay in quarantine for days or even weeks before entering, but others (like England) have recently reduced or eliminated this requirement if you have the right paperwork.

Your travel agent may be able to find out this info for you, or check `www.pettravel.com` for updated pet immigration and quarantine info for more than 100 countries. It can take up to six months to get all the appropriate paperwork for taking a dog into another country, so plan ahead!

put your dog in a crate instead of in a dog seatbelt, he'll be comfortable and in a familiar place. Just take him out every few hours so he can have a bathroom break and stretch his legs a bit.

No matter what happens, never leave your Shih Tzu alone in the car on a warm day — even when the temperature is just 70 degrees and the weather is sunny, a car can heat up to dangerous levels, putting your dog at serious risk of heatstroke. And don't just think cracking the windows or rolling them down will make a huge difference. The car can still get too hot, and a Shih Tzu alone in a car with the windows open is an invitation for dog thieves. Put on the leash and take your dog with you, even if you're just going to the bathroom.

Leaving on a jet plane

I don't normally recommend flying with dogs because too many things can happen when you and the dog get separated and the dog has to ride in the baggage compartment under the plane. Is it too hot down there? Too cold? What if he gets out? But some airlines let small dogs ride in carriers with you in the cabin, and this kind of travel is better. However, before you traipse off to the airport, check into a few things first.

Some airlines, such as Air Canada, specifically forbid pets in the cabin. Others don't put them in cargo. Some allow both. Airlines generally have very specific rules about traveling with pets, and these can change regularly, so be sure to check.

No matter what you see in print or on a Web site about an airline's rules and regulations regarding pets, always call the airline and find out for yourself, in case the rules have changed. Be sure to ask the following questions, and get everything confirmed in writing (bring this info with you to the airport to avoid any misunderstanding):

- Am I allowed to bring my dog in the cabin?
- What are the requirements for the crate or kennel my dog must be in while in the cabin?
- Can I take my dog out of the carrier during the flight?
- Do you have limits on how many pets can ride in a cabin on a single flight?
- Can you guarantee that my dog will have a spot on the flight?
- What's the extra charge for flying with a dog?

Finding pet-friendly lodging

More and more hotels allow dogs, especially small dogs. In fact, many hotels allow dogs and cats weighing less than 20 pounds, so your little Shih Tzu is just fine. Many hotels don't allow any pets, however, and those that do often charge for the privilege, so be prepared to pay extra. The hotel may also charge a damage deposit, which you can have back if your dog doesn't trash the room.

Businesses open and close often and policies change, so always call ahead to confirm information. To guide you in your choices, however, a few good Web sites can help you track down the hotels, motels, and even campgrounds and recreational areas that give a thumbs-up to dogs. Check out these sites:

- `www.dogfriendly.com`: This site includes dog city guides, beach guides, RV park and campground guides, hiking guides, off-leash dog park guides, outdoor dining guides, and state-specific search features for hotels. The site also has a ton of great travel info, links to dog-friendly apartments, and even dog camps as well as road trip prep, traveling etiquette, airline policies, and breed-specific laws. If you like to travel with your dog, you'll love this site.
- `www.petswelcome.com`: This site includes lodging listings by city, travel tips, and even bulletin boards so you can exchange info with other people who travel with their dogs.
- `www.travelpets.com`: This site focuses on pet-friendly lodging in the United States, Canada, and even internationally. You can also sign up for a free newsletter.
- `www.1clickpethotels.com`: This easy-to-navigate site gives you detailed information about pet-friendly lodgings in all the states and provinces in the United States and Canada.

- `www.pets-allowed-hotels.com`: You can search for pet-friendly hotels in the United States and Canada and make reservations.
- `www.petfriendlytravel.com`: This site lists pet-friendly lodging including vacation rentals, as well as dog-friendly beaches, attractions, events, off-leash dog parks, and restaurants with reviews. You can also find out airline policies for pet travel.

No matter what hotel you choose, you should also always keep your Shih Tzu on his leash in any new surroundings like hotel parking lots, parks, rest stops, and recreational areas.

Packing your Shih Tzu's suitcase

Traveling with a dog is much easier if you have everything you need with you. If you travel frequently, make copies of the following list. Before you leave on your trip, check off the important items that you need to bring:

- ❑ **Leash, collar or harness, and identification tags:** Never take off your Shih Tzu's identification tag while traveling. Despite your best efforts, your Shih Tzu can get lost and ID tags ensure that your dog can find his way back to you.
- ❑ **Enough food to last through the trip:** Bring some extra food just in case you run out. Make sure the food is sealed in an airtight container.
- ❑ **Familiar food and water bowls:** Some stressed-out dogs may not want to eat or drink from strange containers.
- ❑ **Water from home:** Water isn't the same everywhere you go. Different chemical makeup and bacteria can cause your dog to get an upset stomach, so bring some water your dog is used to drinking.
- ❑ **Motion sickness remedies:** Some dogs actually do get motion sickness when riding in cars or airplanes. Talk to your vet about medication or natural remedies that can alleviate motion sickness for dogs and what symptoms to look for.
- ❑ **Familiar blankets, pillows, and toys:** These items can make your Shih Tzu feel like he isn't too far from home. They also have familiar scents that your dog will recognize.
- ❑ **First-aid kit, just in case of an emergency:** If you have a kit for humans, it can work for your dog, too.
- ❑ **Copies of paperwork:** Take vaccination records, proof of rabies vaccine, license/registration paperwork, and any other paperwork you may need when crossing borders, boarding

your dog in a different city, or visiting locations where this info is required.

- ❑ **Drugs:** Take along prescriptions or any other medication and/or supplements your dog normally takes.

If you forget to pack something, you may be able to stop at a nearby pet store for some items. However, other items, such as your dog's ID and vaccine records, are vital, so don't leave home without them.

Leaving Your Shih Tzu at Home

If traveling with your pet sounds like a lot of trouble, well, frankly, sometimes it is. The hassle of traveling depends on the kind of trip you take. Sure, Lola *thinks* she wants to go with you, but you might consider making other arrangements for your Shih Tzu if your trip includes any of the following:

- Long periods where you can't be with your dog
- Visits to friends who don't like dogs or are allergic to dogs or don't have accommodations for dogs
- Business trips where you have a lot on your mind and won't be able to be tuned-in to your dog and her needs
- Visits to recreational areas with activities that exclude dogs
- Trips to places that can be dangerous for your dog, such as hot climates where your dog doesn't have air conditioning access

Aside from these considerations, what do *you* want out of your vacation? If you really just want to relax without any responsibilities, you may be better off without your dog. If you decide to leave your Shih Tzu at home, this section helps you make arrangements.

Finding the right dog sitter

Cats might be fine and dandy alone for a week with someone peeking in on them once a day to refill food and water and clean the litter box. Dogs, however, aren't quite the same. They need more attention and more companionship. They need exercise and interaction. And they need to know somebody is nearby and in-charge. That means a neighbor checking in once a day probably isn't sufficient for your dog, unless you're only gone for one day. Gone longer and you need to arrange for more extensive care for your dog, either at home or elsewhere. Fortunately, many individuals and businesses cater to pet owners who travel without their dogs. The following are some options.

The friends-and-family option

If your mom just adores little Samson or you have other friends or family with an already-established relationship with your dog, you may be able to convince them to either live in your house while you're gone or let your Shih Tzu live with them. This experience can be fun for everyone — your family member or friend gets to play Shih Tzu mommy or daddy and your dog gets to hang out with someone he already knows and trusts.

Picking a professional pet sitter

Hiring a professional pet sitter is another great option (especially if you don't have a reliable person in your life who can help out — see the previous section). Pet sitters care for pets when owners can't. They can stop in two or three times a day, and some even spend the night at your house. Prices vary depending on your dog.

Before choosing a professional pet sitter, ask around for recommendations to be sure you choose someone with experience, knowledge of pet safety and pet behavior, and preferably someone who has experience with and loves small dogs. If you haven't heard of anyone, ask your vet if she knows of anyone offering this service. Most cities and even small towns have at least one pet sitter. You can look up *pet sitting* in the phone book, or look at the National Association of Professional Pet Sitters' (NAPPS) Web site at `www.petsitters.org`. You can also call (800) 296-7387.

What your caregiver needs to know

Even though your Shih Tzu is in her own home, the caregiver — whether family member or professional pet sitter — needs to know some important things in your absence. Be sure your caregiver has access to and understands the following:

- Your vet's name, address, and phone number
- A folder with vaccination records and health records
- Info on any medications, including where they are and how to give them
- The location of the leash and collar or harness, with ID tags, for walks or if the caregiver needs to take the dog to the vet
- The location of food, treats, and food and water bowls
- Instructions for how to feed your Shih Tzu (what, how much, and how often) and how often to refill the water bowl and include instructions on treats (how many and how often)
- Instructions on what *not* to feed the dog

- The location of your Shih Tzu's dog bed or crate and instructions on when he should be there
- Instructions on walking the dog, how often the dog must go out and where, or instructions about how the dog is paper trained for inside and how to clean up
- The location of favorite, toys, blankets, and so on
- Instructions on grooming rituals along with brushes, combs, moisturizing eyedrops, or nail clippers (Leave this book out and opened to Chapter 10 for essential grooming info.)
- Your emergency contact info and, if available, a friend's name and phone number who knows your dog

Boarding Your Shih Tzu

Sometimes, the best place for your Shih Tzu while you have to be away isn't at home. If a family member or friend can't take your dog and you can't find a reputable pet sitter, you can have your Shih Tzu boarded, either at a boarding kennel or, even better, at one of the new and wonderful doggy daycare centers. The upside to away-from-home boarding is that your dog gets to have fun with other dogs and other well-trained people. The downside is that some boarding facilities may not offer your dog much attention, and your dog can catch kennel cough or fleas from other dogs.

Before you leave your Shih Tzu, check out any boarding facility thoroughly, and get recommendations. Have a look around for cleanliness and how things are run. You don't want to leave your baby just anywhere. Don't just always judge a place by the cost; if the good boarding facility costs a lot more, it's probably worth it. Some are incredibly posh and high-end, while others are no-frills. This section discusses the pros and cons to boarding your Shih Tzu in a reputable boarding kennel or a doggy daycare and what your Shih Tzu needs while he's away from home.

Finding a good boarding kennel

Boarding kennels can be wonderful or not so wonderful. A good boarding kennel is clean, comfortable, and run by knowledgeable and well-trained staff who take the dogs out often for walks, playtime, and attention. You should be able to bring your dog's regular food, water bowls, and bed or crate, plus comfort items.

Make sure you take the time to ask the kennel owner or manager the following questions:

- What does your insurance and liability cover?
- Do you require dogs to be vaccinated? Do you have other requirements? Can I be sure the other dogs in this facility won't have contagious diseases like kennel cough?
- What's the cost? Do extra services cost extra?
- What's the daily schedule like and how will Lola spend her days and nights?
- Who will care for Lola?
- Can my dog get groomed? If so, what kind and how often?
- Do the dogs spend time on fun training or walking sessions?

Some high-end boarding kennels offer outdoor play sessions in beautiful areas, luxury accommodations, and even spa services for dogs, from high-end grooming to pet massage and plenty of pampering. Of course, this kind of place isn't cheap, but for many pet owners the extra cost is well worth the extra care and pampering.

The doggy daycare option

Doggy daycare provides social time for dogs when their owners are gone. Some centers also provide boarding, grooming facilities, and even training classes. A few places even have Web cams, so you can see from your computer where your dog is. Many facilities can give your dog a chance to really blossom and meet new friends. Some businesses also have dog trainers on staff who can help you with your questions about your dog's behavior and who can work with dogs that may not be entirely comfortable around other dogs at first.

If your dog normally attends a daycare facility during the day, he may be able to stay on around-the-clock when you travel. Or, friends and family can take him at night but take him to daycare during the day. Many doggy daycare facilities are flexible, especially if they already know you and your dog.

To find a reputable doggy daycare, consider these options:

- **Ask your breeder or vet if he can recommend a good daycare.** Many breeders and vets know the local pet community and have heard who is good and reputable.
- **Ask friends and family members for referrals.** If your cousin's Maltese loves a particular daycare facility, your Shih Tzu may love it too, especially if she already has friends there.
- **Look in the phonebook under *pet services* or *dog daycare*.** Ask the daycare for references and check them.

- **Search online for pet care resources.** Just type *dog daycare* and your city and state in your favorite search engine. Many cities have multiple options. Get references and check them.
- **Consult with your local animal shelter or humane society for references.** These organizations may have a good idea about which places are the best, and which to avoid.

Before you decide on a facility, visit the facility. When evaluating a doggy daycare, keep the following in mind:

- **Make sure they require an interview with you and your dog.** During this interview share your dog's health info including his current vaccination history; you can also talk about your dog's personality. If the daycare facility doesn't care how healthy your dog is and how he behaves, they don't care how healthy or well-behaved the other dogs are either, which can put your dog at risk for catching a contagious disease or getting into a run-in with a dangerous dog.
- **Check to see that the facilities are clean and that the play areas are spacious.** Ask for a tour and see if the place looks like somewhere you want your Shih Tzu to spend her day.
- **Verify that the staff is knowledgeable and that the staff provides plenty of supervision so small dogs are safe.** Do the small dogs romp around with the Great Danes? Ask about how the dogs get along, and how the staff handles any issues.

Many good doggie daycares may have a waiting list, so plan ahead, and be prepared and have a backup plan.

You can ask the daycare owner or manager the following questions before deciding to leave Samson, whether overnight or just during the day. (The list of questions in the previous section is good, too.)

- What do you require before a dog can come here?
- Do the dogs have their own rooms? Do you have a special area for small dogs?
- How do you supervise dog play? What if the dogs get in a fight? Do you keep problem dogs in a different area?

Like upscale boarding kennels, many doggy daycare centers offer high-end pet services from fun training sessions to gourmet dog treat bakeries and spa services. Come to think of it, your Shih Tzu may end up having a more relaxing vacation than *you!*

Part IV
Training Your Shih Tzu

"Honey- either the dog is acting erratically, or he's riding the robot–vac again."

In this part . . .

The sweet Shih Tzu doesn't need much training, but you uncover the best methods for training your Shih Tzu in Chapter 15, along with some helpful hints to make you a better trainer so your Shih Tzu can understand what you tell him. Chapter 16 shows you how to housetrain your Shih Tzu so he really does understand where *his* bathroom is. Chapter 17 covers the basic cues like Sit, Stay, and Come, so you can teach your Shih Tzu what these important words mean and how to do what you want him to do (because he really does want to please you).

Chapter 15

Building a Partnership: Rules to Train By

In This Chapter

- Understanding dog language
- Using positive reinforcement for easy training
- Training yourself to train your Shih Tzu

A Shih Tzu breeder once told me that this breed didn't need any training. Although that sounds like a great reason to choose a Shih Tzu, I must disagree. Not only do all dogs need training, but also Shih Tzu have some particular tendencies that can be channeled to make your dog an even more well-behaved and easy pet than Shih Tzu naturally are.

Shih Tzu don't come pre-programmed with info about your house rules or preferences. Lola doesn't know you think the newspaper makes much more sense as a toilet than the new carpet. Samson doesn't know that you don't think his musical barking serenades get tiresome. Through training, dogs discover your preferences, rules for good manners, and much more.

This chapter helps you get inside your dog's head to understand what your dog really wants and needs, so you can communicate better. After all, communication is really what training is all about.

News Flash: Your Shih Tzu Is a Dog

Come here. Get close to the page; I have something to tell you. Lean a little bit closer. I have a secret. Your Shih Tzu is . . . a *dog!* I know, I know, it seems incredible. You thought he was a cute furry little baby. Take a minute to recover from the news.

Just because a Shih Tzu isn't a big slobbery tennis-ball chaser doesn't mean he won't act like a dog — all dogs have certain doggy traits. They all need housetraining. They can all growl, nip, and bite if they aren't trained not to do this or if they feel threatened. They all enjoy living with humans better if they understand who's in charge, what the rules are, and the meaning of a few basic cues like Come, Stay, Sit, and Drop it. (For info on teaching cues, see Chapter 17.)

For the most part, Shih Tzu like to do what you say. It's part of their companion-dog nature. All you have to do is make it clear what you want, and your Shih Tzu is likely to go for it. The trick, then, is to discover how to communicate what you want. After you master the fine art of communicating with a Shih Tzu, teaching basic house rules, good manners, and even tricks will be easy.

How to speak Shih Tzu

The most important point to remember when you're trying to speak Shih Tzu is that because the Shih Tzu is a companion animal, he reflects the behavior, stress level, and personality of the household. In other words, speaking Shih Tzu has a lot to do with tuning in to your own behavior. What is your dog reflecting? What is your dog trying to tell you? Are you stressed? If so, your Shih Tzu will be, too. Are you angry? Your Shih Tzu is probably feeling fearful. Are you calm and relaxed? So is your Shih Tzu.

Take a look at yourself, and then consider these strategies, for a better-behaved dog:

- **Chill out and calm down.** Shih Tzu pick up on your stress and bad mood, and Shih Tzu respond best when your emotions aren't all revved up.
- **Enjoy your dog.** Spend time every day appreciating your dog's best qualities. Let him make you laugh. Notice his beautiful coat. Appreciate how attentive and tuned-in he is to you. Your Shih Tzu will pick up this kind of attention. It makes him feel more secure and confident.
- **Share your life.** If you talk to your dog, take him with you when you leave the house (when possible), and let him be a part of the things you do every day, you'll both discover more about each other and understand each other better. Remember, your dog is a companion dog. Let him be your companion.

How to show (or not show) your dog what behavior is okay

Shih Tzu also need guidance from you. One of the best ways to train your dog is simply to give her feedback about what she does. Remember to:

- **Reward the behavior you like.** Shih Tzu understand rewards, and rewards motivate them.
- **Ignore the behavior you don't like.** Shih Tzu want your attention more than anything else, so ignoring bad behavior sends a powerful message to your dog that if he wants *you,* he'll have to do something differently.
- ***Don't* reward the behavior you don't like by yelling, picking up your dog, or even looking at your dog when she does something you don't like.** These actions reinforce the behavior because she's managed to score your attention.
- **Never yell at or hit your Shih Tzu.** Shih Tzu are sensitive dogs, and rough, loud, or physical behaviors can damage your relationship for good, not to mention injure the dog.
- **Remember that your Shih Tzu is a dog.** Dogs bark, chase things, run around, scratch, whine, and defend themselves with their teeth. You can't erase these instincts out of your Shih Tzu, but you can channel them appropriately . . . with training. (Check out Chapter 17 for specific training pointers.)
- **Don't underestimate the power of your own charisma.** Your Shih Tzu wants to be with you more than anything else. You're your dog's be-all and end-all — that's key to communicating with and training your Shih Tzu.

The Magic of Rewards: Keeping That Paycheck Coming

Positive reinforcement works like a charm with small dogs, as well as other breeds — and even with cats, rabbits, rats, dolphins, and children. And spouses! Really, who doesn't like rewards? But notice that this definition doesn't say anything about punishing naughty behavior. That's because punishment isn't a part of positive reinforcement training. In fact, this kind of training is completely opposed to punishment. The most punishment your dog gets with this method of training is to be ignored — no yelling, no hitting, just the withdrawal of your attention.

For example, say every time you come home, your Shih Tzu jumps up on you, snagging your pantyhose or yipping desperately for your attention. What do you do? You ignore her. In fact, you can even turn your back on her. This isn't what she wants! Because your Shih Tzu wants your attention and her jumping isn't working, she'll try something else. When she stops jumping and sits to figure out what may work, you turn around and kneel down. You pet her and praise her. Your smart little Shih Tzu quickly can figure out that sitting quietly gets your attention, but jumping doesn't.

The problem is that most people reward the behavior they don't like by giving the dog a *lot* of attention. Do you pick up your dog when she jumps to get her to stop? Do you coo and pet her to calm her down? If so, you're rewarding the bad behavior. Ignore her until she sits quietly and looks at you attentively. *Then* pour on the praise, the cooing, and the picking up. It sounds simple, doesn't it? You have to retrain yourself and pay attention to what you're doing in order to master this training method.

The positive reinforcement training method is particularly important for small dogs like Shih Tzu. Small breeds can be seriously injured or at least emotionally traumatized with more traditional training methods like choke chains and shock collars. Shih Tzu don't need these training tools. In fact, I argue most dogs don't *need* them, but Shih Tzu in particular don't benefit from punishment.

In this section, you find a breakdown of the basic concepts of positive reinforcement — how to use it by rewarding the good, ignoring the bad, and understanding why punishment doesn't work. Use these concepts when you start training the cues in Chapter 17, and you can see how easy training a Shih Tzu can be.

Rewarding good behavior

Rewarding good behavior sounds easy, but you can easily forget to do it because people tend to notice their dogs more when the dog's misbehaving.

To effectively reward good behavior, keep the following pointers in mind:

- **Pay attention.** Every time your dog does something good — sitting nicely instead of jumping up on someone's legs, being quiet, coming when called, and doing what you say — you have to remember to reward: "Good dog!" "Here's a treat!" "Here's your favorite toy." "You can sit on my lap now!"
- **Keep changing the reward.** If your Shih Tzu never knows what reward he'll get, he'll stay a lot more focused on you. If

he knows the reward is *always* a piece of dog cookie, he may sometimes decide that the fun of digging in your garden or jumping on a visitor is better than the reward of the dog cookie. But if he knows that sometimes it's a cookie, sometimes it's a game of fetch, sometimes it's a bit of chicken, sometimes it's some focused cuddle time, then you'll be much more interesting than anything naughty he might want to do.

- **Don't reward bad things.** Your dog can interpret you picking him up, petting him, or even yelling at him as rewards. You're *paying attention* to him. Try to never reward any behavior you don't like. (See the next section for more info.)
- **Never miss an opportunity for reinforcement.** Even if your Shih Tzu is just sitting quietly, praise her. When she does anything you ask, praise her. When she stops herself from doing something she shouldn't (like eyeing your shoe, then choosing her chew toy instead), praise her. You can't overdo constantly rewarding and reinforcing good behavior.
- **Mark good behavior with a particular word that you've taught your Shih Tzu.** Every time your dog does something good, use the same word, like "good!" or "yes!" before rewarding with praise or a treat. Your dog learns quickly that this word means something good's coming, and the word itself will become an easy-to-use reward.

Not rewarding bad behavior

Being a good dog trainer requires not only vigilant awareness of rewarding the positive, but a vigilant awareness of *not* accidentally rewarding the negative. Rewarding bad behavior without intending to is easy! For example, say you've been really busy all day, doing whatever it is you do, and you've ignored the dog. To amuse himself he may look out the window and start barking at things wandering into his line of sight. That yip-yip-yipping is driving you crazy, and finally, you explode and yell at him: "Bad dog! Stop barking! Shhhh!!!!!"

Guess what? You just gave your Shih Tzu the attention he's been craving all day. Sure, it wasn't a treat or praise or even necessarily pleasant attention, but to a dog, negative attention is better than no attention. Plus, your dog probably thinks you're just barking right along with him, so in a way, he may feel even more justified in making all that noise.

Your family also plays a significant role. For example, say your Shih Tzu always hangs out under the dining room table during dinner, looking for tidbits the kids drop. Did you know that your second grader is feeding your dog under the table the meat he doesn't want to eat? Did you know your boyfriend is a really sloppy eater and always drops food on the floor? Maybe that's why your Shih Tzu keeps pawing people's legs or jumping on laps or otherwise pestering you at the table.

How do you stop the madness? You have to stop rewarding the dog, and all those scraps of food have been serving as a pretty powerful reward. That means you have to remove the dog from the room during dinner, or tell him to Sit — not under the table but next to you where you can see him — and have him stay in the Sit until you're done eating. If he gets up, out of the room he goes.

Teaching yourself *and your family* not to reward bad behavior takes constant vigilance, especially until you get into better habits. Are the kids sticking their fingers in your puppy's mouth and shrieking when he bites them? Reward. Is your wife cooing and petting the dog when he growls at people who approach *his* human? Reward. Do the neighbor kids come to the fence and tease the dog until he barks? Reward. If you can just stop rewarding the bad behavior (ignore it, or remove the dog from the situation without a word), you have made a lot of progress communicating to your dog. Then you can focus all your energy on teaching your dog good behavior (see Chapter 17 for more info on teaching cues like Sit and Stay).

Dogs sometimes escalate bad behaviors at first, hoping that even more extreme behavior will finally win your loving glance, the sound of your voice, or a treat, but if that doesn't work, eventually your dog will give up that behavior and try something else. When he hits on the right thing (being quiet, sitting instead of jumping, waiting for you to finish eating, lying down when you ask, or whatever you are going for), bingo! Now you really *can* reward! That lesson will stick in your dog's head. You just have to teach it.

Why punishment doesn't work

Grasping the power of positive reinforcement can be difficult at first, especially if you grew up in the old ways of training: scolding, swatting with a newspaper, jerking on a chain, nose flicking, or rubbing the puppy's nose in a housetraining accident. If the dog is good, rewarding make sense. But what do you do when he's bad?

The main problem with punishment is that although it may teach your dog what you don't like, it doesn't tell your dog what you *do* like. Punishment scares a dog, especially a small dog. And unless it occurs within seconds of bad behavior, the dog isn't capable of linking the punishment to the behavior you don't like. If he peed on the carpet two hours ago and suddenly you start yelling, he doesn't know why you're yelling. He only knows that you're loud and scary.

And even if he does know you don't like him to pee on the carpet because you started yelling the second he started peeing, you have taught him what you don't like, but not what you do like. Your dog wants to know what to *do.* This makes more sense to an animal than the negative concept of what *not* to do, which is more complex. Positive reinforcement tells your dog exactly what you want, so he can repeat that behavior by choice. Positive reinforcement is active and makes sense to a dog. Dogs understand: *Do this. Doing so results in good things.*

Another problem with punishment is that it's more likely to make too strong an impression on the sensitive Shih Tzu. He may start to fear you and hide from you rather than love and trust you. Eventually, he may stop responding to you at all, and your loving relationship will be destroyed.

Figuring out how to stop punishing and start rewarding does take some time and a new mindset for many dog owners. Even so, I'm confident you can do it by discovering how to be a good dog trainer. (Check out the next section and Chapter 17 for helpful pointers.)

Who's Training Who?

Humans are easy to train. In fact, your Shih Tzu may have you trained to provide treats on command, supply a warm lap on cue, and shower him with affection. Some humans are so easy to control when it comes to a cute little dog! So you may just want to look at your own situation and ask yourself: Just who's training who?

Nothing's wrong with a little mutual training. You and your Shih Tzu both get rewarded by spending time together, cuddling, petting, and playing. Studies show that petting a dog actually lowers blood pressure and levels of stress hormones in humans, and if I had to guess, I'd wager that petting is probably healthy for dogs, too.

But at some point, if you want your Shih Tzu to do more than just sit on your lap looking cute, you need to be in control. You don't have to quit your job and take up dog training as a profession to be a good dog trainer. Being a good dog trainer isn't difficult, but it does require some practice — every single day. This section helps you remember the important concepts.

Being in charge

Dogs feel more secure with a benevolent leader, so if you can step up to the throne and wear the crown, your Shih Tzu will worship you accordingly.

How can you be in charge? Being in charge doesn't mean you have to be stern or strict or even a disciplinarian. But you do have to make the rules and stick to them, every single time. Your Shih Tzu wants to know the rules and what to do to make you happy enough to give her praise, treats, and loving attention.

If you don't want your Shih Tzu get on the antique sofa, *never let her get up there,* not even once. If you don't want your Shih Tzu to jump on people, never reward her for it. If you want her to use the newspaper for her bathroom, make sure she never has an accident anywhere else (for more on housetraining, see Chapter 16). Being in charge is all about consistency. If you sometimes bend the rules, your Shih Tzu will quickly figure out how to manipulate you so you bend them whenever she wants you to bend them.

Making training a daily habit

If you make training sessions a daily habit, as important as feeding your dog, taking him outside, and giving him water, you build an even stronger and closer bond between you and your dog. Plus, your communication will improve and you'll get to know each other better. And that's rewarding for both of you. Even if you don't have a lot of time to devote to training on some days, you can still find just five or ten minutes once or twice a day to work on different cues.

Another important part of daily training is grooming (for more on grooming, see Chapter 10). A well-trained Shih Tzu knows how to sit nicely for grooming, so when grooming becomes a non-negotiable part of the daily routine, it also becomes a part of training. Whatever your Shih Tzu is used to doing every day, she will learn to do well.

But even if you and your Shih Tzu just prefer to stay home and hang out, you can have great fun teaching simple cues like Sit, Down, Stay, and Come, not to mention cute tricks to show your friends and family. Shih Tzu love to spend time with you this way, especially if it's fun and (you guessed it) rewarding!

Chapter 16

Housetraining Your Shih Tzu: Oops, She Did It Again

In This Chapter

- Understanding housetraining basics
- Creating and sticking with a housetraining schedule
- Using the crate for housetraining success
- Paper training your Shih Tzu
- Housetraining the older Shih Tzu
- Cleaning up those mistakes

Is that a new spot on the carpet? Housetraining any Toy breed, including as a Shih Tzu, can be a real challenge and can try the patience of even the most consistent and fastidious pet owner. Are you destined to endure carpet stains and tiny piles forever?

Your Shih Tzu is a smart little dog, and he has no reason to think that he should *not* use your carpet as a bathroom, unless you tell him otherwise — and that doesn't mean yelling and carrying on whenever your Shih Tzu has an accident.

In this chapter, you discover how to teach your Shih Tzu when and where to relieve himself, how to quit sabotaging your dog's house-training success (yes, you aid in the mistakes!), and how to make housetraining truly rewarding for your Shih Tzu. (You can also check out *Housetraining For Dummies* by Susan McCullough [Wiley] for more extensive info.)

Housetraining from A to Z

A lot of people claim to have the secret to housetraining, but I have a secret for you: All the variations really come down to a few basic methods, and two of them work really well, especially when used together. The two are taking the dog out on a regular schedule, and using a comfy crate when you can't supervise and watch for those signs that your dog needs to pee or poop.

In this chapter, I explain all the tools that can help make housetraining a snap, from crates and leashes to puppy pads and plain old newspaper. I also tell you how to set up a housetraining routine and take your dog out on a schedule so he never, ever has to have an accident (he may have one sometimes anyway, because you forgot or weren't watching — but everyone makes mistakes!).

Whatever method you use, the most important thing to remember when housetraining a Shih Tzu is consistency! Set up a system, make potty time a routine, and your dog will quickly figure out what you expect. This section looks at the tools you can use to housetrain, gives you a pep talk so you don't get discouraged, and helps you notice warning signs that mean your dog is ready to go.

Using tools: Crates, leashes, puppy pads, and more

Housetraining is a lot easier if you use some very effective tools. Take advantage of the following items, and you can save a lot of time, effort, and mess:

- **Crate:** A crate keeps your pup supervised when you can't watch him for signs he has to go potty. For more on using the crate for housetraining, see the section later in this chapter called "The Amazing Crate."
- **Leash:** If you always keep your dog on a leash until he poops or pees, he'll figure out how what he needs to do so he can play. Using a leash takes more time initially, and it means you have to go to the potty spot with your dog (outside or inside, rain or shine), but in the long run, this extra effort pays off in a big way. Your dog will be housetrained more quickly and will understand what you want.
- **Pee pads and paper:** Dogs tend to pee where they peed before. They can smell it. If your dog goes on the paper just once, you can use a tiny scrap of that paper on the fresh paper to remind him of the right spot. Puppy pee pads also come pre-scented with a pee-like aroma to encourage your dog to go in that spot. Find them in the pet store.
- **Litter boxes:** Cats use 'em, but dogs can, too. Just don't use cat litter — use special litter made for dogs, which doesn't get as messy and doesn't stick to your Shih Tzu's coat. You can also line a litter box with newspaper (and/or puppy pads).

Check out the sidebar "Litter boxes aren't just for cats" later in this chapter.

Staying upbeat

Another important aspect of housetraining is to stay positive. If you find a mess, especially one he made more than a few minutes ago, don't yell or get mad at him. He won't know why, and in fact, he'll probably associate your anger and his fear with the presence of a housetraining mishap, but not with the action of peeing or pooping on the floor. He's more likely to think that next time he'd better just pee or poop where you won't see it.

Whenever Samson does the right thing, such as pees in the right place or asks to go out — praise him with happy appreciation. If he has an accident, whisk him outside without saying a word, and then praise him if he finishes in the right place. If you miss the accident and find it, clean it silently, without looking at him, without a word. He won't like being ignored, but he won't get the wrong message.

If you stay relaxed and positive throughout the housetraining process (challenging as this can be), Samson will see the new routine as just one more part of his fun and reassuring life. If you're upset whenever Samson has an accident, he'll get upset, too — but not because he thinks he somehow failed. He'll be upset because he's a companion dog and very tuned-in to your emotions. He worries about *you.* "What's wrong with her? Should I be afraid?"

Sure, you're frustrated when you find a mess, but be frustrated with yourself, not with Samson. He's doing the best he can with the info he has. Be patient and consistent, and you both can succeed.

Watching for warning signs

Dogs don't usually let their bladders fly all over your carpet; they give signs beforehand. You just need to know how to read them. So even when it isn't time for that scheduled pit stop (everyone needs to go to the bathroom out of their normal schedule once in awhile), you must keep an eye on your Shih Tzu, especially when she's a puppy. Doing so is especially important when you're first house-training your dog, no matter what her age. After you figure out her cues, you can pick up on them much more quickly.

Look for these signs that indicate she may need to go potty:

- **Sniffing and circling:** Many dogs sniff the ground and walk in small circles before they actually go.

- **Dancing around:** No, your Shih Tzu doesn't don a little skirt and start doing the cha-cha or hop from one foot to the other whimpering. Rather, dogs generally flit around and squirm and go to the door and then come back to see if you've noticed yet.
- **Whining:** If you had to go to the bathroom and you couldn't open the bathroom door and nobody was helping you, and no one was paying attention to let you go, you'd whine and whimper too. The whine may not be obvious, but if you hear some noises coming from your dog, check it out.
- **Staring:** Some dogs just stare at you. After you figure out the stare, you'll know in a flash that your dog needs to go out.
- **Standing by the door:** Many dogs stand at attention at the door when they need to go out. They don't make any noise, so if you haven't seen your dog in awhile, go check by the door.

If you see any of the preceding signs, immediately whisk your pup to the appropriate spot. When your dog starts to squat or lift a leg, the event is imminent! After she goes in the right spot, praise her.

Sticking to a Schedule

One of the most effective housetraining methods is schedule training. No matter where you train your Shih Tzu to go potty or what other methods you use, housetraining on a schedule makes everything easier. Typically, puppies need to go every three to four hours during the night and both puppies and older dogs need to potty at other predictable times during the day, so training on a schedule takes advantage of this biological reality.

The first thing to know is that most dogs need a bathroom break:

- When they first wake up
- After eating
- After a vigorous play or exercise session
- After a nap
- Right before bed

So, set up a schedule. If you aren't available for all these potty breaks, find someone else who can be (another family member, a pet sitter, a dog walker, or a friend).

As an example, your housetraining schedule may go something like this (I assume you're feeding your Shih Tzu three times per day, but if you feed your dog on a different schedule, just remember to take her out 15 to 30 minutes after a meal — for more on feeding schedules, see Chapter 9):

1. **Take Lola to her potty spot as soon as she wakes up in the morning.**

   Is Lola an early riser? If so, take her to her pee spot, and then go back to bed — she'll probably be glad to join you.

2. **Take her to her potty spot again about 15 minutes after she's eaten her first meal, snack, or treat of the day.**

   If she doesn't eat in the morning, take her about three hours after her first potty break.

3. **Go again midmorning, around the time when most people would have a coffee or bathroom break.**

4. **Take her to the spot about 15 minutes after any midday meal, snack, or treat.**

5. **Take her to potty in the mid-afternoon, after she's had a nap.**

6. **Head for a potty break 15 minutes after she's eaten dinner.**

7. **Take her after any particularly frisky play or training sessions.**

8. **Make one last trip to the potty spot just before bed.**

9. **If Lola is still a puppy, plan to wake up once or twice during the night when she wakes up and starts stirring and whining.**

In general, shoot for taking your dog to her potty spot about every three to four hours during the day (every one to two hours for puppies under 12 weeks and for the first couple of weeks of housetraining, just to get the concept firmly in place). Even more importantly than how often you take her is that you take her *at the same time every day.* This is the heart of schedule training, so make your schedule in whatever way works for you and your dog, and then stick to it like glue.

Hold on! Do you think I'm living in a dream world? You think I'm nuts right now, don't you? You're thinking there's no *way* you have that kind of time. Yes, taking your Shih Tzu outside or over to the newspapers every two hours and standing there waiting for him to decide to pee isn't convenient. You have a life! You're busy! Time is money! But this is the very reason why most Toy dogs take so long to get housetrained and why some of them *never* get fully house-trained. Those tiny bladders need to empty themselves often. Who has the time to supervise and direct each urination? Doing so is important, and you must make time for it, or enlist others to help.

Your level of consistency is up to you. As long as you realize that housetraining takes longer when *you* mess up, and that housetraining mistakes are usually *your* mistakes, you won't feel so compelled to yell at Lola because you forgot to take her out or didn't notice that she was circling and sniffing or staring mournfully at the back door (see the section "Watching for warning signs" earlier in this chapter). You're in charge, so be a good manager. The more consistent you are, the faster your dog will be housetrained, and you'll completely forget how much time it took.

The Amazing Crate

To housetrain your Shih Tzu quickly and effectively, you have to do two things: Make sure he goes to the bathroom in the right place, and make sure he doesn't go to the bathroom in the wrong place. Sounds simple, but unless you can watch your Shih Tzu every second of the day, how will you always prevent him from doing the right thing? By using a crate.

Even the most disciplined pet owners can't watch a dog every minute of every day, and despite your best efforts at maintaining a perfect routine, sometimes your Shih Tzu will relieve himself when you aren't looking or don't expect it, so most trainers recommend crate training, especially for Toy breeds.

The *crate* is a tool that helps with housetraining when coordinated with a regular schedule of meals and potty breaks. (Refer to the previous section for how to specifically housetrain your dog.) People sometimes get confused about what a crate is supposed to teach a dog. The answer: Nothing! The purpose of crate training isn't to teach your Shih Tzu anything. It just keeps him from having an accident until you're ready to take him to his potty spot again.

Here's how to use it:

1. **Whenever you can't play with or directly watch your Shih Tzu, put him in his crate for a rest.**

   Most dogs won't have an accident in the crate. See the sidebar, "All about natural instinct: Why crate training works," for the reasons why.

2. **Fill the crate with soft bedding and the occasional treat, to help make your dog feel comfortable and happy in there.**

   Remember that dogs like their dens and you want this to feel comfortable there.

All about natural instinct: Why crate training works

Crate training works because it takes advantage of a natural instinct dogs have: Den animals understand instinctually that it would be unsanitary, not to mention uncomfortable, to use their own beds as toilets, so den animals don't normally relieve themselves in their dens, unless they're sick or can't get out. In most cases, dogs will work hard to hold it until they can get away from the place they sleep.

If your dog has accidents in his crate, even when he hasn't been in there very long, and you never leave him in the crate for more than three or four hours at a time, see your vet to rule out a health problem such as a urinary tract infection. If your dog is healthy, talk to a trainer or behaviorist about other possible security or anxiety issues (for more info on finding a behaviorist, see Chapter 11). Never scold the dog for soiling his crate — if he does, it wasn't on purpose, and he has a more serious problem.

3. **Whenever you take your dog out of the crate, take him directly to his potty spot.**

   Most dogs need to go after a nap, and most dogs nap when in their crates. When your dog isn't in the crate, you *must stick to the schedule and watch him!* The crate only works as well as your efforts when the dog isn't in the crate. The crate can't help you remember to stick to the schedule or let the dog out when he has to go. You still have to do your part.

   And that's it! It doesn't take long for most dogs to figure out where their own personal bathrooms are located, and how to use them, as long as they don't keep making mistakes in the wrong places.

Crates can backfire into abuse. Don't just put your puppy in a crate and expect him to hold his bladder for six or eight hours at a time — his bladder is too small. He'll inevitably have an accident in the crate, feel miserable, and hate the crate. Then he won't want to go in there, and he'll be much harder to train. Plus, what kind of life is that for a little companion dog to be locked up in a crate for hours on end? Your Shih Tzu certainly doesn't want to spend his day that way. And after your puppy has made a mistake and soiled his crate, he's confined to the mess until you clean him and the crate.

Paper or Litter Box Training

If you decide that your Shih Tzu's potty spot should be indoors rather than out, you can paper or litter box train him pretty easily.

(Check out the nearby sidebar, "Litter boxes aren't just for cats" for more info.) Just follow all the same instructions in this chapter (training on a schedule, using the leash, using the crate), but when it's time to take your dog to her potty spot, take her to her newspaper or litter box, on the leash, and wait for her to do her business (see Figure 16-1). (Check out the "Sticking to a Schedule" section for specific housetraining steps.) When she does, praise her.

Figure 16-1: You can use newspaper to housetrain your puppy.

The following tips can help you with paper or litter training:

- **Use pre-scented puppy pee pads because dogs tend to pee where they smell pee.** (Check out the section, "Using tools: Crates, leashes, puppy pads, and more" earlier in this chapter for more about pads.)
- **If your dog has a favorite pee spot, move the paper to that spot.** If the spot isn't a good place, wait until your dog pees there reliably on the paper, then move the paper, one or two feet each day, to the place you want your dog to go. He should follow the potty spot.
- **Always clean up any pee and poop in the house immediately and thoroughly.** You don't want you dog to smell her previous accident and continue to use the wrong spot.
- **Never forget to praise your dog for going in the right spot, every time.** Good dog!

Paper or litter training is very convenient if you can't take your dog outside easily or conveniently, and if your dog is trained to use a certain area of the house for her potty, you don't have to worry about coming home to let her out on time (although you still need to come home to spend time with her!).

Litter boxes aren't just for cats

Some people have great success litter box training their Shih Tzu. Litter box training is especially useful if you live in high-rise apartments or condominiums and can't quickly get outside or if you're housebound. Litter boxes make clean-up easy, and although you can use a litter box made for a cat, some companies also make litter boxes for dogs.

However, you don't use the same litter as you would use for a cat. You can buy special dog litter that's designed to absorb odor and wetness (like kitty litter), or you can also just line the litter box with newspaper. If your Shih Tzu has a long coat, newspaper works better than litter because the litter can get caught in the hair. You may end up spending extra grooming time just combing out the litter!

If you can't find dog litter boxes or litter in your local pet store, you can purchase them online. Here are some good sources:

- **Puppy-Go-Potty:** `www.puppygopotty.com`
- **Wizdog Indoor Dog Potty:** `www.wizdog.com`
- **Pet-a-Potty:** `www.petapotty.com`
- **Doggy Solutions:** `www.doggysolutions.com/doglitterbox.htm`

Some people paper or litter box train their dogs easily without using a crate, but you can still use the crate (see the preceding section) if you're paper or litter box training your Shih Tzu, especially in the beginning when you're still teaching her where to go. Let her rest in the crate when you aren't watching her, and then take her out and straight to her paper or litter box, on a leash, for her to "go."

Dealing with Setbacks

Sometimes, a perfectly housetrained Shih Tzu suddenly begins having accidents in the house. You may catch little Samson taking a piddle right there in your living room for no apparent reason. But he was housetrained! What gives?

This section helps you deal with setbacks in a relaxed and calm manner. This section also helps you measure whether your dog is really trained, especially if he's gone a few days without a setback.

Why your dog had an accident

Everybody makes mistakes, but if your Shih Tzu seems to forget he's housetrained and starts having accidents in the house every day for more than a few days, see your vet first. Your dog may have a medical problem, such as a kidney infection or diabetes.

If your vet rules out a medical problem, consider these other reasons why your Shih Tzu's housetraining has seemingly disappeared:

- **Your Shih Tzu is stressed.** Changes in routine can stress your dog. The birth of a child, a divorce, a death in the family, a new home or job, and even the furniture rearranged can stress dogs, causing a housetraining setback (the same as with small children and potty training). Shih Tzu tend to take on the household's personality, so look at what's going on at home.
- **You're stressed.** Think about how things are going in the family. Are you particularly stressed out about work? Are certain family members depressed or arguing a lot? Shih Tzu tune in to people in their family. If someone is stressed, your Shih Tzu is probably stressing, too.

  The best way to address this problem is to spend quiet, together-time with your Shih Tzu, and also make sure you're keeping a regular schedule of meals and potty breaks. Remember, routines reassure dogs and help alleviate stress. Also, take measure to reduce *your* stress. (Routines and clearing your schedule can help you — so can petting a Shih Tzu!)
- **You weren't paying attention.** Did you miss the signs that your dog had to go, or were you too busy sitting at the computer that you forgot to let her out? Check for warning signs (refer to "Watch for warning signs" earlier in this chapter). You may have been really busy lately, and the problem is your neglect.
- **Your dog smelled the scent of an accident.** One accident can lead to more, especially if you don't see it and never clean it up. Always clean any housetraining errors thoroughly with an enzyme cleaner that removes the odor. When a dog smells a previous pee spot, she's more likely to pee there again.
- **Your dog has a behavior problem.** Sometimes dogs develop behavior problems like anxiety that need professional help. Housetraining problems related to behavior happen often in rescued dogs who may have endured abuse or neglect in the past. Consult an animal behaviorist for an evaluation if you can't resolve housetraining issues. For more on finding an animal behaviorist, see Chapter 11.

Whether the problem is physical or emotional, you obviously need to do something about it. No matter how old your Shih Tzu is, you can start back at square one, cheerfully and calmly, housetraining as if your Shih Tzu has never had these lessons before. (Check out "Housetraining from A to Z," earlier in this chapter.)

Catching your dog in the act

If you catch your dog in a piddle, how you respond can make all the difference. If you see your Shih Tzu doing her business, follow these steps:

1. **Clap your hands once or say, "No."**

   Don't shout. You just want to get the dog's attention. You don't want to scold or give a lecture; you just want to remind him of the proper spot.

2. **Pick him up and take him to the designated bathroom area.**

   When he goes, praise him.

3. **Make sure to thoroughly clean the mess up off the floor.**

   Old stains can lead to new accidents. Check out "Cleaning Up after Your Shih Tzu" later in this chapter for ways to clean properly.

When your dog forgets his housetraining, you feel frustrated, but don't take it out on your dog. He isn't peeing and pooping in the house to get back at you (even if it seems like that). Your Shih Tzu really is having a problem, and even if you don't know exactly what the problem is, your Shih Tzu needs your help, your gentle reminders, and your leadership — not your wrath.

Determining if your dog is trained

New pet owners commonly assume that their dogs are house-trained before they really are. If your puppy hasn't had any accidents in the house for two weeks, congratulate yourself! *You* haven't messed up. But that doesn't mean your puppy is housetrained.

Toy dogs can't be reliably housetrained before 16 to 20 weeks of age, and many of them take even longer (especially if the schedule and supervision aren't always consistent). Stick to the schedule, even after you think she understands. And don't forget to keep rewarding her for doing her business.

By the time your puppy is 6 months old, you'll probably be able to take her outside without the leash, or even let her outside by herself. If she's paper trained, she'll probably begin to go to the paper on her own when she needs to go. She'll be used to the routine now.

Housetraining an Older Dog

Adopting an older Shih Tzu comes with many joys, one of which is that older dogs are usually housetrained. However, sometimes a rescued Shih Tzu never really grasped housetraining because no one ever communicated the concept correctly. In other cases, a formerly housetrained Shih Tzu has endured so much stress from losing his home and family that his housetraining may have lapsed, or he may not be sure what the new rules are in this new situation with you.

The best way to housetrain an older Shih Tzu is to do exactly the same thing you would housetrain a puppy. (Check out "Sticking to a Schedule" earlier in this chapter for tips.) When you bring a Shih Tzu into a new home, start a new housetraining schedule right away. Your dog will more readily accept any new routines you set up.

Problems are more likely to arise when you bring home an older Shih Tzu and wait to start the routine, hoping to let her get settled. She wants to know what's what right off the bat, so don't delay. If your older Shih Tzu has trouble understanding, just proceed with housetraining as if she were a puppy. You *can* teach an old dog housetraining, but remember to be patient, consistent, and gentle.

Cleaning Up after Your Shih Tzu

Accidents happen. Sometimes, you forget to take the dog outside. Sometimes you just can't bear to get up in the morning when your Shih Tzu does. Or you got delayed coming home and Samson left you a little present on your rug. Lucky for you, your Shih Tzu is tiny and leaves tiny messes. Not to worry. This section explains how to remove the mess and odor and which cleaning products to use.

When your Shih Tzu has an accident, you must clean it thoroughly so no lingering odor remains, which would signal to your dog that this spot is okay for future bathroom use. To do so, you need a product that removes the scent completely. Many odor-removing products exist; some are more effective than others, so you may have to experiment to find one that works. Ask your local pet store employees for a recommendation, or look online. Just search *pet odor remover.*

For messes on hard surfaces like tile, wipe and spray with a deodorizing cleaner. For messes on wood, you can buy special products that penetrate the grain. For messes on carpet or fabric, get a product that penetrates down through all the layers. Look for a product that removes both the odor *and* the stain.

Chapter 17

Mastering the Cues: Sit, Stay, Come, and Others

In This Chapter

- Finding the training method that works for you and your dog
- Teaching the basic cues
- Training for tricks, competitions, titles, and therapy work

Imagine Lola standing wide-eyed in front of you. "Sit," you say. Lola blinks, innocently. "Sit," you repeat. Lola wags her tail, as if to ask whether you might not pick her up now. "Sit!" you say yet again, a hint of irritability creeping into your voice. Lola turns around and walks away. Clearly, she isn't going to get what she wants from you right now, so she may as well leave you and your strange, mysterious words.

You can't really expect your Shih Tzu to understand the meaning of cues like Sit and Down and Stay without some coaching. But your Shih Tzu is smart and she'll pick up the cue quickly, if you communicate the right info to her. This chapter shows you how.

Choosing Your Training Methods

You can train a dog in many different ways. Different dog training instructors teach different methods, and many of them work just fine. But some methods work better for teaching certain cues, while other methods work better for other things. The next few sections fill you in on some of the more popular training methods, how they work, and what they work best for. Consider this your Shih Tzu training methods smorgasbord.

Luring and rewarding

This classic and easy training method really is simple. Using a treat or a toy, you lure your dog into the position you want while saying "Sit" or "Down." When the dog is in place, you reward the dog.

Lure-and-reward training is the easiest way to teach cues like Sit and Down. Dogs follow a treat with their noses, so you just have to move the treat in a way that coaxes the dog into the right position, such as holding the treat in front of the dog's nose, then moving it slowly up and back so the dog follows the treat with his nose and automatically sits down. The word "Sit" and the reward seal the deal, and the position and the word into your dog's memory. (For a more detailed lesson on using lure-and-reward training to teach an actual cue, see the section "Sit," later in this chapter.)

Clicker training

Clicker training is a popular training technique first used by people who trained marine mammals like dolphins and killer whales. But clicker training works for dogs, too. Clicker training uses a small plastic device, called a *clicker,* to precisely mark a desirable behavior. The clicker has a button and when you press it, it makes a clicking sound.

Using a clicker

Incorporating a clicker into your dog's training isn't too difficult. In fact, follow these steps and click away.

1. **Load or charge the clicker by clicking it and then giving the dog a treat.**

   Do this step a few times, several times a day. Dogs catch on quickly and soon understand that a click means a treat.

2. **Carry the clicker with you and use it often.**

   Don't just reserve the clicker for training sessions. Make clicking a part of everyday life.

3. **Every time your dog does something good, click the clicker at the exact moment the dog is doing the behavior, and then give the dog a treat.**

   A clicker can mark a behavior faster than a word and definitely faster than the clumsy ritual of giving a treat. Sit-click! The click means the reward is coming, and your dog knows it.

To mark small behaviors as part of training for complex work, tricks, or sports, you have to be quick and observant, but if you do it right, you get immediate results. Click, and then give the dog a treat. This direct communication tells the dog that the particular behavior is something you like a lot — something that gets a reward. And the dog remembers.

Clicker training isn't for everyone. Not everybody enjoys it or feels the need for it. Some people like to rely on a well-placed verbal cue like "Good!" or "Yes!" Sometimes Shih Tzu seem to grasp good behavior with hardly any training because they're so good at knowing what you want. But if you want to teach more advanced behaviors for competitive obedience, agility, or other dog sports or for training a dog for the show ring, the clicker may just be the key.

Taking a clicker class

If you're interested in pursuing clicker training, the best way to understand the basics is to take a class with a clicker training instructor. The teacher can show you how to use this method to teach all kinds of cool and complex tricks and useful behaviors, such as turning a light switch on and off, ringing a bell to ask to go out, or even doing choreographed dance routines.

Many dog training instructors offer classes on clicker training, so you can get professional guidance. You can also read more about clicker training online, and you can purchase a clicker online, too. Here are my two favorite clicker training sites, from two of the best-known names in the clicker-training field:

- **Karen Pryor's Clicker Training (www.clickertraining.com):** A former marine mammal trainer, Karen Pryor made clicker training famous in the dog world, and she's always working to expand the field and give dog trainers new information.
- **Gary Wilkes' Click and Treat (www.clickandtreat.com):** Gary Wilkes gives training seminars and lectures all over the world. He takes a practical and sensible approach to clicker training and his site has info about dog care and behavior, in addition to articles about clicker training.

Catching the good stuff

One of the very easiest ways to train a Shih Tzu to do things you like is to catch her in the act of doing something useful, interesting, or good, and mark that behavior, either with the click of a clicker (for clicker info, see the preceding section) or with praise or some other reward like a treat or a toy.

For example, say your Shih Tzu has a really cute little yawn. Every time she yawns, say "Yawn!" or click the clicker, and then reward her with a treat or a "good dog!" Before long, Lola will figure out that you like the yawn. Then, she'll figure out that the word "Yawn" refers to that thing she does. Pretty soon, she'll do it for you, on cue. This takes some patience and a lot of repetition — she won't understand what you want the very first time — but with persistence, it works. (And don't be surprised if she comes up to you and starts yawning, just to get the reward!)

Shih Tzu do a lot of cute, comical things so if you can catch them with a reward and mark them with a cue, you may soon have a whole arsenal of cute behaviors and tricks that your Shih Tzu came up with all by herself. You can impress your friends with fun tricks.

Starting with the Basic Cues

Before you start aiming for agility titles or really complicated tricks, you need to get some basic moves under your belt. Most complex tricks and even dog sports are based on some elemental moves that every good dog, whether canine athlete or happy pet, should know. This section delves into these basics, using the training method that, in my opinion, is the most appropriate.

Most of these cues work best if you train with treats. If your Shih Tzu shows no interest in the treat, try the cue again later when he's hungry, or make the treat even better — a tiny bit of turkey, perhaps, or maybe a liver snap. However, many dogs are so eager for your praise that a warm "Good dog!" is just as good as a treat.

Also remember to keep treats very small so you aren't adding too many calories and too much fat to your little dog's diet. (Check out Chapter 9 for good snack ideas.)

Sit

Sit (see Figure 17-1) just may be the most useful cue to teach your Shih Tzu because you can use it to stop most bad behaviors. So fortunately, teaching the Sit cue is also one of the easiest cues to teach, especially if you use the lure-and-reward training method (check out "Luring and rewarding" earlier in this chapter). Just follow these steps:

1. **Put your Shih Tzu in front of you, standing, and touch a small treat to his nose.**

2. **Slowly raise the treat up and over his head.**

   As he follows the treat and his head goes up, his rear will go down.

3. **Say "Sit" as he sits.**

   If your Shih Tzu doesn't sit, you can gently guide his rear down with your other hand as you say "Sit."

4. **Praise him and give him the treat.**

   As soon as your dog sits, praise him with a "Good dog!" and give him the treat he's been following so closely.

5. **Repeat often — at least a few times each day.**

   Your Shih Tzu will pick this cue up quickly and frequent reminders make your little guy feel good about getting this easy trick right.

Sit can be incredibly useful. If Samson barks when the phone rings or if Lola jumps up on people when they come to visit, then teach the Sit cue. You can solve many problems with a simple Sit.

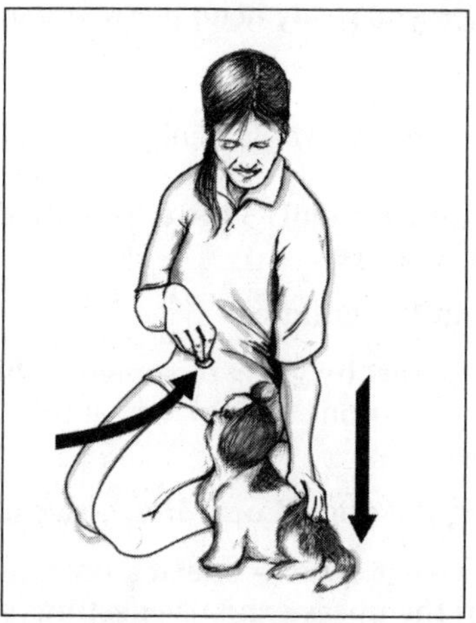

Figure 17-1: You can teach your dog to sit.

Come Here

If your Shih Tzu starts out an open front door toward a busy street, you can understand the power of the Come Here cue. A dog that comes back to you reliably when you call her (dog trainers call this *having good recall*) is a much safer dog. Recall also comes in handy in other situations like exiting the dog park when playtime is over or learning the moves required for competitive obedience.

Teaching this cue is simple. Just follow these steps:

1. **Whenever you notice your Shih Tzu coming toward you (which she'll want to do often because she likes to be with you), say "Come Here!" or "Come!"**

   Or, you can whistle or make some other noise that you want to represent the Come Here cue.

2. **When Lola gets to you, praise her.**

   Every so often, add a small treat to the praise.

3. **Repeat at least several times a day, or even more.**

   You can't overdo it. After practicing it for two or three days, start offering the cue when Lola *isn't* coming toward you. Call her to you, with or without her name: "Lola, come here!" or "Lola, Come!" or just "Come!" (Or, use the whistle or other cue you've devised.) If she comes, praise her and give her a treat. If she doesn't, do nothing.

4. **Practice the cue at least several times a day, every day.**

   The more you do it, the more chances she has to be successful. Then, when you really need her to come, you can be sure she will.

You can also teach Come with the whole family. Try this fun game:

1. **Have everyone in your family hide a treat behind his or her back, and sit in a circle.**

2. **Put the Shih Tzu in the middle.**

   Your Shih Tzu may start by going to someone, but don't make eye contact. Everyone should have a treat hidden behind their backs.

3. **Take turns calling the dog: "Come Here, Samson!"**

   Don't everybody yell at once — one at a time, please. The person can repeat the phrase and use gestures and an animated face when calling the dog. Anything to get the dog to come! When the dog comes to the person who called him, that person praises the dog and gives him the treat. If he comes to someone who didn't call him, that person must ignore him (no matter how hard that is).

4. **Keep going around the circle, only rewarding Samson when he comes to the person who called.**

   It only works if the people who aren't calling truly ignore the dog, and the person who is calling rewards the dog when he comes. Shih Tzu are smart — they'll soon figure out the score.

5. **After the dog masters the game, change your voice's inflection.**

This game teaches your dog to come to anyone, not just the person who feeds him. It also links the words "Come Here" to the reward of actually coming, no matter who says the cue and no matter what inflection they use.

Stay

If your Shih Tzu gets away and crosses a busy street, you'll be glad he knows the cue Stay, so he doesn't see you and come dashing back in front of traffic. Stay can also be an important safety cue in many other situations, such as when your dog wants to run up to greet a larger dog who may be aggressive, when you drop something on the floor that may be dangerous for your Shih Tzu to eat (such as medication), and when people come to visit.

Stay is harder for a Shih Tzu than Come Here or even Sit, because a Shih Tzu wants to be with you, and if Stay means staying somewhere apart from you, she isn't going to like it. But that doesn't mean she can't learn Stay, and she should.

Here's how to train your Shih Tzu Stay:

1. **Stand in front of your Shih Tzu and say "Sit."**

   I cover Sit earlier in this chapter.

2. **Take one step back and hold up your hand, palm facing your dog, and say, "Stay."**

   If your Shih Tzu gets up and comes to you, act like nothing happened, and don't reward him. Step back in front of him and ask him to sit again. Then step back with palm up and say, "Stay."

3. **Keep repeating Steps 1 and 2 until your Shih Tzu gives up and stops coming to you.**

   As soon as he stays put, step back to him right away and give him a treat. When first teaching this cue, reward him after just a few seconds. He'll learn how to stay longer, later on. You always come back to your Shih Tzu to reward him with the treat and praise, so he doesn't have to break his stay to come get the reward — otherwise, he may confuse the Stay and Come cues.

4. **After your Shih Tzu reliably stays when you take one step back, try taking *two* steps back as you say "Stay" and continue to keep your palm out.**

Your Shih Tzu will figure out that the word Stay and the hand signal mean he shouldn't move. If he stays put, step back to him and reward him.

5. **Keep adding more steps backwards, just one at a time.**

   Don't move farther away until your Shih Tzu reliably stays at each level. If you practice this in small steps and exercise a lot of patience, your Shih Tzu can figure out this trick easily. Keep practicing Stay, for a few minutes several times each day, until you can say "Stay" and walk all the way out of the room without your Shih Tzu following you to see where you went. If he's really mastered his lesson, he knows perfectly well that you'll be back soon to reward him for being such a good boy.

When training Stay, always reward your Shih Tzu by coming back to him to give him his treat. This part is crucial. Don't let your dog come to you when training this cue. That will be confusing for him. If you come back to *him* to reward him, you reinforce that Stay means Stay, not "Stay for a minute and then come as soon as I say 'Good dog.'" After all, "Good dog" doesn't mean "Come Here!" (although a lot of dogs seem to think it does!).

Down

Down is incredibly useful when you need your Shih Tzu to stop bothering people, stop jumping on people, or when you just need her to settle down a little and chill out. Down means *lie down.* Your dog sits, belly on the ground, elbows and paws on the ground, but with his head up to look at you. Or, he can rest his little chin on his paws. Dogs can hold Down longer than Sit because it's more comfortable and takes more effort to get back up. Sit is for short periods, but a well-trained dog can stay in a Down position throughout an entire family dinner, television program, or visit with friends.

The best way to teach Down is usually the lure-and-reward method. Here's how to do it:

1. **Stand or sit in front of your Shih Tzu holding a yummy treat.**
2. **Touch the treat to his nose.**
3. **Move the treat forward and down in a long diagonal line away from your dog, toward the floor.**

   Some dogs sink into a down position to follow the treat. If yours does, say "Down" and reward her with the treat. If your dog just creeps along after the treat, take the treat away (put it behind your back) and start over. This time, guide the treat down while gently guiding her rear end down, and then her front legs down. If she goes easily into the down position, say "Down" and reward her!

If your Shih Tzu resists going into Down, that's okay. Keep working on this cue, but also keep a sharp eye out. That active little puppy is bound to lie down eventually. As soon as she does, say "Down" and reward her profusely. Catching this behavior enough times makes her see exactly what you mean when you say "Down."

Down is harder for younger dogs than for older dogs because they have so much energy and they want to stay up. However, practicing this cue early comes in handy later because Down is the basis for many tricks and lessons you may want to teach your Shih Tzu. A Long Down or Down-Stay (teaching your Shih Tzu to hold the down position for an extended period of time) can also be great when you have company over or you're having dinner and you need your dog to calm down and behave herself.

Drop It

Shih Tzu got your shoe? Your sandwich? If so, you'll be glad he knows Drop It! The trick to teaching a Shih Tzu to drop something is to convince him that something else — a toy, a treat, or more attention — is better if he drops what's in his teeth.

The best way to teach Drop It isn't to wait until your Shih Tzu gets something he isn't supposed to have, but to teach Drop It ahead of time. Set up your Shih Tzu on purpose to practice this cue. Enough practice and he'll know exactly what the word means when he has something you really *need* him to drop.

To teach Drop It, follow these steps:

1. **Before you call your dog, collect three different items.**

   Pick one item that your Shih Tzu likes, one he loves, and one he *really* loves. These items may be toys or chew sticks or bones or whatever. Don't use food.

2. **Hold out the object toward the dog and try to get him to take it in his mouth.**

   If he doesn't take it, find something else he'll take (or try again later when he's in a more receptive mood).

3. **When your Shih Tzu has the item in his mouth, immediately show him the next best item.**

   Most dogs drop any item for an item they like better. Doing so makes dropping it easy and nonthreatening. Instead of thinking you're taking something from him, the dog understands that giving up the object means getting something better.

4. **When your Shih Tzu drops the item to get the better item, say "Drop It" exactly *as* he's dropping the item.**

5. **Immediately give him the better item and praise him.**

   If he doesn't drop the item, try taking it away (gently). If he relinquishes the item, say "Drop It" and then give him the treat and praise him.

6. **Trade up again, offering your Shih Tzu the very best item**.

   As he drops the item, say "Drop It," and then immediately give him the upgrade and praise him.

   Some dogs do these steps right away, but training is always easier if you know your Shih Tzu wants the item you have in your hand more than the item he has in his mouth — getting your Shih Tzu to trade up willingly. Practice these steps a few times each day, always saying "Drop It" *as* he drops the item.

As your Shih Tzu gets better, try using different items. After he gets the idea, you can give him a favorite toy and get him to drop it for a treat. Keep trying different ways to get your Shih Tzu to give up the goods, but always say "Drop It" the second he does, and reward him immediately with something better. After much practice (some dogs master this cue faster than others), you'll be ready when your Shih Tzu runs off with your new shoe.

Leash walking

Walking on a leash is the safest way to walk your dog outside. If a squirrel happens to dash in front of you, Lola may be tempted to run off to say hello; you'll be glad that you have her securely on a leash.

Traditional training taught leash walking with a choke collar, but this method simply doesn't work for Shih Tzu and can even injure their delicate necks, possibly contributing to health problems like collapsing trachea (a condition to which many Toy breeds are prone — for more on this condition, see Chapter 13).

So how do you get your eager little Shih Tzu to walk nicely beside you without pulling? Frankly, many Shih Tzu do this naturally. They don't need training to stay beside you because they already want to do this. But if you have a leash puller, you can quickly train him out of this bad habit the same way you train everything else: You must make walking nicely more rewarding than pulling. You do that by making pulling unappealing but not in a punishment sort of way. Follow these steps:

1. **Clip the leash to your dog's collar or harness for a walk.**

   You can even walk around the house or the backyard. The point is to practice walking correctly, not to get anywhere.

2. **When your Shih Tzu pulls, stop moving.**

   Don't look at her.

3. **Stop and look the other way.**

   When you stop, your Shih Tzu may sniff around for awhile, but eventually she'll want to keep going.

4. **As soon as she looks at you thinking, "What the heck are you doing just standing there?", say "Good girl!" and start walking again.**

   You want to reward her paying attention to you. The second she starts pulling, stop again. Only walk when she isn't pulling, and be sure to praise her for walking without pulling. This training method teaches Lola that focusing on you and sticking close by your side result in movement. She'll soon figure out what keeps the walk moving along.

A what? A walk? No way

Some Shih Tzu really don't care much about walking. If so, you may just let her get her exercise at home or in the backyard and forget the leash training. Every Shih Tzu should be accustomed to wearing a leash if necessary, but Toy dogs don't necessarily need to know how to hold a perfect *heel* (walking next to you on the leash without pulling) unless they're also involved in some kind of show dog or other competitive activity that requires this.

If you and your Shih Tzu love walks, figuring out how to leash walk can be a big priority. If you both couldn't really care less about walking, and your dog gets plenty of exercise romping around the living room, don't worry about it.

Don't get me wrong; these steps can be tedious. But you can do them. Mastering them will be worth the good behavior and pleasant walks the two of you enjoy.

Trying a Few Good Tricks

What's cuter than a Shih Tzu who can do tricks? At the moment, I can't think of a single thing. Because Shih Tzu are so sweetly attentive, some tricks are easy to teach them. Others, not so much. After all, your Shih Tzu is a small heavily coated toy dog, not a Labrador. Don't send him into the river after a big stick. But shake? Speak? Roll over? Now you're talking. This section shows you how you can teach your little Lola or sweet Samson to play these adorable games with you.

Shake

Some Shih Tzu use their paws a lot and these dogs are easy to teach how to shake. Every time your Shih Tzu lifts up a paw to touch you, capture this spontaneous behavior by saying "Shake" as you take his paw gently, and then reward him. Do this a few times every day and your Shih Tzu will soon lift up his paw on cue.

To teach Shake to dogs that don't naturally use their paws much, follow these steps:

1. **While petting your dog, gently touch his paw and then immediately remove your hand.**

   You're getting your Shih Tzu used to having you touch his paw.

2. **As you touch the paw, say a word like "good" or click the clicker, and then reward him.**
3. **Repeat until he doesn't seem to mind you touching his paw.**
4. **Touch his paw for longer and mark the touch with the click or word and then reward.**
5. **Practice picking up his paw, just for a moment.**

   As you do this, say "Shake" and then reward. Repeat this many times each day, and always let go of the paw right away. Some dogs start to volunteer their paws at this point to get the reward. If yours does, fantastic!

6. **Practice saying "Shake" and holding out your hand to get your Shih Tzu to lift up his paw on his own.**

Keep going back and forth between lifting up the paw and rewarding, and holding out your hand for your Shih Tzu to lift up his own paw. He should know by now what you want, and after that solidifies in his mind, if he really wants that tiny bit of dog cookie, he'll shake.

If you've been diligently trimming your Shih Tzu's nails or at least touching his feet every day as part of your daily grooming ritual (for more on this, see Chapter 10), Samson is probably perfectly happy to let you touch his paws from the beginning. However, some dogs just don't like it. For these little guys, Shake may simply be a trick you don't want to bother with. On the other hand, practicing Shake often and making it super rewarding, may just cure your dog's nail-trimming apprehension.

Speak and Shush

Some Shih Tzu don't bark much, and that's exactly the way their owners like it! So why would you want to teach your Shih Tzu to *start* barking or to bark *more?* Actually, the point of teaching Speak is to get your Shih Tzu to bark on cue. This trick can be a fun way to show off your Shih Tzu at parties, which some dogs love (and the party guests love it too).

The danger of this trick is that many dogs like to volunteer the Speak just because they know it gets them the treat. If your Shih Tzu is always volunteering a Speak, you may feel like you've created a monster. That's why it's also good to teach the Shush cue.

On the day you start training this trick, your goal is to capture every bark with a Speak cue and then reward, and also to capture every single post-bark moment with a Shush cue, and then reward.

Ideally, you should say "Speak" to barks aimed at *you.* Your Shih Tzu will be focused on you and more likely to understand the cue than if she is busy barking at the mail carrier.

After you've linked the words "Speak" and "Shush" with the right behaviors as often as possible for several days — "Speak!" "Shush!" "Speak!" "Shush!" — start requesting your Shih Tzu to Speak and Shush. Here's how:

1. **Hold a treat in front of your Shih Tzu so she can see it, and say "Speak!"**

   If your Shih Tzu rarely barks, you may be able to get her wound up enough with a toy or a good game of tag to get her to bark. If she does, immediately stop, say "Speak!" and then reward her.

2. **If she barks, give her the treat and praise her.**

   She did it! If she doesn't bark, don't give her the treat.

3. **If she barks a second time, in the hope of getting another treat, say "Shush!"**

4. **If she keeps barking, don't give her the treat.**

5. **If she stops barking and looks at you, wondering why she isn't getting the treat this time, give her the treat and praise her profusely.**

   She got it! But you have to practice these cues a lot so your dog can master the difference between Speak and Shush. For the fastest results, always say "Speak" when your dog barks, or "Shush" when you want her to stop, until you're sure she knows the cues. The more you practice this, the faster she'll master it. After she reliably speaks and shushes on cue, you can stop capturing her random barks. She's understood you.

It may take awhile for your Shih Tzu to understand what you mean when you say "Speak" and "Shush" because you can't say the cue *while* she's barking. She won't hear you because she's too busy barking. But she probably will notice that your response and the treat must have to do with something.

The more barks and post-bark silences you mark with a cue and reward the faster she'll understand. Just be patient and keep at it. If you start to feel frustrated, stop. This trick should *always* be fun or your Shih Tzu won't want to play, either.

Roll Over

Teaching Roll Over is easy for your Shih Tzu because he's already close to the ground. Teach Roll Over using the lure-and-reward method, like this:

1. **Put your Shih Tzu into a Down.**

   See instructions for how to teach Down earlier in this chapter.

2. **Hold the treat in front of his nose so he sees that you have it.**

3. **Move the treat just above his head, keeping it very close to his nose, and try to move it in a slow circle so he follows the treat and rolls over.**

   As he does it, say "Roll Over," and then reward him with the treat. If you can't get him to roll over, don't give him the treat. You want to be very clear that he hasn't quite done what you want yet.

4. **Keep luring him until he understands what you want him to do.**

   You can also help him roll over with your hands, if he doesn't mind. As soon as he gets it, reward him!

Some dogs are very resistant to this trick because a dog becomes very vulnerable when exposing his belly. Only a very secure dog exposes his belly, but if your dog does, then great! However, if your dog feels too vulnerable or insecure rolling over, that's fine, too. No point in forcing the issue. You can teach him other tricks. But if it's just a matter of not getting it, be patient. Work on this trick for just a few minutes, a few times each day.

You can also start teaching this trick when your dog already happens to be lying on his side or stretched out on his back. Lure him back around to his stomach with a treat as you say "Roll Over," then praise him and give him the treat. When Samson finally gets what you want and gets that reward, the moment will be sweet for both of you. Now, keep practicing so he knows exactly what you mean when you request it of him: "Roll Over, Samson. *Good* dog!"

Moving Up with the Truly Talented, Trainable Shih Tzu

If your Shih Tzu masters tricks easily and loves new tricks, you may want to consider training your Shih Tzu for more advanced activities, including competitive obedience, agility, or therapy work. If so, this section can give you some ins and outs in case you want to take your Shih Tzu to the next level in training.

Making a Canine Good Citizen

The Canine Good Citizen (CGC) program tests a dog's obedience skills and rewards those dogs who pass the test with a CGC title. This unofficial, but impressive, title shows that your dog has what it takes to be a model canine citizen, and some programs, such as dog therapy certification programs, use this test as a prerequisite.

The AKC trains testers to test dogs, usually through local obedience clubs. Your dog must prove she can perform ten specific behaviors in front of the tester. These tests include

- Accepting a friendly stranger talking to the pet owner
- Sitting politely for petting

- Being well groomed
- Walking on a leash without pulling
- Walking through a crowd without getting distracted or agitated
- Sitting and staying on cue
- Coming when called
- Reacting appropriately to another friendly dog
- Reacting appropriately to a distraction
- Waiting with a trusted person while the pet owner walks out of sight for a few minutes

If you want your Shih Tzu to earn a CGC and you think she can pass this test or you can train her to pass this test, check with your local dog club to see if they have testers. Some local dog clubs and trainers even have training classes specifically to help dogs pass this test. To find a local club and other CGC-related information, including a more detailed description of the ten tests and where your dog can get tested, check the AKC's Web page dedicated to the Canine Good Citizen program at `www.akc.org/events/cgc`.

Performing competitive obedience

Competitive obedience tests your dog's ability to perform a set of exercises like retrieving a dumbbell, jumping over a hurdle, and staying in place when you walk away. Judges score these exercises. In each exercise, your dog must score more than 50 percent of the possible points and get a total score of at least 170 out of a possible 200. Find out about the AKC's qualifications and rules of competitive obedience at `www.akc.org/events/obedience/index.cfm`. If your dog is registered with the United Kennel Club (UKC), you can get more info at `www.ukcdogs.com/Obedience.htm`.

Taking things less seriously: Rally

For less serious competitors, the new Rally program takes a more informal, fun approach to competition. *Rally* is a sport where the dog and handler complete a designed course, proceeding at their own pace through 10 to 20 stations. At each station a sign is posted with instructions regarding the next skill to be performed. Scoring isn't as rigorous as traditional obedience.

Many pet owners particularly enjoy Rally when they aren't so concerned with putting highfalutin titles on their dogs. Find out about the qualifications and rules of Rally for AKC-registered Shih Tzu at www.akc.org/events/rally/index.cfm. (The UKC doesn't hold Rally competitions.)

Considering agility: That Shih Tzu sure can jump!

Agility is a rip-roaring and rollicking good time. Dogs love to do it, and people love to watch it. In agility, a dog demonstrates athletic ability by following cues through a timed obstacle course. For Shih Tzu who seem particularly coordinated and agile, you may consider this fun obstacle course race, which has dogs literally jumping through hoops as well as barreling through tunnels, sailing over see-saws, and navigating weave poles (see Figure 17-2).

Figure 17-2: Your Shih Tzu may enjoy agility competition.

Don't worry about all those record-breaking Border Collies, either (the breed famous for dominating this sport). Shih Tzu only compete against other dogs of similar height. For more info on agility, check out AKC agility at www.akc.org/events/agility/index.cfm. UKC has a registered agility course as well: www.ukcdogs.com/Agility.htm.

Conformation shows

If you purchased a show dog, or even if you didn't but you think your gorgeous guy or girl would wow 'em in the ring, you can get involved in conformation showing. *Conformation showing* is a sport that judges how a dog is built to encourage bettering the breeds. Dogs parade around a ring with their handlers, and a judge examines them for good structure, coat, head shape, and other physical qualities, as described in the official breed standard (see Chapter 2). Traditionally, conformation shows reward good breeding stock, so dogs can't be spayed or neutered to compete.

AKC show dogs must be registered with the AKC to compete in conformation, and UKC shows require dogs be UKC-registered. For more info on conformation showings, check out these sources:

- www.akc.org/events/conformation/index.cfm
- www.akc.org/events/conformation/beginners.cfm
- www.ukcdogs.com/conformation.htm

If your pup isn't registered with these organizations (or is spayed or neutered), you can still participate in fun matches, pet beauty contests, and other less formal conformation shows. Local training clubs often train dogs for the show ring, too, so you'll know exactly what to expect. They also tend to hold the occasional fun match, so if you want to find out how to participate in these events, give your local club a call. (To find a local club, look in the phone book under *dog training* or *dog club,* or look for a local or regional AKC club at www.akc.org/clubs/search/index.cfm.)

Training a certified therapy dog

Smaller breeds often make excellent therapy dogs. Therapy dogs go, with their owners, to nursing homes, children's hospitals, or other places where people may feel better petting a sweet, soft dog. And they do make people feel better! Therapy dogs are incredibly popular and if you get involved in this fun hobby, you'll likely hear some pretty amazing stories about the impact therapy dogs make.

The best therapy dogs are quiet, gentle, and intuitive. That also describes most well-bred and well-trained Shih Tzu. If you think your Shih Tzu may be the perfect dog to brighten someone else's life, check out these links to the two most well-known and reputable therapy dog certification organizations:

- Therapy Dogs International, Inc.: www.tdi-dog.org
- Delta Society Pet Partners Program: www.deltasociety.org

You can get your dog officially certified through these programs, which allows you to visit establishments with a pet therapy dog program. Or, you may be able to start a program in conjunction with a local hospital or nursing home.

Part V
The Part of Tens

"It's definitely Shizis Gigantis – prehistoric predecessor to the Shih Tzu. You can tell by the bony topknot."

In this part . . .

The ancient Shih Tzu comes with many fascinating stories about his origin and the things he used to do in Tibetan temples and Chinese palaces. Get the top ten Shih Tzu myths and legends in Chapter 18. If you think you have a serious show dog prospect or if you just want more info on dog shows and how to get started, turn to Chapter 19 for ten tips on showing your Shih Tzu.

Chapter 18

Ten Shih Tzu Legends: Believe Them or Not!

In This Chapter

- Exploring Shih Tzu spirituality
- Bowing down to the Shih Tzu's royal past
- Understanding the Shih Tzu, historically speaking

Everybody loves a good story, and in this age of reality TV, does anyone really know (or care) whether the fantastic stories you hear, see, or experience are absolutely accurate? When it comes to Shih Tzu history, much of what breed historians know or think they know or suspect can't be proven. But that doesn't stop people from formulating theories, interpreting historical documents, and just plain guessing about the fascinating history and, yes, mythology behind your favorite little long-coated dogs.

Add to the confusion the fact that the histories of several breeds today — Shih Tzu, Lhasa Apso, Pekingese, Pugs — are intertwined, and much of the mythology crosses over. Were those temple watchdogs Shih Tzu or Lhasa Apso? Were those tiny sleeve dogs Shih Tzu or Pekingese? But just because there's no proof that the Buddha had a Shih Tzu as a pet — a Shih Tzu that could *shapeshift* (a change from human form to animal form and vice versa) into a lion at will, no less — doesn't mean you can't enjoy the story. With these cautions in mind, this chapter contains ten myths about Shih Tzu or their ancestors. Believe them . . . or not!

Buddha's Pet

Even the spiritually enlightened can benefit from the ultimate companion dog. Legend says that the Buddha himself had a Shih Tzu with him all the time, and the little dog could magically transform into a lion, which the Buddha rode.

As a lion, the dog protected and shielded his master from harm. As a dog, he was most useful as a foot warmer and meditation companion. (Some versions of this story claim that the Buddha in question wasn't *the* original Buddha but another Buddhist god.) Chinese and Tibetan breeders emphasized breeding for traits that would liken the Shih Tzu to the Buddha. There were 32 superior marks of the Buddha that these breeders sought. Some of these included

- A little shining circle of silver between the eyebrows
- A topknot and a white blaze, or white marking down the forehead and between the eyes
- A long large tongue and the square jaws of a lion
- A coat with a touch of pale yellow, because yellow was the color of royalty
- The marking of a saddle — particularly prized because of the association of the Buddha riding on the Shih Tzu's back

Because China Doesn't Have Lions

The lion is one of Buddhism's sacred symbols, but lions aren't native to China, so legend has it that the Chinese bred and groomed their little lion dogs to resemble that kingly beast, lending a particularly noble and commanding air to the tiny Shih Tzu.

Some folks also say that the famous Chinese lion sculptures standing imposingly outside palace doors (and Chinese restaurants) look more like dogs than like lions because the artists had only the dogs themselves and paintings from royal dog books as models, because each succeeding ruler had his favorite dogs painted. From these dubious sources, the artists guessed what lions looked like.

Prayer Wheel Duty

Shih Tzu probably evolved when the Chinese bred the Tibetan Spaniels or Lhasa Apsos with the Chinese Pekingese. The Tibetan Spaniel's head more closely resembles the Shih Tzu than the more flat and narrow skull shape of the Lhasa, but historical records say Lhasas were also crossed in at some point. Either way, the Shih Tzu's origins must certainly be in Tibet, where small dogs guarded the Buddhist temples and turned the prayer wheels in the monastery's daily ritual to release prayers to the heavens.

Watch Dog for the Guard Dogs

Shih Tzu, or their ancestors, did more than provide cuddly companionship for the Tibetan monks. The small Asian dogs of Tibet were probably larger than today's Shih Tzu and tough enough to withstand the harsh conditions in the mountains of Tibet.

These little dogs also served an important function. Large, ferocious dogs (possibly related to the Tibetan Mastiff) guarded the temples, but the Shih Tzu, with its keen and alert senses, noticed intruders first and barked to alert the guard dogs to attack. They were like the trip wire that sets off an alarm. Even today, Shih Tzu have very acute hearing.

Shih Tzu Means Chrysanthemum Dog

Shih Tzu means *little lion* in Mandarin Chinese, but the Shih Tzu is also sometimes called the "Chrysanthemum Dog" because the Shih Tzu's sweet little face looks like the chrysanthemum flower, with hair sprouting in all directions like flower petals. Lady Brownrigg, who brought the first Shih Tzu into England, coined the phrase *Chrysanthemum Dog.*

The Wet Nurses Did What?

Shih Tzu were so prized and honored in China that human servants were employed to nurse the puppies on human milk to elevate their status to the human level. Talk about treating your dog like a baby.

Sleeve Dogs: A Fashion Statement

Shih Tzu and their ancestors have come in many sizes, as fashions changed during different periods of history. Sometimes, the very smallest Shih Tzu were all the rage, particularly in the mid-19th century, and Chinese ladies kept these tiny furballs in the huge sleeves of their kimonos. This practice spurred the term *sleeve dogs* to refer to the tiniest Shih Tzu, Pekingese, and Pugs (although most of the sleeve dogs were probably Pekingese). When the Dowager Empress Tzu Hsi reigned in China, after 1900, she put a stop to the artificial dwarfing of her favorite little dogs and bred them to a more normal and healthier size.

For Royalty Only

Back as far as the 17th century, legend tells that the Chinese emperor deemed his small dogs much smarter than any humans and bestowed royal ranking on all the dogs in his court. The dogs wore the hats befitting of their station, and the female dogs wore the ladies' hats appropriate for a wife of a ranking official.

The Dowager Empress Tzu Hsi of China did more than anyone else to advance and refine the Shih Tzu breed in particular. The Empress so prized her little Shih Tzu that only royalty were allowed to own Shih Tzu. In fact, selling a Shih Tzu to a commoner resulted in a death sentence for the offender, and some say the Empress would have the most beloved Shih Tzu killed instead of letting it suffer the horrible fate of being owned by a commoner.

Bred by Palace Eunuchs

During the reign of the Dowager Empress Tzu Hsi, her most trusted servants were the palace eunuchs. Some were loyal and some were traitorous, but these eunuchs were in charge of the breeding programs for the Empress's favorite little dogs. They competed to produce the best and most beautifully marked Shih Tzu. Some people say that the eunuchs secretly sold the less promising puppies to commoners for a great price, even though this practice was strictly forbidden and punishable by death. Historians also believe that much of the damage to the royal palace after the death of the Old Empress was done by the eunuchs to cover up their stealing and selling of her dogs.

Obliterated by Communists

Throughout history, China has been invaded many times, but when the Communists took over the government, owning pets was strongly discouraged and many Chinese breeds almost died out completely. Luckily, Shih Tzu had been stolen, smuggled, or otherwise secretly transported from China to Europe and the United States, where the Shih Tzu was able to thrive.

The first Shih Tzu to reach the western world was brought into England by Miss Hutchins in 1930. The dog was owned by Miss Hutchins and Lady Brownrigg. However, only one import reaching the West was a dog actually bred in the Imperial palace — a single black Shih Tzu, one of three dogs Madame Henrik Kauffman, wife of the Danish Ambassador to China, brought to Europe in 1932. Mme. Kauffman registered all three of these dogs with the Norwegian Kennel Club in 1934.

Chapter 19

Ten Tips for Showing Your Shih Tzu

In This Chapter

- Sizing up your Shih Tzu's show potential
- Checking out the show scene in person
- Training and grooming for the big time
- Figuring out dog show lingo

You know that your Shih Tzu has that extra-special something and he deserves a shelf full of silver cups and blue ribbons. You may be right. Showing your Shih Tzu can be fun and extremely rewarding, but it can also be highly competitive and incredibly frustrating, depending on how much potential your dog really has, how much you dedicate to the pursuit, and how serious you really are about putting titles on your little Lola or Samson.

I could write an entire book, just on showing your Shih Tzu. Although I've tried to focus this book on your pet Shih Tzu and not your show dog, some of you may still want to show. So even if you're a teeny bit interested in showing your Shih Tzu, this chapter gives you tips on showing and can whet your appetite — or convince you that you don't really want to show after all.

But if you do have a show prospect, books aren't the best way to understand the art of showing your dog. Go check out the real thing, in person, to get a clue about this strange and wonderful world. To find dog shows near you, check out this chapter.

Know the Breed Standards

At its very heart, the dog show is about rewarding the dog that most closely fits the written *breed standard,* which describes the ideal specimen of an individual breed that breeders should aim for in their breeding programs.

Show dogs can't be spayed or neutered (except for less formal pet dog shows, which can also be fun). If Shih Tzu are judged to be great potential breeders, then the point is to breed them. But you don't have to want to breed your dog to show your dog. You can do it just for fun. Even so, if your Shih Tzu doesn't match the standard very closely, you probably won't get very far. (Check out Chapter 2 for a complete discussion on breed standard.)

Read the standard carefully and take a good hard look at your Shih Tzu. If she deviates from the standard in any obvious way, like being smaller than eight inches or taller than 11 inches at the shoulder or having a very shy temperament, she probably won't do well in the show ring.

Check for "Faults"

Of course your little baby doesn't have faults, right? But if you want to show, you need to know that the breed standard lists faults that disqualify your pup from the show ring. *Faults* are qualities that don't live up to the *ideal,* and they affect a judge's assessment of the dog in the show ring. Occasionally, a dog with faults may win if all the other qualities are superior, but in general, faults don't pass the test for a Best-in-Show hopeful.

For the extreme lowdown on what the breed standard has to say about faults, check out `www.akc.org`. The AKC's Web site is a wealth of info about all parts of dog shows and standards. You can also flip to Chapter 2. If your dog does have a fault but you really want to get involved in an activity with him, consider pet therapy, Rally, or something else that isn't based on perfect conformation. Of course, a physically imperfect Shih Tzu can and often does make a perfect pet.

Visit Dog Shows

If you like the idea of dog shows, but aren't sure about the reality, then take time to attend a dog show. They may not be what you imagine at all! Visiting a dog show gives you a glimpse into the world from the spectator side, and that can tell you a lot about what it would be like to show your Shih Tzu. Visiting a dog show may also convince you that you aren't so interested after all.

When you visit, choose a benched show if possible that allows you to look at the dogs and talk to the breeders when they aren't in the ring. In some outdoor shows and indoor ring shows, you can also talk to the breeders. Ask questions about showing. You can't bring your dog into the show if he isn't part of the show or if he's less than 6 months old, but if you bring a good picture of him, some helpful exhibitors may even be able to advise you about your dog's prospects as a show dog.

To find dog shows near you, check out the AKC Web site at www.akc.org/events/search. Click the *Conformation* tab, select your state, and click the *Search* button. You can also subscribe to the AKC Gazette to get updated, first-hand information on dog shows. The Gazette comes in two sections. One is the journal with articles, and one is the Events Calendar, which lists shows, dates, judges, and breed seminars, usually three months in advance. For subscriptions go online at www.akc.org/pubs/index.cfm or call (800) 533-7323.

Find a Mentor

A mentor is a dog show expert — a breeder and/or exhibitor — who takes you under her wing, guides you through the process of doing your first few shows, and gives you advice to save you a lot of time and keep you from making some common beginner mistakes.

If your Shih Tzu's breeder shows her dogs frequently (most of the best breeders do or used to), she may be able to give you some great advice and even take you to some shows. If she can't commit to that, she may be able to recommend show people to help you. If you don't know any other Shih Tzu folks, when you attend dog shows, ask around. Someone may be able to hook you up with just the right person to show you the ropes. A good way to start would be to join the American Shih Tzu Club (ASTC). Check them out at www.shihtzu.org.

Attend a Training Class

When you watch a dog show, you probably notice that the handlers all seem to know just what to do with their dogs: when to move, when to stop, and how to help the dogs show themselves off most effectively. Where do those handlers learn those skills?

After you're in the ring, the judge tells you (and everyone else) how to move, when to move, and where to move. Most judges use down and back so they can view the rear and front movement of the dog and the triangle pattern to best see the side, front, and rear, for side movement. Many exhibitors pick up these patterns from others or by attending a lot of shows, but many people also take conformation classes that teach you everything you need to know to navigate a dog show with ease. You'll get a lot of practice before you jump into the real thing.

Check with your local dog club to see if they offer conformation training classes. You can also find nearby conformation clubs online at `www.akc.org/clubs/search/index.cfm`.

Practice Handling Techniques

Even though Shih Tzu take to handling better than some breeds, not all of them like to be poked, prodded, and examined by strangers. But that's just what happens in a dog show. Shih Tzu are judged on a table. Often, if a dog has never been set up on a table before a dog show, the dog will get spooked. You want your little show dog to stand up there with confidence.

The best way to get your Shih Tzu used to the kind of hands-on examination she'll experience in a show is to practice the things that the judges will do. This examination may include

- Petting
- Looking in the ears
- Pulling back the lips
- Examining the eyes
- Picking up the feet
- Pressing the paw pads
- Lifting up the tail
- Running hands down both sides of the body

Have other family members and friends do these actions, too, a few times every day. And before long, your Shih Tzu will be used to people handling her. Dogs don't fear what they're used to experiencing.

If your little show prospect really hates the poking and prodding, resists the table, and just doesn't seem to enjoy any of it, you may consider passing on the conformation ring idea. Some dogs get used to showing and learn to love it, but some never do. Maybe your Shih Tzu would have more fun doing something else, like Rally.

Practice for Perfection

The age-old advice of practice makes perfect applies to more than piano lessons and soccer practice. Conformation training classes can give you a lot of specific activities to practice to make your dog show experience easier and more pleasurable.

Although some people get lucky right away and their dogs take to the activity immediately, other dog owners need to persevere so their dogs feel comfortable in the show ring. Try out these tips for your practice times:

- Work at home every day, training your dog to walk beside you on the leash without pulling. (For more on how to do this, see Chapter 17.)
- Practice the right grooming for the show ring.
- Practice handling the dog like the judge would.
- Practice spending time together to improve your communication.

Before you know it, the two of you will be dog show pros. And don't forget that competing in dog shows counts as practice, too!

Master the Art of Stacking

Stacking is a dog show term that means the handler poses the dog's body to show it off the best, although many show dogs are trained how to stack themselves. Shih Tzu are stacked both on the judging table and on the ground, although the judge rarely examines a Shih Tzu on the ground. He'll stand back and look at him, instead, and if the judge wants a closer look, he'll ask you to put the dog on the table again.

When dogs stand alert and look up at you and seem to pose on their own, that's called *free stacking,* but many handlers stack their dogs in the ring by moving their feet a little, pulling up at the tail, and generally adjusting the pose — sort of like a photographer does during a photo shoot.

When you attend a dog show, watch the handlers and what they do to the Shih Tzu when the dogs are standing at attention and when they're up on the table. Look how they pick up and put down the Shih Tzu on the table. Some handlers don't stack their dogs, but many do. At dog shows, you can ask handlers about how to do this, but make sure to wait until they're out of the show ring. Some helpful people are happy to give advice.

Check Out the Groom Room

Different handlers groom dogs in slightly different ways, but to be competitive, Shih Tzu have to be groomed a certain way for the show ring. Although Shih Tzu don't need the exacting and meticulous grooming of the Poodle or the Bichon, they do require extensive grooming and a long coat for showing.

The best way to discover how to perfect the Shih Tzu coat is to train under someone who already knows how. Then you can take the lessons and develop your own style and flair. If you're on friendly terms with your professional groomer, he may even give you some tips. You can also watch in the grooming area of some indoor and outdoor dog shows.

You can find out grooming tips on your own, too. The ASTC has a grooming page on their Web site at `www.shihtzu.org/Articles/article_list.asp?menu=Articles&ART_TYPE=Grooming`. Or, consult Chapter 10.

Know the Lingo

Dog show lingo can get pretty confusing, and to newbies, it may even sound like a foreign language. You can do more research on the AKC Web site or read about dog shows in books dedicated to the subject, but here are a few things you should know:

- Dogs shows can be all-breed shows, specialty shows of just one breed, or group shows with only, for example, Toy breeds.
- To compete in a dog show, dogs must be at least 6 months old, registered with the AKC, and not spayed or neutered.
- Each dog must be entered into a particular class: *Puppy* (for dogs age from 6 to 12 months), *Novice* (for dogs older than 6 months who haven't won three first prizes), or *Open* (for any dog 6 months or older). Male and female dogs compete separately in most classes.
- Dog shows typically have several levels. All-breed and group shows have breed competitions and then group competitions, where the winning breeds compete against each other.
- Several other rules and regulations exist for a number of shows. If you're interested in finding out more, check out `www.akc.org/events/conformation/beginners.cfm`.

Index

• A •

• B •

• C •

• I •

• J •

• K •

• L •

• M •

• N •

• O •

• Q •

• R •

• S •

• T •

• U •

• V •

• W •

• Y •